THE
BEST
SHORT
PLAYS 1989

edited and introduced by
RAMON DELGADO

Best Short Plays Series

APPLAUSE
THEATRE BOOK PUBLISHERS
211 West 71 St. New York, N.Y. 10023

for Charles C. Ritter

Copyright © 1989 by Ramon Delgado
All Rights Reserved
Published in New York, by Applause Theatre Books
Library of Congress Catalog Card No. 38–8006
ISBN 1–55783–045–2 (cloth), 1–55783–044–4 (paper)
ISSN 0067–6284
Manufactured in the United States of America

1 2 3 4 5 6 7 8 9 0 4 3 2 1 0 9 8 7 6 5

CONTENTS

BOOKS AND PLAYS BY RAMON DELGADO

The Best Short Plays 1981 (with Stanley Richards)
The Best Short Plays 1982
The Best Short Plays 1983
The Best Short Plays 1984
The Best Short Plays 1985
The Best Short Plays 1986
The Best Short Plays 1987
The Best Short Plays 1988
Acting With Both Sides of Your Brain

The Youngest Child of Pablo Peco
Waiting for the Bus
The Little Toy Dog
Once Below a Lighthouse
Sparrows of the Field
The Knight-Mare's Nest
Omega's Ninth
Listen, My Children
A Little Holy Water
The Fabulous Jeromes
The Jerusalem Thorn
Stones
The Flight of the Dodo
An Actor Named Booth

INTRODUCTION

After this volume—my ninth year of editing the annual *Best Short Plays*—the present editor is stepping aside to concentrate on other professional pursuits. The series will be continued, however, under the protective wings of Glenn Young, publisher of Applause Theatre Books. To commemorate the changing of the guard I have included one extra play, eleven, instead of the traditional ten. Here, again, are the best representatives of the short play form as currently presented on the stages of America's theatres: from the topical social problems of AIDS in Lanford Wilson's *A Poster of the Cosmos* and spouse abuse in Edward Alan Baker's *Dolores*; to the lyrical spiritual exploration in Ernest Ferlita's *The Mask of Hiroshima*; through the trenchant character studies of an aging writer in *April Snow* by Romulus Linney and the confrontation of an alcoholic nun and a voice-over actor in *Penguin Blues* by Ethan Phillips; to the sharp black comedy in Andrew Foster's toxic waste play, *Chemical Reactions*; to a bit of 1930s Black music history in Willy Holtzman's *San Antonio Sunset*; to the tender romance of ordinary people in Ernest A. Joselovitz's *There Is No John Garfield*; through the sensitive study of maternal love for the exceptional child in Katherine Snodgrass's *Haiku*; to the philosophical contemplation of fishin' in William R. Lewis's *Trout*; to the bittersweet fantasy of a young author confronting his muse in Richard Greenberg's *The Author's Voice*.

The series has been a source of great satisfaction as I have seen many of the playwrights included here continue to develop their careers. In the 1987–88 theatre season alone professionally produced writers included within the volumes of this series include: Martin Jones (*Old Soldiers, B.S.P. '83*) with *West Memphis Mojo* at the Negro Ensemble Theatre; Harry Kondoleon (*Self Torture and Strenuous Exercise, B.S.P. '84*) with *Zero Positive* at Joseph Papp's Public Theatre; Milcha Sanchez-Scott (*Dog Lady, B.S.P. '86*) with *Roosters* at the INTAR Theatre; David Henry Hwang (*The Dance and the Railroad, B.S.P. '82*, and *The Sound of A Voice, B.S.P. '85*) with *M. Butterfly* on Broadway receiving the 1988 Tony Award for Best Play and numerous nominations for other awards; Lee Blessing (*Nice People Dancing to Good Country Music, B.S.P. '84*) with *A Walk in the Woods*, another award winner on Broadway; David Mamet (*Reunion, B.S.P. '81*) with *Speed the*

Plow on Broadway; and Lanford Wilson (*Thymus Vulgaris, B.S.P. '82; A Betrothal, B.S.P. '87;* and *A Poster of the Cosmos, B.S.P. '89*) with *Burn This* on Broadway. Undoubtedly, the future work of these playwrights and others preparing in the wings through these volumes will be visible on the future stages of American Theatre.

From the beginning of this series the past and present editors have sought to include a balance among three categories of playwrights: 1) established playwrights who continue to practice the art and craft of the short play, 2) emerging playwrights whose record of productions indicate both initial achievement and continuing artistic productivity, and 3) talented new playwrights whose work may not have had much exposure but evidences promise for the future. An effort has also been made to select plays not anthologized elsewhere and, when possible, plays that are making their debut in print. Notably for the 1989 edition only one of the eleven plays was in print at the time of selection. The value of these considerations is to honor the artistry of the established playwrights, encourage the emerging, acknowledge the promising, and offer a varied selection of new plays in one volume.

There are a number of groups and individuals that I would like to thank for their support of the short play over the years: at the top of the list is the Actors Theatre of Louisville, where Producing Director Jon Jory sponsored an annual SHORTS Festival (1980–85) and Literary Manager Julie Beckett Crutcher, and her successor Michael Bigelow Dixon, have supervised the reading and evaluations of thousands of short plays; the Ensemble Studio Theatre, where Artistic Director Curt Dempster's annual Marathon since 1977 has generated excitement for the short play in Manhattan; and the Philadelphia Festival Theatre for New Plays, where short plays have been fostered under the leadership of Artistic and Producing Director Carol Rocamora.

Other individuals who have encouraged our efforts through the years include Alan Turner and Elsie Comninos at Chilton Books; publisher Glenn Young at Applause Theatre Books; agents Clyde Taylor and Henry Dunow at Curtis Brown, Ltd.; Robert Main, editor of Fireside Theatre Books, whose selection of three double volumes for distribution through the Fireside Theatre Book Club helped boost my spirits between individual annual volumes; Christian H. Moe, Professor of Theatre at Southern Illinois University at Carbondale; and my theatre-going friend, Ellen Kauffman, who must hold a record for the number of plays she has seen in her eighty-plus years.

Thanks also to those loyal readers, theatre buffs, and librarians, who have taken the collection in hand over the years. And, of course, a deeply felt thanks to the many playwrights and agents who have sent their plays for consideration and waited patiently for decisions.

Finally, a note of acknowledgment and thanks to Charles C. Ritter, to whom this volume is dedicated. Dr. Ritter, Professor of Theatre at Ohio State University, was my first playwrighting teacher over thirty years ago at Stetson University, and the skills he introduced, through writing and rewriting, have been a valuable asset in my own progress as a playwright and editor. Thanks, Charlie.

RAMON DELGADO
Montclair, New Jersey

Richard Greenberg

THE AUTHOR'S VOICE

Richard Greenberg

Richard Greenberg's *The Author's Voice* was one of the hits of New York City's Ensemble Studio Theatre's (E.S.T.) Marathon '87. *New York Times* reviewer Mel Gussow praised the play thus: "This comic gem deals with the ambiguous relationship between the writer and his muse, while also commenting on *Beauty and the Beast* and *The Hunchback of Notre Dame,* among other literary precedents. *The Author's Voice* is a shaggy yarn about the headlong pursuit of 15-minute fame."

Mr. Greenberg's earlier short play *Life Under Water,* a story of two fragile love affairs bathed by the restless waves of summer in the Hamptons, Long Island, appeared in the 1987 edition of *Best Short Plays.* Frank Rich, reviewing that play for the *New York Times,* showered the play with praise: "*Life Under Water* ... is no mere gem. It is a full-bodied 45-minute work that marks the arrival of a young playwright with a big future. ... It is Mr. Greenberg's own arresting sensibility that informs every pungent line and bristling scene."

One of Mr. Greenberg's full-length plays, *The Maderati,* was presented in the winter of 1987 at Manhattan's Playwrights Horizons. He also wrote the text for Martha Clarke's 1987 performance art piece, *The Hunger Artist,* based on Franz Kafka's short story, performed by the Music Theatre Group at St. Clements. E.S.T. also presented another new short play by Mr. Greenberg entitled *Neptune's Hips* in Marathon '88, and his full-length play *Eastern Standard* premiered in May 1988 at the Seattle Repertory Theatre Mainstage and was under option for the New York 1988–89 theatre season. His adaptation of Laurie Colwin's short story, "An Old-Fashioned Story," was produced for American Playhouse on PBS television.

Mr. Greenberg grew up in East Meadow, New York, the son of second-generation, ex-urban, Jewish parents. The first professional production of his work was in the fall of 1984, when the E.S.T. presented his play, *Bloodletters,* a family comedy laced with biting wit. *Bloodletters* brought Mr. Greenberg the *Newsday* award for "Best New Playwright" in 1985. E.S.T. also produced his short play, *Vanishing Act,* in Marathon '86.

While an undergraduate at Princeton, where he received his B.A. magna cum laude in English in 1980, Mr. Greenberg wrote a novel for his senior thesis. The work was graded by novelist Joyce Carol Oates, who dubbed Greenberg, " ... a young novelist of genuine promise." Also at Princeton Mr. Greenberg received the Ward Mathis Prize in short fiction in 1980. After a year of graduate work in literature at Harvard, Mr. Greenberg entered the Master of Fine Arts playwrighting program at Yale School of Drama, where he was awarded the coveted Molly Kazan Playwrighting Award in 1984.

Among his current writing projects are a screenplay for 20th Century Fox, TV pilots for Orion and Viacom, two full-length plays entitled *Refugees* and *Nothing Human*. Another full-length play, *Sweeter Music*, received its premiere at Sarah Lawrence College in the spring of 1988.

Characters:

PORTIA, *young, beautiful, and dressy*
TODD, *young, beautiful, and dressy*
GENE, *a gnome*

Setting:

Todd's apartment. Strangely shadowed. A door in the back wall. A bed obliquely angled into the room. Two chairs and a table—both dark wood.

Scene One:

Lights up on Todd and Portia.

PORTIA: The author's lair ...
TODD: All right, you've seen it, let's go.
PORTIA: You're joking.
TODD: I ...
PORTIA: You're serious?
TODD: Well ...
PORTIA: What? What are you?
TODD: Portia.
PORTIA: I'm looking for clues.
TODD: ... Hm.
PORTIA: Tips.
TODD: Yes.
PORTIA: Leads.
TODD: None here.
PORTIA: It's not ... exactly ...
TODD: No ...
PORTIA: ... *forthcoming* ...
TODD: This ...
PORTIA: ... room.
TODD: (*Sighs with relief*) No.

PORTIA: You're strange, Todd.

TODD: I'm not, not at all.

PORTIA: What's behind that door?

TODD: Another apartment. Neighbors.

PORTIA: Really?

TODD: Railroad flat. Tenement.

PORTIA: Curious smell.

TODD: The neighbors.

PORTIA: Food become flesh, somehow, you know?

TODD: (*Stymied*) Of course.

PORTIA: Well, you know those people who trap cooking odors? In their hair—in their down vests—in their—all over, all over themselves?

TODD: They're sloppy people, the neighbors.

PORTIA: Do you know them?

TODD: We've never met.

PORTIA: They *must* be sloppy people.

TODD: Yes. (*He looks puzzled*)

PORTIA: This isn't what I expected, I must say.

TODD: What did you ... ?

PORTIA: Something cleaner, more pared down, geometric, somehow, I don't know, I can't say. But not this ... I don't know ... House of Usher. Do you like living here?

TODD: (*Curiously mechanical*) Sometimes the walls feel like predators, they roam and idle, grow mouths and tongues, close in and bare their teeth; this is what loneliness is to me—living beasts.

PORTIA: (*A beat*) I've noticed you quote from yourself an awful lot.

TODD: What?

PORTIA: That, just now, that was a quotation, wasn't it?

TODD: ... Yes.

PORTIA: From this book of ours, wasn't it?

TODD: ... Yes.

PORTIA: Well, of course I'd realize that, wouldn't I?

TODD: ... Yes. Look, why don't you just go home now, I need ...

PORTIA: I've also noticed that, in general, when you're not quoting from yourself, your conversation tends towards the ...

TODD: ... Towards the ... ?

PORTIA: Bland.

TODD: Ah, the bland, yes.

PORTIA: You're not one of our *glib* authors.

TODD: Perhaps ... (*Searches for the word*) *not.*

PORTIA: You're beautiful, though.

TODD: So are you.

PORTIA: And you write like an angel. How do you write so beautifully?

TODD: My writing ...

PORTIA: Yes?

TODD: It ... burns in the smithy of my ... in my smithy.

PORTIA: The torment, I love it. Beauty and pain, what a parlay! Tell me the truth—those aren't the neighbors behind that door. Behind that door, there's some horribly twisted gnome who does all your writing for you ...

TODD: You had too much to drink tonight ...

PORTIA: I'm celebrating!

TODD: Celebrating what?

PORTIA: Us ... this teaming, this partnership. Success is absolutely assured. Todd, no, I want you to know that. Those pages you've shown us ... God, they're incredible. And the jacket photograph *alone* will be a classic. No, I'm sincere. I think you have something important to contribute to literature.

TODD: Thank you.

PORTIA: Why are you so nervous?

TODD: I'm embarrassed by the smell.

PORTIA: ... I don't mind.

TODD: It embarrasses me.

PORTIA: I think it's sexy.

TODD: It's not.

PORTIA: It is ...

TODD: No ...

PORTIA: I swear ...

TODD: Tonight it's not.

PORTIA: (*A beat*) You want me to go.

TODD: You've noticed.

PORTIA: You're the fevered type.

TODD: A little.

PORTIA: And tomorrow you must rise early and have your job and your protein shake and then spill your pain at the typewriter. Hours and hours of wiggling the loosened tooth of your despair.

TODD: I guess.

PORTIA: I'm sorry I've invaded your territory. I needed to see, though. I'm not one of those casual editors. I can't just tighten your syntax. I need to *see*, to *know*, to *absorb*, to *live through*, to *live with*, to *contemplate*, to *understand*. To *understand*. (*She kisses him passionately*) Good night. (*She exits. Todd sits at the table for a long moment. The door in the back creaks opens. A horribly twisted gnome emerges, carrying a sheaf of papers. He goes to Todd and hands him the pages. Todd accepts them. They look at each other. Fadeout*)

Scene Two:

Todd reading. The gnome, Gene, watches.

GENE: You *balked*.

TODD: This is wonderful. Is it?

GENE: The moment came—the decisive moment—and you let it slip by. That's unforgivable.

TODD: The pain, the sheer ... *pain*; it's painful, right?

GENE: Was it because of me?

TODD: I'll send this off first thing tomorrow. Portia will think she inspired me. Will she like it?

GENE: What?

TODD: The chapter.

GENE: Yes. She will.

TODD: You're sure?

GENE: I'm sure ...

TODD: Because I can't tell ...

GENE: I'm sure ...

TODD: Because I don't seem to have a feel for ...

GENE: I'M SURE!

TODD: Touchy, touchy, touchy.

GENE: She was beautiful, wasn't she?

TODD: Who?

GENE: The girl.

TODD: Which ... ?

GENE: Tonight.

TODD: Portia.

GENE: Yes.

TODD: (*Thinks a moment*) Yes. I think so. Yes.

GENE: You *think* so?

TODD: I wasn't paying close attention. That sort of thing gets stale. (*Gene lets out a strangled howl*)

GENE: You *appall* me.

TODD: She was beautiful.

GENE: I saw.

TODD: *What?*

GENE: There's a keyhole, you know. A slit at the bottom of the door. Slants of light. This room made visible. I moved, I watched, I saw ...

TODD: Son of a bitch ...

GENE: Not the whole picture, but ... hair and ...

TODD: Son of a bitch ...

GENE: ... Calves and ankles and once, I think ...

TODD: I told you

GENE: ... an elbow—

TODD: I told you not to move when she was here. I told you to act like church mouse.

GENE: I *am* a church mouse ...

TODD: She was curious enough without hearing sounds ...

GENE: She was curious, you ...

TODD: Don't you know how fragile this whole deal is ...

GENE: You nipped that curiosity in the bud, I noticed—the *neighbors!*

TODD: She can't find out about this, Gene, or it's over, all over, we're through.

GENE: Is that a *bad* thing?

TODD: Not again, please. Not again. That damned ... what is it called, something you say over and over?

GENE: Litany.

TODD: That damned litany, over and over! Yes, it would be a bad thing. What we have, this is a good thing. If it ended, it would be a bad thing.

GENE: Not for me.

TODD: Oh, please ...

GENE: Despised, sequestered, denied even the standard compensations, I would relish the termination of all ...

TODD: Do you want me to put you back where I found you?

(*A beat*)

GENE: (*Quietly*) No.

TODD: In the gutter.

GENE: In the gutter! What a cliché. I was in an alley.

TODD: Starving and crying ...

GENE: And carrying pages of precious material which you promptly sold to the highest ...

TODD: I took you in!

GENE: You took me for everything I had; it was not Nightingale in the Crimea.

TODD: I brought the pages to a party—could you have done that? I met Portia there—could you have done that? She said, "This is work of ... this is a work of ..."

GENE: Genius ...

TODD: Genius! Yes! I let her take me to lunch, I worked my charm, I finessed her into a contract ...

GENE: Thus began my stellar career!

TODD: And it's good! (*Gene stares at him fiercely, then lets out a beastly roar. A beat*) That sort of thing has got to stop.

GENE: Why did you let her go tonight?

TODD: I wasn't interested.

GENE: How can you not be interested?

TODD: These things repeat themselves.

GENE: *They ... !*

TODD: ... Get dull ...

GENE: *I ...*

TODD: My libido wavers.

GENE: *Use mine!*

TODD: I'm going to bed.

GENE: You never bring anyone home! Some nights you don't come home yourself! I wait. I sit. I don't move. It hurts to move anyway. My body is sore. My muscles ache from disuse and misshapenness. I sit in that patch of darkness, that cupboard that has been allotted me, and stare out at an airshaft and wait for some noise from the hallway, some stirring, for *you* ... and you don't come. Why don't you bring one home? I'd be still as a church mouse. I'd hold my breath. I want to hear it, to peek through the keyhole and see it. Live. Unrehearsed. The whole event. I would be so grateful.

TODD: Please stop talking and go to sleep before I say something true that will hurt you.

GENE: I *wash*. Hour after hour, I scrub, I pumice! I'm meticulously clean. The smell comes from *airlessness*. From being alone with myself in a dark room. It's the smell of *imprisonment*, let me out and it will go away!

TODD: You can't go out!

GENE: You don't let me.

TODD: Don't dare.

GENE: Just for a stroll. A walk on the street. I need books! If I'm to live in a purely verbal universe, I must have my vocabulary replenished every now and then, let me buy books and I'll come right back and be happy ...

TODD: I get you whatever books you need, you know that ...

GENE: I need to see people walking on the street ...

TODD: No fits, tonight, I'm too tired.

GENE: My needs are not being attended to!

TODD: You don't want to go out, you know you don't, you know it ...

GENE: Just for an afternoon ...

TODD: They *laugh* at you on the street.

GENE: *Not always.*

TODD: *Mostly they do!* (*A beat*)

GENE: (*Softly*) Mostly they do. (*He goes quietly to his room, closes the door. Todd lies down on bed. A knocking starts from behind the door. Pauses. Starts again. Pauses. From behind the closed door*) Todd ... ?

TODD: Yes ... ?

GENE: What's in it for you? (*Todd puts pillow over his head and turns over. Fadeout*)

Scene Three:

A flash goes off in the dark. Lights up. Portia is taking Polaroids of Todd.

PORTIA: Now, don't get offended!

TODD: I'm not offended.

PORTIA: The higher-ups simply think—and in a way I agree with them—they simply think—here, hold this. (*She hands him photo*) They simply think the book, as it stands, is a little *spineless*, that's all—pose. (*He poses*)

TODD: Spineless?

PORTIA: Lacking a spine.

TODD: Ah!

PORTIA: The quality of the—of the what?—of the *feeling*, of the emotional, you know, *milieu* is immaculately rendered, but there seems to be no, no thrust, no action, no event. Right now it's sort of lumpy, sort of pudding-y, a kind of *mousse* of despair, if you know what I—not that that's *bad*—we're all agreed despair is due for a revival. Here, hold this. (*She hands him photo*) We're simply suggesting you incorporate more of the, you know, you make it less *endoscopic*, if you know what I—pose. (*He poses*)

TODD: I don't know how to do that.

PORTIA: Oh, Todd, oh, Todd ...

TODD: What does that mean, oh, Todd, oh, Todd?

PORTIA: I know your night life.

TODD: That's irrelevant.

PORTIA: It's superficial; it's not irrelevant.

TODD: I could never possibly ... write ... I could never possibly write that.

PORTIA: Hold this. (*She hands him photo*)

TODD: These are grotesque.

PORTIA: They're just jacket ideas, they're not the real thing.

TODD: Do I look like this?

PORTIA: Of course not.

TODD: How do I look?

PORTIA: Like Todd.

TODD: I mean, how do I look to *you?* (*Portia sits on him*)

PORTIA: Nice.

TODD: Portia ...

PORTIA: Todd.

TODD: Please get off me.

PORTIA: Aren't you attracted to me?

TODD: I don't remember.

PORTIA: What?

TODD: I sometimes empty out.

PORTIA: What?

TODD: I can't muster enthusiasm. I forget. My body remembers but I forget.

PORTIA: Is that, what, is that some sort of Zen *koan* or something, what is that?

TODD: Please.

PORTIA: What is it with you, Todd?

TODD: Portia ...

PORTIA: Don't hide from me, Todd. There's no need. Don't you know? There is nothing about you too dark, too hideous, no single thing too ugly for me to accept, embrace, and love. (*She moves to kiss him*)

TODD: I need to do rewrites.

PORTIA: It's come over you?

TODD: What ...

PORTIA: Inspiration?

TODD: Yes!

PORTIA: I'll go. (*Dismounts him*) Now, remember: a story, a spine, facts! Bring in your club days, bring in your sex life! Make me a book I can sell!

TODD: Yes.

PORTIA: Wait a second.

TODD: What?

PORTIA: Have the neighbors moved?

TODD: ... Why?

PORTIA: The smell is gone. (*She kisses two fingers, waves with them, and exits*)

TODD: ... Gene? (*He approaches Gene's room*) Gene! (*He opens the door, bangs violently around in the room*) GENE! (*Blackout*)

Scene Four:

Todd is seated at the table. Gene wears a long coat, dark glasses, a fedora. By his side, there is a package of books.

GENE: It came to me: why not? (*A beat*) You were gone and I wasn't physically restrained. The outside world might be a painful place but every place is a painful one, so why not? (*A beat*) I put on your greatcoat and your glasses and your fedora and looked almost hardly abnormal at all. I was careful, Todd, don't look at me like that, I was so careful, no neighbor saw, not the super, no one, I walked in shadows *exclusively*. (*He smiles hopefully*) I know you've taken me on at great financial and personal sacrifice to yourself, I know I've altered your life completely, I know with me on your hands no sane life is possible, I'm grateful, I truly am, I'm not an ingrate, *don't look at me like that!* (*A beat. He picks up the books*) I got these at a used book store, a place, I swear to you, as musty as myself. I fit right in. (*A beat*) Todd, I had to do this for both of us. I was forgetting things; words lost their attachments. Without this little trip, this one, one-time-only little trip, you would have had a book full of nonsense, a mere *crunch* of syllables. (*A beat*) It's not a place I want to go to any more, the world. I promise. (*A beat*) *This isn't fair!* (*A beat*) Look: burn this coat, buy another on our royalties! Another hat, too, and new glasses, I know I'm an infection, I won't be insulted! Please, please talk! I'm sure I must have been laughed at on the street, you don't have to worry ... (*A beat*) Please ... (*A beat*)

TODD: (*Quietly*) Come here ...

GENE: Why?

TODD: Come here ...

GENE: Why?

TODD: I want to hug you. (*Pause*)

GENE: ... Todd?

TODD: Please. (*Gene approaches gingerly as Todd stretches out his arms. Gene is about to enter them when Todd grabs his wrist and wrestles him to the ground, getting him in a hammerlock. Gene howls, tries to twist his way out of the lock, rolls.*

Todd rolls with him, gets him into the lock again) SON-OF-A-
BITCH! *(Gene cries out in blinding pain)* NEVER DO THAT
AGAIN! *(Gene cries out)* DO YOU HEAR ME? *(Gene cries
out again)* DO YOU HEAR ME! *(Gene utters a strangled, rat-
tling cry, manages to dodge out of Todd's grip and crawl a few
inches away. Todd leaps on top of him, lies flat on him, crushing
him into the ground) Do you hear me?*
    GENE: Y-E-E-E-E-S!!!!!!!!!!!!!! *(Todd springs off him,
falls panting onto the bed. Gene crawls to his room, as quickly
as he can from fear, but still haltingly, jerkily. He kicks the door
shut. A long moment)*
    TODD: Gene ... ? *(A beat)* Gene ... ? *(A beat)* Gene ... ?
    GENE: We're over. *(Fadeout)*

Scene Five:

*Todd stands at the door, a liquor bottle in his hand. From
Gene's room, an incessant keening, a mournful, animal
sound. Todd knocks his palm against the door. Again.
Again. Again. Again.*

    TODD: Christ, I'm sorry! *(A beat)* I didn't mean to hurt you.
Please come out. *(A beat)* Please come out. *(A beat)* I'm not a
cruel person. I'm not ... I don't ... *(A beat. The keening subsides)* Gene? *(It starts again)* Gene, I'm sorry, I'm sorry, I'm
sorry, I'm sorry, I'm ... *(He is now almost climbing the door,
almost caressing it, pacifying)* Listen ... Listen ... Listen ...
Gene? Gene? ... Gene? ... *(The keening subsides again)* Gene,
are you all right, now? *(A beat. Still quiet)* Are you better?
(Still quiet) Are you better? *(Still quiet)* You sound better
Gene, what can we do? Can we be friends? Can we ... ? *(A
beat)* Gene, listen, I'm going to do like we used to, okay?
Remember? I'm going to tell you something that happened to
me and you can tell me what it means, remember? Okay? *(A
beat)* Is that okay? *(A beat)* Is that okay? *(A beat)* Okay. *(He
sits with his back against the door)* This happened the other day
at the Health Club. You know, where I go? *(A beat)* Right.

Well, I was going to take a swim. I'd never used the pool there
before, but I wanted to swim. So I was getting suited up when a
man at the row of lockers across from me started talking to his
friend. This man, he was balding, but he seemed pretty fit, and
he was pleased with himself, you could tell, like he didn't even
mind being bald, and I thought, well, if I feel like that at his age, I
won't be doing half bad. And his friend looked pretty good, too,
and it sort of cheered me up. Anyway, they went to the pool. I
finished getting ready, and then I went to the pool. It was just
the three of us and an attendant. The attendant yelled at me,
"No trunks!" I didn't understand. Then I looked at the two men
swimming in the pool. They were naked. It was policy. When
they were naked like that, they didn't look so good. They looked
fat. They looked like fish—large ... extinct ... fish ... I bent to
take off my trunks. As I did, the bald man came up for air. For a
second, he was completely still, frozen solid in the water. He
looked at me and kept looking. I dove in, a perfect dive with a
flip and a spin. When I came up for air, the bald man wasn't in
the pool any more. He was standing by the poolside, crying
hysterically. His friend was next to him, trying to calm him
down, but the bald-headed man wouldn't stop crying. "Why are
you crying?" his friend kept asking. "It was the dive." he said.
"It was the dive." (*A beat*) Gene ... ? (*A beat*) Gene, why did
that make him cry? (*A beat*) Why? ... Why did that make him
cry? (*A beat*) Gene ... ? Gene ... ? Why?

GENE: (*From the bedroom; braying*) BECAUSE IT WAS
SAD! (*A beat*)

TODD: Oh. (*A beat*) I need you to tell me these sorts of
things, Gene. I can't figure them out on my own. (*A beat*) My
life isn't good. You think it is, but it's not. Once it was, but it's
not any more. (*A beat*) I used to be made happy by ... stupid
things. Parties! People around me. I was vain. I was a pea-
cock. I looked in the mirror. I looked so hard I didn't recognize
myself. I didn't recognize anything. I forgot why I did things. I
got scared, Gene! I got scared outside, I got scared in my room.
I didn't know where I was half the time. I wanted to drown, I
wanted to be covered over ... Then I found you. (*A beat*) Make
me famous, Gene. I want to be famous. People will photograph
me and write about me. I'll study how they see me and live in-

side it ... Fame will be a kind of home. But I need you to get it for me. Only they can't know it's you, they can't know it's *you*; if they ever see you, it will die like *that*. (*Snaps his fingers. A beat*) It panics me when you leave and it panics me when you're here. You're the whole problem of my life, but without you I don't have any life. (*A beat*) I'll give you what you want. I won't deny you any more. Anything I can, I'll give you. (*A beat. Gene emerges from the room. He embraces Todd. Todd moans. Fadeout*)

Scene Six:

Todd and Gene. Todd dressing for the evening.

GENE: The scene must be played beautifully.

TODD: I don't know if I can do this.

GENE: You don't have a choice. I'll stop writing if you don't. I'll go back to the streets, find another benefactor. Or die, I don't care which.

TODD: All right. But what do I say? It's been a long time ...

GENE: I'll write the scene for you. You simply play it out.

TODD: Jesus.

GENE: You come up behind Portia ...

TODD: Yes ...

GENE: Fling an arm across her chest ...

TODD: That's melodramatic ...

GENE: *You fling an arm across her chest* ...

TODD: Yes, yes, all right, fine ...

GENE: And you say, "Darling, I want you." (*A beat*)

TODD: I say, what?

GENE: "Darling, I want you."

TODD: I don't say that.

GENE: You do.

TODD: She'd laugh in my face.

GENE: Never.

TODD: You're insane.

GENE: (*Insistently*) "Darling, I want you."

TODD: The only words I could possibly get away with in that whole sentence are "I" and "you."

GENE: You will say this! You will say, "Darling, I want you." She will be moved by the poetic simplicity of your expression! (*A beat*)

TODD: Fine.

GENE: Then—you will turn her towards you, kiss each shoulder, her neck, then rise ever so slowly till your lips meet hers. You will kiss her, and say, "Be mine." (*A beat. Todd looks at him skeptically*) Then ...

TODD: Wait a minute ...

GENE: What?

TODD: That won't work.

GENE: It will work like a *dream* ...

TODD: Trust me on this ...

GENE: Like a *dream* ...

TODD: She will be out of here in fourteen seconds flat.

GENE: Nonsense.

TODD: I promise you.

GENE: Nonsense.

TODD: I *promise* you. (*A beat*)

GENE: What would you say—what *do* you say, then, in circumstances like these? There's a woman, there's a bed, you're alone, you're enchanted, what do you say? (*A beat*)

TODD: Do you want to sleep with me?

GENE: A-A-A-R-G-H!!!!

TODD: I'm sorry.

GENE: You don't understand.

TODD: I do ...

GENE: You don't understand the situation.

TODD: Inform me.

GENE: You are *enraptured*. You are ... *transported*. This is no common *lay*. This is no cheap *one-nighter*. The finest fibers of your being quiver in expectancy. Poetry floods your soul. "Do you want to sleep with me?" simply will not suffice, not this night. What do you say, then? When all the beauty of the universe churns inside you. (*A beat. Todd thinks*)

TODD: Are you staying?

GENE: A-A-A-A-R-G-H!!!!!!

TODD: Gene ...

GENE: A-A-A-R-G-H!!!!!

TODD: Gene ...

GENE: The world *requires* me ...

TODD: Gene ...

GENE: ... to rewrite its wretched *dialogue!*

TODD: Gene ...

GENE: You will make it beautiful. You will proceed as I describe. You will *say*, "Darling, I want you." You will say, "Be mine," you will be tender and slow and romantic. You will *make it work!* (*A beat*)

TODD: Not a word from you.

GENE: ... I know.

TODD: Not a peep.

GENE: I promise.

TODD: For your own good as well as mine. You know I act for both of us, don't you? You know I want the best for both of us?

GENE: ... Yes.

TODD: I'll be back soon. (*He exits. Gene looks after him, waits until he's sure he's gone. Then he approaches Todd's bed. He touches it carefully*)

GENE: Todd ... ? (*Gene runs his hands across the bed, feeling the smooth, silky textures*) Todd ... it wouldn't be bad if she saw me. Not so bad. (*He climbs onto the bed*) Often beautiful women come upon hideous men and love them. They uncover an inner beauty, oh, and crowns of light weave into canopies over their heads and the carbuncles and the cicatrices, the humps and wens miraculously disappear. The beasts are replaced by angels. She'll see me, Todd, she'll see. And you'll be loved for me. (*Fadeout*)

Scene Seven:

Todd's room in half-light—a golden shaft spilled across the floor. Todd and Portia enter. The picture they make in this light is burnished and lovely. Lights come up slightly fuller.

PORTIA: You were brilliant tonight. You didn't even have to *speak* is how brilliant you were. I loved when we went to that place with the flashing lights and your face came floating up at me in patches, it was poetry, truly poetry. I was speaking to the big boys today, Todd. They want to take you to lunch; they're very excited, really thrilled. Everything's mapped out, your whole itinerary. The book jacket's designed, there are display cases ready, and we're putting your photograph on billboards all over the city. All we need now is a book ...

TODD: I'm working slowly.

PORTIA: No matter. I have faith in you. I believe in you. (*A beat*) This night has been sensational. You actually invited me in. (*A beat*) Todd?

TODD: (*Grabbing her from behind*) Darling, I want you ...

PORTIA: What? (*A beat*)

TODD: Darling, I want you. (*She turns, laughs in his face, and in one blindingly quick motion, whips her dress off over her head*) Hey ... (*She starts undressing him*)

PORTIA: This will have to be quick; I have an early day tomorrow.

TODD: Wait! I have to kiss you slowly, I have to ...

PORTIA: I've been wondering what your problem was ...

TODD: Portia, I ... (*She has his shirt off, is starting on his pants*)

PORTIA: I was beginning to think you were gay ...

TODD: Turn around ...

PORTIA: You always wonder about that. Could you shrug out of these? (*He shrugs out of his pants. Portia lies on the bed*) Thank you. Now be careful, I'm getting my period, I'm a little sensitive ...

TODD: Wait ...

PORTIA: I know this is not the best time to start some sort of blazing romance, but you were just so damned *slow*.

TODD: (*Kneels on bed, grabs her hand*) Be mine! (*A beat. She laughs in his face*)

PORTIA: Christ, Todd, where are you getting these lines? Come on. (*She starts to pull off his underpants; he stops her, moves away from her*)

TODD: Wait!

PORTIA: What?

TODD: This is not going well ...

PORTIA: I think it's going pretty well. I think most people would think it was going pretty well ...

TODD: (*Pulling her off the bed*) You don't understand.

PORTIA: What?

TODD: Turn around ...

PORTIA: Todd ...

TODD: *Turn around. (A beat. She turns around. He puts his arm across her chest*) Be mine.

PORTIA: Look, do you want to sleep with me?

TODD: Portia ...

PORTIA: Am I staying?

TODD: You're doing everything wrong!

PORTIA: What are you talking about?

GENE: (*From his room*) IT'S SUPPOSED TO BE BEAUTI-FUL! (*A deathless pause*)

PORTIA: Todd ...

TODD: Oh, Jesus ...

PORTIA: What was that, Todd?

TODD: Nothing.

PORTIA: That wasn't nothing. That was a voice, saying ...

GENE: (*From bedroom*) IT'S SUPPOSED TO BE BEAUTIFUL!

PORTIA: Jesus Christ, what's the deal here? (*Gene flings open the door*)

GENE: Am I the only one left with a sense of loveliness? (*Portia stares at him in horror*)

PORTIA: Oh, my God ... oh, my God ...

TODD: Gene ...

GENE: (*Coming out of the room*) Look at the two of you ... You are ... trustees of beauty ... You shine with grace ... How have you managed to avoid a minimal interior fineness?

PORTIA: Todd ... (*Gene approaches her*)

GENE: Don't you know what you're supposed to do now? Don't you know your part?

PORTIA: Todd ...

TODD: Oh, Jesus ...

GENE: You see me and you are not repelled. You draw in. You come closer and closer. The closer you get, the handsomer I become. You touch me. You kiss me. (*He kisses her*) I stand tall. (*She faints. Todd catches her*) No. You don't know your part at all. (*He closes his eyes. Fadeout*)

Scene Eight:

Gene is bent half on a chair, half on the table, hands spread flat before him almost in an attitude of supplication. He is moaning softly, his eyes closed. Todd laces into him.

TODD: I *lied*. I *finessed* the situation. I said you were an *intruder*. The crazed, hideous neighbor breaking down the door between us. I *calmed* her down. I said this was an *unprecedented* event. I said I was contacting the authorities *immediately*. I said it would *never* happen again.

GENE: O-o-o-o-h-h ...

TODD: And it's not going to, either. There aren't going to be any more little jaunts, Gene. No more charming trips into the street. No more expeditions into the living room. From now on, you lock yourself in that room, and you don't come out until there's a book, a goddamn publishable item! *Do you understand me!*

GENE: I can't ...

TODD: What are you talking about?

GENE: I can't go on ...

TODD: *What are you talking about!*

GENE: ... She fainted ...

TODD: Oh, Jesus ...

GENE: I lived for the moment when I would blossom at a kiss and she fainted!

TODD: I don't want to hear this, now!

GENE: I can't, I can't possibly go on ...

TODD: *Listen to me!* You *will* go on. You will ... do what I demand of you! You will find a story and ... pick the words you need and ... get a *spine* and *make me a book!* Do you *under-*

stand?
    GENE: ... I can't ...
    TODD: You will *do it! Do you understand!* (*He slaps him*)
Do you understand! (*He slaps him again*)
    GENE: (*Roaring it out*) YES! (*Todd pulls Gene up out of the chair*)
    TODD: Then *start!* (*Todd throws Gene toward his room. He lands hunched in the doorway, his back to us. Todd sits, controls himself*) Gene ...?
    GENE: ... What?
    TODD: I didn't mean to be harsh.
    GENE: ... Ah.
    TODD: I just wanted you to know that. (*Gene turns sharply; looks at Todd. Fadeout*)

Scene Nine:

Gene sits at the table, smiling. A small gift-wrapped package is on the table. Todd bursts in, effusive.

    TODD: I just got word! We're already into a second printing. That's extremely unusual on a publication day.
    GENE: Ah!
    TODD: And three reviews came out—all raves!
    GENE: Lovely.
    TODD: (*Reading*) "When a book receives as much hype as *Drift* has, and when, in addition, its author looks more like a model for cologne that like Herman Melville, this critic is naturally inclined to skepticism. That proves unfounded here, however, because *Drift* is a knockout, far and away the best first novel of the season, perhaps the decade." Do you believe it?
    GENE: Very nice.
    TODD: I have to thank you.
    GENE: Oh, no ...
    TODD: No, I do. I know things weren't always ... pleasant ... between us, but look what it got you to do! Gene, I can say it now. I was amazed how you worked! Once you got started, it

took you, what, three weeks? And that from scratch! You ditched all the material you had before and just started. I used to listen, I can tell you this now, I listened at the door to the typewriter clattering away, nonstop, it just *thundered* out of you!

GENE: Yes.

TODD: When I go on talk shows, Gene—I want you to know this—I'm always asked, "How do you write?" And do you know what I say? I say, "A demon lives with me." I mean, you. I want you to know that. For vanity's sake ...

GENE: You're very kind.

TODD: This review starts by quoting the entire opening paragraph! "I live alone. There are no neighbors. There is no neighborhood. Brick has vanished. Tree and sky, too. When I peer through the narrow, grimy shaft that is my window, I see horizon and murk." He says it's the most memorable opening since, "Call me Ishmael."

GENE: (*Indicating package*) This is for you.

TODD: What?

GENE: For you.

TODD: What?

GENE: A present.

TODD: (*Touched*) ... Gene!

GENE: Open it.

TODD: I don't know what to say ...

GENE: I wanted to give you this for publication day. A momento.

TODD: (*Unwraps it*) A book. *Layaway*. Thank you.

GENE: I found it that day I was a bad boy ... remember ... It's very obscure. Canadian. It was out-of-print but it called to me. I used the phone when you were out. I was so moved, I tracked the author down and spoke to him.

TODD: Really?

GENE: I hope you don't mind.

TODD: Of course not. I'm very touched that you'd think of me.

GENE: Read some.

TODD: Now?

GENE: Yes, please. It's one of my favorite books, ever. I think I'm the only one who's ever read it, but it may gain shortly in prestige.

TODD: (*Reads*) "I live alone. There are no neighbors. There is no neighborhood ..."

GENE: That resonates, doesn't it?

TODD: (*Reading on in horror*) "Brick has vanished. Tree and sky, too. When I peer through the narrow, grimy shaft that is my window ..."

GENE: So Canadian ...

TODD: " ... I see horizon and murk ..."

GENE: Do you like it?

TODD: (*Flipping in horror through the book*) Every word ... You stole every word!

GENE: The author has such a strong voice, don't you think? Truly distinctive. It comes right out of him. He's sickly, he told me. Stooped and scarred. Unpleasant looking. He should be calling any minute. Be kind to him. (*Todd doubles over, clutches himself, lets out an almost silent cry*) I hear he's in tremendous pain. (*Gene looks at Todd. Fadeout*)

The End

Willy Holtzman

SAN ANTONIO SUNSET

Willy Holtzman

One of the hits of Manhattan's Working Theatre 1987 One-act Festival, Willy Holtzman's *San Antonio Sunset,* was singled out by Mel Gussow, theatre reviewer for the *New York Times,* as " ... a contemplative look at the blues. A talent scout (Bill Mitchelson) tracks down an unknown guitarist-singer (Dennis Green) and turns him into a recording artist. The guitarist is black, and because this is the late 1930s, he is limited to making 'race' records." Gussow also observed that the play " ... establishes the bleak, blues-like atmosphere of the period and takes a prismatic view of its characters." The play appears here in print for the first time.

San Antonio Sunset received a second production at the Bush Theatre in London. Another play, *The Last Temptation of Joe Hill,* had its premiere in the Working Theatre's One-acts '88 and is being expanded for both the Philadelphia Theatre Company and the Working Theatre. A short comedy, *White Trash,* received productions at New York's West Bank Downstairs and at the Williams Carlos Williams Center at Rutherford, New Jersey. Mr. Holtzman's full-length play, *Bovver Boys,* was first seen at the Philadelphia Theatre Company and received subsequent productions at the Berkshire Theatre Festival and the Cleveland Play House. Another play, *Inside Out,* based on work with teen mothers in the South Bronx, was awarded a production by Theatre for a New Audience at New York's New Federal Theatre.

Along with composer Skip Kennon, Mr. Holtzman has been commissioned by the Mark Taper Forum and the American Music Theatre Festival for a musical adaptation of the George Bernard Shaw play, *The Shewing Up of Blanco Posnet.* A new play, *Evenings with Mr. Eddie,* was recently optioned for film. Mr. Holtzman also has received grants from the Chelsea Theatre Crawford Foundation and the National Endowment for the Arts.

Mr. Holtzman was born in St. Louis in 1951. He attended Wesleyan University. He is a member of the New Dramatists and the Dramatists Guild. He lives in Connecticut with his wife Silvia Shepard and their two daughters, Katie and Josie.

Characters:

MR. STONE, *white, around thirty, looks older*
MR. JOHNSON, *Black, early to mid-twenties*
HOTEL CLERK, *white, middle-aged*

Setting:

A hotel, San Antonio, Texas. 1936–1938.

Scene One:

November 1936. Lights up on adjoining hotel rooms. They are run-down but orderly. Each has a window and a door to the hallway. The connecting door is closed.

The stage left room has a badly sagging single bed, a thread-bare armchair, a straightback wooden chair and a standing ashtray.

The stage right room is more or less the same, with the addition of a small wooden work table.

The Hotel Clerk enters the stage right room followed by Stone, who carries a squat, square, black case. Both men are damp with sweat. Stone keeps his coat on.

CLERK: This is it.
STONE: Eh.
CLERK: It ain't the Ritz. But the sheets are clean. And you get a passable look at the sunset from that window. Here, let me help you with that. (*He lifts the box onto the bed, is surprised at its weight. Stone looks over the room. He is tense, nervous*) Whew. What you got in there? Stones?
STONE: Hey—be careful. (*A beat*) What?
CLERK: Stones. Your name's Stone, right? It's a joke. Or it started out to be. It's heavy, is all.

STONE: Sure it is. It's a recording machine.

CLERK: Well, sure. (*Pause*) What you do with that?

STONE: Record. I'm the A and R man. And you know what else I am?

CLERK: What?

STONE: I'm the man who booked the rooms.

CLERK: Rooms. That's right. I was getting to that. (*Opens the connecting door*) There you go.

STONE: (*Steps in, looks around*) Same thing.

CLERK: One's like the next. (*Makes up bed stage right*) We try to maintain standards.

STONE: Anybody can see that.

CLERK: About that machine ...

STONE: What about it?

CLERK: I'm not clear what you mean to do.

STONE: What's it to you?

CLERK: Just a damn minute. I been desk-clerking this hotel near about five years. This is my place. What goes on here is my business. And if you all don't like it, there's plenty other hotels in San Antone.

STONE: Sure, sure. You got a job to do.

CLERK: I got a job to do. (*A beat*) A job.

STONE: It's to make a record.

CLERK: Here? No shit. Why didn't you say so? I got no quarrel with that. Goddamn. Why didn't you say so?

STONE: (*Lies in bed stage left*) I thought you knew.

CLERK: People always think you know. Out-of-the-way people. (*Pause*) You're not from around here.

STONE: New York.

CLERK: I can spot a ... New Yorker a mile off. In my line, you get a feel for these things. Front desk, you watch people. In, out. Up, down. And change. Sometimes you watch them change. Just like that. Come one way, go another. That fast. You'd be amazed.

STONE: Right. Amazing.

(*Stone sets up the equipment The recording machine is in the room stage right, the microphone stage left, the two eventually connected by a black wire. It takes a while. The Clerk continues to talk. Stone is more concerned with setting up*)

CLERK: What you say your name was?

STONE: Stone. Anything wrong?

CLERK: Just a name. (*A beat*) First time in San Antonio?

STONE: I've been through.

CLERK: Because you don't look familiar. It's not such a big town. And I'm good with faces. Did I say that?

STONE: Probably did.

CLERK: Been to the Alamo?

STONE: No. Why?

CLERK: It's what people generally do. People passing through. (*Makes up bed stage left*) About this A and R ...

STONE: Artists and Repertory. Fancy, huh?

CLERK: As a six dollar suit. (*A beat*) You always been a A and R man?

STONE: What's always? I been at it. And I'll tell you this—it's all sales. Just now south central territory.

CLERK: Little out of your way.

STONE: I made an exception.

CLERK: But you know your way around these parts.

STONE: I mighta' worked the Southwest, once.

CLERK: Got to work the territory. That's what they tell me, the ones stay here. The salesmen. (*Stone pulls the sheets off the second bed, leans it up against the wall*) The wiseguys. Like that fella we passed on the stairs. He's with Miracle-Stitch.

STONE: Don't know the line.

CLERK: Yard goods. (*A beat*) Funny—he seemed to know you.

STONE: You think so?

CLERK: Said "howdy."

STONE: Maybe he was being polite.

CLERK: You walked right past. Didn't "howdy" him back.

STONE: Maybe I was being impolite.

CLERK: Takes all kinds. (*A beat*) What you sell?

STONE: Records. Ones I make. And others. Records. The last three years or so.

CLERK: There's a living in that?

STONE: I get by. No complaints. A salesman sells. And it's not just selling. It's finding, too. The record company needs to make records. They need somebody found for that, they come to me.

CLERK: I talent scout.

STONE: "A and—" ... finding. I'm good at it. And when I'm not finding, I'm selling. Sell the records right out of the trunk of my car. No middleman. Take the merchandise straight to the customers.

CLERK: And where's that?

STONE: Wherever you find them. Barrelhouses. Jukes.

CLERK: Wait another damn minute. You don't sell them nigger records?

STONE: Records. Far as I know, money comes in one color.

CLERK: There's plenty folk hereabout don't approve that sort a thing. Call it the devil's music.

STONE: Coloreds can't get on the white labels. So give them their own damn labels. Where's the harm?

CLERK: You spread money.

STONE: Nobody's going to retire.

CLERK: You spread other things. Music. There's harm enough. That's what some people think. I'm not saying I'm one of them. (*A beat*) Jukes, barrel ... a nice man like yourself, mixin'. A man could get lost.

STONE: Good and lost.

CLERK: This fella you aim to record here. What's his name?

STONE: Johnson.

CLERK: Nigger?

STONE: Is there some problem?

CLERK: Is there a problem? A problem? (*A beat*) You one of them radicals? (*Stone laughs to himself, lights a cigarette*) It's just that a certain kind of establishment, a certain price of establishment, don't have a lot to offer. But one thing you can offer is the way it ought to be. The way it is. (*A beat*) We don't let shines upstairs.

STONE: I didn't see any signs.

CLERK: Now a salesman knows that. No niggers. No Messicans. And while I'm on the subject, I can do just fine without Jews, thank you.

STONE: Yeh?

CLERK: Most Jews. As a general rule. There are standards.

STONE: Mr. Johnson won't be staying except to sing.

CLERK: Not in my hotel, he won't.

(*Stone folds cash into the Clerk's pocket*)

STONE: He'll have a guitar. He's very shy, they tell me. I wonder could you deliver him up the back stairs?

CLERK: Whose nigger am I?

STONE: This man in town told me—he could be wrong—he told me he's seen some of your guests take local talent up to their rooms. Some of them colored girls.

CLERK: That could be. That's different.

STONE: I hope so. I do.

CLERK: I don't like it.

(*Stone counts out more money into the Clerk's hand*)

STONE: He should be here any minute.

CLERK: (*Crosses to stage right hallway door*) He don't sing Messican music? I won't have that.

STONE: He sings blues.

CLERK: And what the hell is that?

STONE: Search me.

CLERK: Look—I don't believe in coming between a man and a dollar, rightly earned. But no Messican music. Understand?

STONE: Understand.

CLERK: You just tell me one thing, Mr. Stone—what's this world coming to?

(*The Clerk exits. Stone checks the equipment, is satisfied. He removes a pint bottle of whiskey from his bag, then searches the room until he turns up two glasses, which he takes care to wipe clean. He pours himself a drink, goes over the equipment once more.*

A Black Man appears at the door, quietly waits. He carries a guitar wrapped in a blanket. He is bruised over one eye. Stone finally notices him)

STONE: Mr. Johnson? Come in, come in. I'm Stone. I saw you at the El Cantina, last night. Come in. (*Stone offers a hand in greeting. Johnson is unsure what to do. Stone grabs his hand and shakes it*) What do you say to a drink? Rye is all.

JOHNSON: Rye.

STONE: (*Pours*) Some heat. What do you think? Eighty? Eighty-five? Eighty-five in November. I can't ever remember it that way in San Antonio. In November. (*Hands Johnson a glass*) To your health, Mr. Johnson. (*They drink. Johnson sets down the glass, which draws him more into the light. Stone notices the bruise*) Rough night?

JOHNSON: Well. You know.

STONE: Bar fights. You got to pick your spot and score. Can't tap dance. You come up under that one, boy, you'da sent him into next week.

JOHNSON: You think so?

STONE: I know so.

JOHNSON: There was bail.

STONE: Forget it.

JOHNSON: You was in and out so fas—...

STONE: (*Interrupts*) We move fast, where I come from. I'm from New York. (*He shakes a cigarette out of the pack, offers it to Johnson, who declines, then smokes it himself*) You been to New York?

JOHNSON: Some.

STONE: Uhuh. I heard you been around. Hoboed. Memphis, St. Louis, Chicago, Cleveland, Pittsburgh. New York.

JOHNSON: I rode the blinds.

STONE: That's what I heard.

JOHNSON: Must be so.

STONE: I've been to those places. Not to see. To do business. (*A beat*) I heard this story. From a player in Mississippi. This was a couple years back—the story was. Him and his friend were playing a Saturday night dance outside Clarksdale, somewhere. A good house. Good players. Good times. And you come in with a harmonica. What kind of instrument is that?

JOHNSON: Mostly for them what can't play nothin' else.

STONE: So he said. So he said. But at the breaks, you picked up a guitar. Kept playing. Kept trying. So I heard.

JOHNSON: You heard it, it must be so.

STONE: And the playing—not too good?

JOHNSON: Not good at all.

STONE: I heard people started to laugh. More they laughed, worse you played, more they laughed ... till they laughed you right out of the damn place. Then you disappeared. Or so I heard.

JOHNSON: No tellin' what you liable to hear these days.

STONE: Did you disappear?

JOHNSON: No, sir. Man don't disappear from hisself.

STONE: Where'd you go?

JOHNSON: Away.

STONE: How long?

JOHNSON: You could put it into time. Uhuh. You could do that. (*A beat*) Year. Half that.

STONE: Seven months was what I heard. And there was one last thing I heard: when you came back, you could play.

JOHNSON: I learned some.

STONE: Not just play. Play like nobody ever heard.

JOHNSON: That's my no nevermind. I learned.

STONE: And what you learned ... you ever thought about making a record, Mr. Johnson?

JOHNSON: What do I need with that?

STONE: If you have a gift for music—a kind of music—why not share it?

JOHNSON: I do my sharin' at jukes and such.

STONE: Also there's money in it.

JOHNSON: For who?

STONE: For you. The record company. For me? Some change. But for you.

JOHNSON: What did you hear last night?

STONE: There was a lot of noise.

JOHNSON: Did you hear my music?

STONE: Sure, sure. Music. But what was I hearing? It's hard to say. It's not my music.

JOHNSON: No?

STONE: My taste runs more to ... other music.

JOHNSON: I hear other music. You hear mine?

STONE: What do I know about it? I know it sells. Blues? What is that? Some words, over and over.

JOHNSON: Just words.

STONE: Words. (*A beat*) Only last night ...

JOHNSON: Uhuh?

STONE: It's loud, it's drinks, it's Saturday night, it's nothing new, seen it a hundred times in a hundred places, and the people there—who the hell's listening. Only last night, they were listening ... like there was something to hear. Something.

JOHNSON: Maybe you heard.

STONE: Shit—nothing. Words. (*A beat*) The point is, and this is the point—will you make a record?

JOHNSON: (*Stands*) I best be goin'.

STONE: What? What? You're shy?

JOHNSON: Oh, I'm shy enough.

STONE: Because it won't be but you. You there. Me in this room. I'll take care of everything. There's nothing can't be taken care of. So if you're afraid ...

JOHNSON: I ain't

STONE: If you were ...

JOHNSON: I ain't. Anyway, no more than you.

STONE: Me? Afraid of what?

JOHNSON: That ain't for me to say.

STONE: This is some kind of bullshit.

JOHNSON: Uhuh. Well, no use showin' fear. I seen a hog run from a cat what didn't show fear. And I seen a rat kill a cat what showed. But you know that. (*A beat*) Man o' your sort in south Texas know that.

STONE: My sort?

JOHNSON: Just a man. (*A beat*) Trying to be a man.

(*Stone walks to the microphone*)

STONE: There's nothing to it. You sit down and sing into this. When you're done, they get the record, you get the money.

JOHNSON: And what you get?

STONE: We can do this. We can. You and me.

JOHNSON: What you get?

STONE: Jesus. I got to be out of my mind. The heat. The goddamn fucking heat. And you dicking me around. Pissing up my leg, when we could be doing business.

JOHNSON: This about business?

STONE: Nothing more.

JOHNSON: You're a businessman—that's plain to see.

STONE: Now you're talking.

JOHNSON: One of us talkin'.

STONE: I coulda' left you in there. You coulda' got hurt.

JOHNSON: What you know 'bout a nigger's hurt? (*A beat*) You wanna get inside. Walk 'round.

(*They are in separate rooms*)

STONE: You're crazy. You know that?

JOHNSON: I know that. 'Cause there's enough hurt in me to plain swallow a man up. A man can go all the way crazy with that. You got to push it down. Throw you in jail. Push it down. Send you up the back stairs. Push it down. Play the nigger to the man. Push it down. Push it down, till you got to let some out. And maybe the rest just pour out on its own. Then, there you are. Soul and all, in plain sight. Down the road. On the corner. In a room. On a record.

STONE: Do you make the record or not? I'm telling you, there's money in it.

JOHNSON: Live by the nickel, die by the dime. I got better ways.

STONE: All I want is for you to put your music on a record.

JOHNSON: Could be that's the way.

STONE: (*Agitated*) This whole business ... I shouldn't have come here, you want to know the truth. Texas ... at all. It's poison to me. What I put on the line to cross over. I don't have all night. I shouldn't be here. Any place but here. (*Joins Johnson stage right*) And you, back and forth. I mean, what the hell is this? WHAT IS THIS?

JOHNSON: What's this?! (*Johnson balls up his fist, waves it under Stone's chin. Stone is ready to fight*) I said, what's this?

STONE: A fist, goddamnit.

JOHNSON: And what come out of yours?

STONE: You might find out!

(*Johnson slowly unballs his fist, smiles*)

JOHNSON: Well, now. So happens notes come out of mine. Music. And what's a man to do? What's a man to do? (*Johnson carefully unwraps his guitar, pulls a chair to the microphone stage left, sits*) So, Mr. Stone. Show me the way. I been 'xpectin' you for some time.

(*Johnson faces the corner, the microphone, his back to the room. Stone stands stage right, stares a moment, turns on the recording machine*)

STONE: Let's go.

(*Lights fade. A few sliding chords on the guitar, then ...*)

JOHNSON: (*Singing*)

I GOT TO KEEP MOVIN', GOT TO KEEP MOVIN',

BLUES FALLIN' DOWN LIKE HAIL (BLUES FALLIN' DOWN LIKE HAIL).

HMMM, BLUES FALLIN' DOWN LIKE HAIL.

AND THE DAY KEEPS ON MONDAY, WITH A HELLHOUND ON MY TRAIL (HELLBOUND ON MY TRAIL, HELLHOUND ON MY TRAIL).

(*Lights fade quickly to black*)

Scene Two:

June 1937. Lights up on the hotel rooms. Johnson sits stage left, drinks from a pint bottle, and sings a cappella.

JOHNSON:
THE LAST FAIR DEAL GOIN' DOWN,
THE LAST FAIR DEAL GOIN' DOWN,
THE LAST FAIR DEAL GOIN' DOWN GOOD LORD,
IT'S THE LAST FAIR DEAL GOIN' DOWN.
(*As Johnson continues into the next verse, Stone enters from the hallway, stage right, carrying a paper bag with two Coca-Colas. He stops, listens to Johnson, smiles. Johnson eventually notices Stone, stops singing. They laugh, shake hands*) Have mercy.
STONE: What is it, a half a year? Half a year. Record got made. And here you are. You're here.
JOHNSON: Seven months. Yessir. Seven months. A record. And I ain't died once.
STONE: Don't start that again.
(*They laugh*)
JOHNSON: Some heat we're havin', Mr. Stone.
STONE: What do you think? A hundred? A hundred, easy.
JOHNSON: They's folk died in their beds. That's a special kind o' heat. Cooks up out of the ground, and pulls you down. Like gravity. The heat of hell is pure gravity. It's damn hot.
STONE: That's Texas for you. The sun comes out, there's no getting away. It finds you. (*A beat*) Is it hot where you come from?
JOHNSON: Hazelhurst, Mississippi. Copiah County. 'Bout eighty miles down the Pearl from Jackson.
STONE: I know the general area. Delta.
JOHNSON: Prime Delta country. Earth so rich, so black, no tellin' what's liable to sprout. (*Johnson offers a drink to Stone, who passes. Johnson drinks*) A fella told me once—don't know it for myself—told me delta is a letter in the Greek alphabet. Shaped like a triangle.
STONE: I might've heard that.

JOHNSON: Funny thing. You take a triangle and tip it on its end, you got something looks like a part of a lady. Part you is likely to sing 'bout when t'ain't none handy. Song says: Blues ain't nothin' but a good woman on your mind.

STONE: I had my share of women.

JOHNSON: Then more 'n likely you had your share o' blues. (*A beat*) And how is our "blues" record doin'?

(*Stone pulls a "78" from his bag*)

STONE: What do you think?

JOHNSON: Don't look like much.

STONE: Not to look at. But to play?

(*Stone crosses stage right, puts the record on the turntable. "Me and the Devil Blues" plays. This disturbs Johnson. He crosses, takes the record off*)

JOHNSON: And most anybody can. Anybody's got the money, the machine—they can have the music. But the man makes the music? Where he at?

(*Johnson crosses back stage left, holding the record. Stone follows*)

STONE: You want to know how the record's doing. Of course you do. You have a right to know. How's it doing—it's hard to say. The music part—there's nothing to apologize for there.

JOHNSON: And the business part?

STONE: They moved. Don't get me wrong. The records moved.

JOHNSON: But no matter how many get sold, what I get ...

STONE: I didn't make it that way. Race labels. They don't pay a royalty. It's not like the majors, the white labels. I didn't make it that way. But it's the music matters. And there's resistance, you know. Here and there. (*A beat*) There's some call it the devil's music.

JOHNSON: And you?

STONE: I call it a payday. Past that? I don't know. The blues.

JOHNSON: And who's blues that?

STONE: Whoever goes the price. Whoever pays.

JOHNSON: Oh, yes. Pay, Mr. Stone.

STONE: It adds up. Dollars.

JOHNSON: Dues. This the blues we talkin'.

STONE: And a white man can't know nothing about that.

JOHNSON: Man's got to find his own. On his own. Because, you see, blues is a let out. And what you don't let out, you take out. Which is why white folks is got to have niggers.

STONE: You just about got it all figured out, don't you, Mr. Johnson?

JOHNSON: Mr. Stone—you believe there's a part of ever' man that's hid? Hid from that man?

STONE: Like what?

JOHNSON: Could be soul. Could be God. Could be Satan. Call it what you like.

STONE: What do you call it?

JOHNSON: Music.

STONE: Music?

JOHNSON: Why not? It's everyplace. They say if you tilt your head just so, you can even hear the planets sing. Do you believe it?

STONE: What are you getting at?

JOHNSON: Seems to me, more you run from things, more they chase you. More you hide, more things show.

STONE: You think you know something about me? You got something to say? Say it.

JOHNSON: Ain't for me to say. But the damnedest things can pull a man out o' himself. Pull the music out. The oppositest damned things. Pull a man clean inside out. And ain't it a bitch. A son of a bitch.

STONE: You're drunk.

JOHNSON: Might could be. But there it is. For you to see. (*Tosses record to the floor*)

STONE: What do you see?

JOHNSON: Just a man in a room. A man with a guitar, a bottle, and some hoodoo runnin' 'round his brain. (*A beat*) We met before.

STONE: Last November.

JOHNSON: Before that.

STONE: We've both been around.

JOHNSON: Round and round.

STONE: I'm here. Now. And I'm a busy man.

JOHNSON: And here I am, talkin' triangles and souls and such. Talkin' shit. 'Cause you a busy man. A business man.

Do business with niggers. Hidin' out in the dark. And all you want from me ... got ... want more of, is for me to come out into the light. And what you lookin' for?

STONE: I'm not looking. I'm not looking for shit. Put two dollars together. And two more to that. And make the dollars add up to a day. A day to a week to a month to a year. And more than that, I do not know. Do not want to know. (*A beat*) I was in Philadelphia. No place to be. A place to do. Business. I do my business, and I'm looking at the road. The road—I don't have to tell you—it gets to where it's looking back. And about this time you get thirsty. Find a joint. Rough joint? Who gives a shit? The rougher the better. You only want a few. And, fuck it, you close the place. (*A beat*)

And the weather ... is ... hot. Not Texas hot, but hot enough. The type of weather where dogs fall over on the street; the neighbor comes at you with a bread knife. What I mean to say is—no buck-a-throw sweatbox fleabag tonight. No, sir. Got to be moving. Get the air running past you. Push the poison through the pores. Moving ... to ... music. But the radio, weather like that ... the radio finds things ... things you didn't set out to find. (*A beat*)

And that night, the radio ... how do you figure? ... the radio waves had to be jumping like a june bug ... because, because I'm in the car, on the road, and I'm doing the knobs, looking for my music. Something out of New York. And Jesus Christ, next thing I know, I'm listening to a station in Mississippi, a place so small, I never heard, and I've been to the smallest ... and, what am I hearing? What am I hearing? Because my hands on the damn knob ... and what's coming out ... my hand just falls away ... because the music coming out, it's washing over me like the hot night air. I'm ... surrounded ... filled with it. (*A beat*)

And what comes at me ... right at me ... right between the goddamn eyes is ... slide guitar. Ride hard on the high notes. Tickle the lows with the thumb. And the voice ... like nothing I ever heard before ... like somebody big had ahold of him. (*A beat*)

Like somebody big had a hold of you. (*A beat*)

What was I thinking? I never should've come back. What was I thinking? Crossing over.

JOHNSON: You got what you come for. (*Holds up record*) Get some more. (*Stone takes record, smashes it. Johnson holds up another record*) And more. (*Again*) And more. And more, till there ain't no more left in me. Then go find you the next boy. There's always the next boy. (*A beat*) But that's future things. Businessman's got to live in the present. So let's get to work.

STONE: No records, Mr. Johnson. No more records. (*Decides to pack up*)

JOHNSON: It's a little late for that, Mr. Stone.

STONE: I'm through with it. You want to stay, that's your business. I don't want any part of it.

JOHNSON: I do believe you done played your part already. Now let's have some music.

(*Johnson plays a few notes on the guitar. Stone covers the strings with his hand*)

STONE: Damn you. Damn you. Goddamn you. It's what they say. What they all say. What the clerk said: it's the devil's music.

JOHNSON: (*Pulls free of Stone*) Well, sir. I give you more credit than to think that. But then, what are you gonna think? Just another dumb nigger, ain't got but a child's mind. (*Blacking up ...*) "Hep me. Hep me. Do hep me, Lawd. Da Debil's after me. Shootin' dem flames. Hep me. Hep m—... "

STONE: Look—you misunderstood me ...

JOHNSON: We gonna talk white now? I can do that, too.

STONE: I'm through talking.

JOHNSON: Then maybe you just better listen. 'Cause maybe we just got something to tell each other. Each the other. About the devil.

STONE: I thought you said ...

JOHNSON: I know what I said. But say there is a devil. And he told me not to play into the record.

STONE: That doesn't make sense.

JOHNSON: Do if you the devil. See, the devil like to keep us down. Makes us think this life is all there is. And mostly we go on thinkin' just that. But ever' once in a while, somebody dig down into that part o' hisself where the devil can't get. The music part. That fill the devil with envy. That make the devil unhappy. And when he unhappy, he the unhappiest son of a bitch in creation. (*A beat*) It's blackness, Mr. Stone.

STONE: What?

JOHNSON: It's all that blackness, ain't it? Oh, the devil, he's a craft one. Get folks to thinkin' soul's a white thing, all air and alabaster. But we know better, you and me. We know that's how the devil holds on to folks—get them to thinkin' they movin' closer to heaven, when all they doin' is stayin' bodily longer. Get folks to lookin' up find God, when all the time God's right here under foot. (*Stomps the floor*)

But you and me, Mr. Stone, we know better. It's all that blackness. All my days, been told it's a' ugly thing, a whippin' thing, a hatin' thing, a hangin' thing, till it sends you inside yourself. Deep inside. And what you find, well, black ain't the color o' hate. Black the color of the soul. You, me, ever'body. You, Mr. Stone, it's a black piece. Hid. Hid real good. But not so good you didn't find it. And find it again. First bad. Then good. And, good Lord, with me, it's a little closer to the surface. The skin itself. All that blackness. Sometimes think if I was to prick my finger, soul'd come runnin' out the hole, so close it's to the surface. (*Pause*)

All that blackness. The soul itself. And it passes out, don't need no body no more, it don't float up like a damn balloon. Hell no—that's the devil's foolery. No sir. The soul runs into the earth. The black earth. 'Cause that's where God is. That's where heaven is. Why there's more heaven in one lump of mud than in a mile of sky. But we know that, you and me.

STONE: You don't know me. You don't know the first thing about me.

JOHNSON: First and last. And like I said, I been 'xpectin' you.

STONE: You're going to sing into the record.

JOHNSON: Don't see as I got much choice.

STONE: And after?

JOHNSON: Got to take what comes.

STONE: Will I see you again?

JOHNSON: There's the music.

STONE: After the music?

JOHNSON: We maybe met once before. World's not such a big place. Wouldn't be a bit surprised we meet again.

(*Johnson sits in front of the microphone, tunes his guitar. Stone walks to the next room, switches on the machine. Lights fade as Johnson sings*)
AND THE BLUES GRABBED MAMMA CHILD,
TORE IT ALL UPSIDE DOWN,
BLUES GRABBED MAMMA CHILD,
AND THEY TORE ME ALL UPSIDE DOWN.
TRAVEL ON, POOR BOB, JUST CAN'T TURN YOU 'ROUND.
(*Lights fade to black*)

Scene Three:

August 1938. The rooms as at rise. Furniture in place, no recording equipment. It is late afternoon, almost evening. Stone enters stage right, crosses stage left, stares out a window. The Clerk enters stage right.

STONE: He's not here.

CLERK: Told you I didn't see him. I don't miss much.

STONE: Thought he'd be here. (*A beat*) That's some sunset. Something in the air.

CLERK: S'posed to be a chill tonight.

STONE: It's funny, isn't it?

CLERK: Might be. If I knew what the damn hell you was talkin' about.

STONE: You take two men. Opposite ends of the earth. And they could have something to say to each other.

CLERK: You mean you? Him?

STONE: Well.

CLERK: That ain't funny. That's laughable.

STONE: Yeh? While you're laughing—I'm taking Mr. Johnson back to New York City with me. Tonight.

CLERK: That his idea?

STONE: No. He doesn't even know, yet. But when I lay it out for him ...

CLERK: You ain't got enough his sort up yonder?

STONE: Could be he's one of a kind.

CLERK: You think that?

STONE: Never mind what I think. There's another man. A man with money. I mean money. He thinks that. (*Emphatically*) And he wants Mr. Johnson to sing at Carnegie Hall.

CLERK: Like where C'ruso sung? That Carnegie Hall?

STONE: You know another?

CLERK: You are bullshittin' me.

STONE: This is me you're talking to.

CLERK: Yeh—we're practically blood relations. (*Disbelief*) Carnegie Hall? (*Stone nods*) Shit. If that ain't New York.

STONE: This is where we start—me and Mr. Johnson. And it started with this. (*Stone takes a "78" from his case, holds it up*)

CLERK: This what all the damn fuss's over?

STONE: (*Offers the "78" to the Clerk*) Go ahead. It's yours.

CLERK: (*Takes it*) You're too generous.

STONE: That's me.

CLERK: I'll give it a listen, sometime. But I don't expect to hear nothin'.

STONE: You might surprise yourself.

CLERK: I might grow titties, too.

STONE: You ever had water from a deep spring? The sort that runs down maybe miles?

CLERK: Course.

STONE: How'd it taste?

CLERK: Clear, cool. Tad bitter.

STONE: Like it's been hid deep a long time?

CLERK: Damned silly.

STONE: No, no. That's how Mr. Johnson's music came to me. There I was in my damn car. In goddamn Philadelphia. And it came ... at me ... out of nowhere ... struck me. I can't get it out of my ears. It stays. Stuck.

CLERK: There's no accounting for taste.

STONE: (*Removes a liquor bottle from the case*) Hey—buy you a drink.

CLERK: I don't know. (*A beat*) What the hell? It's a slow day. (*The Clerk joins him stage left. Stone pours two drinks*) What do we drink to?

STONE: People have to drink to something. Why can't you drink against?

CLERK: Okay. What do we drink against?

STONE: Texas.

CLERK: That don't seem fair.

STONE: You think of something.

CLERK: New York?

STONE: Fair enough. (*They raise their glasses*) Fuck Texas.

CLERK: And fuck New York.

(*They drink*)

STONE: How's that?

CLERK: Satisfying. I may never drink to anything ever again. (*Walks the room, looks into the adjoining room*) It can get on your mind.

STONE: Yeh?

CLERK: Downstairs, at the desk. What goes on upstairs— that can get on your mind.

STONE: The women of the town?

CLERK: There's them. Only ain't much mystery there. But the little guy rolls in with a big bag full of samples. The couple rolls in no bags at all. Then there's the gal takes a room on the top floor, gets up in her best duds, and that first step is a lulu, honeychild. Seems I seen it all. And what I ain't seen, I can pretty well guess at. Fill in. But here ... these rooms ... and here, believe me, buddy boy, it got on my mind good. And I guessed. And I ain't filled in shit. As to what goes on.

STONE: It's records.

CLERK: That takes up all the time?

STONE: More than you think.

CLERK: But not every minute?

STONE: No.

CLERK: And those spare minutes?

STONE: You pass the time. Talk.

CLERK: About what?

STONE: You find things.

CLERK: So what you do up here, when, you know, it ain't business ... it's ...

STONE: Talk. Stories.

CLERK: How's that?

STONE: One of you tells something. One, then the other. And what's told—maybe it happened. Maybe it never did. Maybe it doesn't much matter. Because there can be truth in a story, whether it's true or not.

CLERK: Ever feel like you been on the road too long?

STONE: Well, that's another story, isn't it. (*Stone tosses him the bottle. The Clerk pours them both another drink*)

CLERK: You hear stories all the time in my line of work. Most ain't worth the hearing. A few stay with you. (*A beat*) Like this yard goods man. Southwest territory. Through time to time. Talk you straight to sleep in no time at all. You know, it occurs to me he was here your very first time. That guy in the hallway. Miracle-Stitch? (*No response*) Anyways, he was through again just last week. And he recalled this story—held my attention. Seems he was down in Corpus Christi three, four years back. And he come across this one salesman. From up north.

STONE: North Texas?

CLERK: Norther than that. Thought he said New York, but I could be mistaken. Anyway, this fella—the fella in the story— was in Corpus selling one thing or another. Nice enough, but kinda kept to himself. Mind his own business.

STONE: Nothing wrong with that.

CLERK: No. But then, folks don't always leave you to yourself. See, this fella had finished a day's work. And he was for a drink before he put back on the road. (*A beat*) Did I say his name?

STONE: No.

CLERK: Well, he was having this drink ...

STONE: Minding his own business?

CLERK: Minding his own business. Could be he stayed for another drink. Stayed longer than he meant. 'Cause in come these oil riggers to get drunk. I mean, they was most likely mostway drunk when they come in. A few months in the west Texas oil fields and, well, you know ... Texans just learn to steer clear of riggers on a drunk.

STONE: And the salesman?

CLERK: Like I said, he wasn't from around here. Anyway, one of the riggers got it into his head this fella is a Jew. And the three of them—there were three riggers, according to the man from Corpus—the three of them get going about Jews and all.

STONE: Jews?

CLERK: Well, you know, they ain't exactly given over to niceties. They mighta said "kikes." Kikes. I'm only guessing. But one thing I do know—they got to riding this salesman fella pretty good.

STONE: Why didn't he just walk away?

CLERK: Reckon he tried. They wouldn't have it. Havin' too much fun.

STONE: What happened?

CLERK: Eventually ... there was words. I mean, a Texan woulda' knowed better. Maybe in New York words don't count for much.

STONE: Talk is cheap all over.

CLERK: Who'm I to say? (*A beat*) But as I understand it, this salesman eventually said the wrong word, and the riggers did him over.

STONE: It was a bar fight?

CLERK: A stretch more than that. See, they dragged him out back.

STONE: Nobody tried to stop them?

CLERK: I told you. They was riggers. And he was a Jew. (*A beat*) They've got him behind the place. Two of the riggers hold him. The third takes out his jackknife and carves him up, some.

STONE: Kills him?

CLERK: Well, no. (*A beat*) Just marks him, somehow. Marks him good.

STONE: Marks him how?

CLERK: The yard goods man was not certain. (*Looks at Stone*) He believes it was recognizable. Lasting.

STONE: That was all?

CLERK: You'da' thought so. You see, the riggers have their sport, and they let this fella up. Mind you, he's not a big man. (*Looks Stone up and down*) Head shorter than the shortest of 'em. Just the same, he hauls off and hits this one boy a shot— the one done the carvin'—hits him! Smack in the face. Smack! (*Pounds his fist into his palm*) Broke the sum'bitch's neck. (*A beat*) Who'da' figured it? A short-ass Jew salesman from New York? Hit like that? How would you figure it?

STONE: I'd say he had to swing from real deep. (*A beat*) What became of him?

CLERK: That's just it. Nobody knows. (*A beat*) Did I mention his name?

STONE: You did not.

CLERK: Rothstein. Goldstein. Like that. A Jew name. The man from Corpus was not good with names. Some *stein*—that much he remembered. Stein. (*A beat*) Names. It can get confusing. Like the telegram come this morning. (*Removes a telegram from his hip pocket*) From the record company. (*Stone reaches for it, the Clerk pulls it away*) But ain't to your name. Don't say nothin' 'bout no "Stone" anywhere on it. And the name on it—who could that be?

(*The Clerk holds the telegram in front of Stone's face. Stone stares a moment, then reaches for it. The Clerk does not pull away. Stone reads, slowly lowers the telegram*)

STONE: He's dead.

CLERK: The little nigger?

STONE: Mr. Johnson is dead.

CLERK: Well, I'll be. Who did it?

STONE: They're not sure. It was over in Three Forks, Mississippi. At a juke.

CLERK: If that ain't niggers for you. Boy gets himself killed, and nobody even knows how.

STONE: What's it matter, who?

CLERK: I don't know. Just seems somebody'd know. Look, I had nothin' against the boy. Can't say as I heard anything in his music. But that's no reason to want him dead. (*A beat*) Too bad. Too bad, for you.

STONE: Yeh. Too bad for me.

CLERK: I wonder—where do you go from here?

STONE: That depends. (*Crosses to Clerk, face to face*) You never finished your story. The salesman—was he ever found?

CLERK: You know, I ain't positively sure. I mean, that's where the story ends.

STONE: Is it ended?

CLERK: Like I said—a man in my line of work hears a lot of stories. It's hard to keep 'em straight for long. After a time, they all start to come together.

(*Stone crosses to the window, stares out at the fading glow of a sunset. The Clerk crosses to the stage right door, opens it, turns back*)

CLERK: What do you think it was?

STONE: What?

CLERK: What do you think it was killed him?

STONE: You know, it's just about gone, the sun. Just about sunk out of sight. After the sunset? Night. Black night. When the sun sets one place, it rises another. That's how it goes. So they say. But you can't know firsthand for certain. A man can't be two places at once. (*Pause*) What do I think took Mr. Johnson? Blackness.

CLERK: I guess that about says it ... Mr. Stone.

STONE: That about says it.

(*The Clerk exits. Stone sees that he has forgotten the record, crosses to it, then to the hall door. But rather than call out, he turns back to the stage right room, sits on the bed, and looks down at the record. Lights slowly fade as a recording plays*)

JOHNSON: (*On record*)

I WENT TO THE CROSSROADS, FELL DOWN ON MY KNEES,

I WENT TO THE CROSSROADS, FELL DOWN ON MY KNEES,

ASKED THE LORD ABOVE FOR MERCY,

SAY BOY, IF YOU PLEASE.

(*The lights fade to black*)

The End

Ernest A. Joselovitz

THERE IS NO JOHN GARFIELD

Ernest A. Joselovitz

The publication of *There Is No John Garfield* marks the second appearance of Ernest A. Joselovitz's work in the *Best Short Plays* series. The 1976 edition carried his play, *Sammi*, which then editor Stanley Richard described as "an eloquent and inventive memory play, in which 'character transformation' is imaginatively and affectingly employed to recreate a man's life at several crucial stages." *There Is No John Garfield*, published here for the first time, has received a number of productions including one by the West Coast Ensemble at the Playbill Theatre in Hollywood, California. In reviewing the Hollywood production, Polly Warfield observes that the play, as "directed by Larry Harpel, is a gently comedic non-romance about two non-beautiful people, a warmly tender, clear-eyed and intimate glimpse into ordinary lonely lives. ... Margo and Edgar's very imperfections make them endearing." The play premiered at the American Line Theatre in New York City and was further developed at the Silver Spring Stage in Maryland and at the Washington Smallbeer Theatre Company.

Ernest A. Joselovitz attended the University of California, where he earned a B.A. degree in English, and the University of Minnesota, where he received a Master of Fine Arts in Playwriting. A member of the Phi Beta Kappa honor society, he was awarded a Sam Shubert Foundation Playwriting Fellowship (1965–66) and a John Golden Traveling Fellowship from the Yale School of Drama (1966). In 1971 he also was awarded the Starr Playwriting Prize from the University of California.

In addition to *There Is No John Garfield* and *Sammi*, his other published and/or produced plays include: *Hagar's Children*, *Righting*, *Cry Uncle*, *Parable*, *Woodie Guthrie*, *California Travelin'*, *The Inheritance*, *Nicky and the Theatre for a New World*, *Splendid Rebels*, and *Flesh Eaters*.

Mr. Joselovitz's two most recent one-act plays, *Romance* and *The Day I Met William Inge*, are under option to the Philadelphia New Plays Festival Theatre. His most recent full-length play was recently given staged readings at Arena Stage in Washington, D.C., and the Jewish Repertory Theatre in New York City. His full-length play *Jessie's Land* won the first

Weissberger Best Plays Award as judged by three prominent New York City critics after its production at the American Jewish Theatre.

The playwright is the recipient of two grants from the National Endowment for the Arts, and he has received four Individual Writer grants from the D.C. Commission on the Arts (the most recent in 1987–88), three of their Artist-in-Education grants, and their first annual Larry Neal Writers Award (1984).

Mr. Joselovitz also founded and is currently Administrator/ Dramaturg for the Playwrights' Unit, a non-profit organization which involves about seventy Washington, D.C., area playwrights in developmental activities. Two members of his group have had their plays published in *Best Short Plays*: Bruce Bonafede with *Advice to the Players* in the 1986 edition, and Deborah Pryor with *The Love Talker* in the 1988 edition. Additionally, Mr. Joselovitz teaches playwriting in Georgetown University's Continuing Education program.

Characters:

MARGO FELD
EDGAR SCHUSTER

Time:

The present.

Setting:

Washington, D.C.
While the action of this play takes place in three locations, the suggestion is made for the single realistic set to be that of Margo Feld's efficiency apartment living room/ bedroom, with the simplest props and lighting to indicate the locations of other scenes.

Scene One:

Downstage, a red padded bench, as if in a movie lobby. Behind it, a movie poster of the original 1946, The Postman Always Rings Twice. *On this bench sits Margo Feld. Margo is considered "cute" because she exhibits an overabundant roundness, the result of constantly frustrated diets. She is eating from a box of buttered popcorn as she reads a hardcover novel. She frequently raises her eyes to survey the lobby.*

Entering stage right, Edgar Schuster. Edgar wears a dark suit and tie. He's too short and prematurely balding to be thought handsome. Margo sees him: a moment's recognition before she returns with special intensity to her book. He scans the lobby; he checks his watch; he sees the one bench, sits on the edge opposite Margo, his eyes on the lobby.

MARGO: Edgar.

EDGAR: (*Turning to her*) Huh?

MARGO: Margo. Feld. We met at the film club.

EDGAR: Film club ... Oh, right, Feld.

MARGO: The last two weeks—we ushered together.

EDGAR: That's right, we did.

(*An empty moment; she returns to her book. He turns back to checking his watch, then the lobby*)

MARGO: It's a way of being helpful, I think. Ushering. It's still such a small group; still—you know—personal. (*She waits for a reply*)

EDGAR: (*Shrugging*) It saves the cost of a ticket. (*Pause*) Actually, I have hopes of learning to work the projector, when they get to know who I am.

MARGO: They will, I'm sure of it, as soon as they know you ... Edgar. (*He nods. Silence. Then, showing her book*) Updike. (*Shrugging*) Book-of-the-Month. I'm waiting for something to happen. Nothing ever seems to happen to these people. (*Pause; offering it*) Popcorn? (*He shakes his head*) You like forties films.

EDGAR: Do you have the time?

MARGO: (*She glances at his watch, before pointing*) The clock's over there.

(*He walks to stage right, looks to his side*)

EDGAR: (*Resetting and rewinding his watch*) I keep winding it. I'm all thumbs with watches. They break down on me. Like this one's too slow. (*Instead of returning to his seat, he decides to remain standing*) It's late.

MARGO: Four more minutes.

EDGAR: I'm waiting for some friends.

MARGO: Me too. (*An empty moment*) John Garfield's my favorite. This is one of his greatest hits.

EDGAR: Lana Turner's my ... her performance was very good.

MARGO: She's beautiful. I mean, *The Postman Always Rings Twice*—one chance on the big screen and that's all. I wouldn't miss it for the life of me.

EDGAR: (*Checking his watch*) Three more minutes. If you spot a man and a woman—he's tall, with dark curly hair, an ugly scar over his right eyebrow; she has long blonde hair ...

MARGO: And she's thin and has one continual eyebrow ...

EDGAR: Sally.

MARGO: And Phil?

EDGAR: Cafritz.

MARGO: Right.

EDGAR: I know him from school.

MARGO: I know her from work.

EDGAR: And the film club.

MARGO: Those two times, she asked me to usher.

EDGAR: Me too. (*After pause*) But they didn't tell me there'd be another person here.

MARGO: Me neither. Look, I'm really surprised; believe me, I had no idea. Maybe they just forgot to say.

EDGAR: No. I specifically told them ...

(*Silence*)

MARGO: Two minutes. What if they're late?

EDGAR: I bought my ticket. There's no refund.

MARGO: Me too. Garfield's my favorite. They'll get here, I'm sure of it.

EDGAR: Maybe something has happened to them.

MARGO: They'd have called one of us, if they needed.

EDGAR: Well, what could happen?

MARGO: Nothing, I guess; nothing ever happens.

EDGAR: They should have mentioned ... I mean, none of this is like them.

MARGO: They normally know just what they're doing.

EDGAR: That's right. (*Silence*) We can't just go in without them.

MARGO: No. Of course not. (*Pause*) I can hear the credits starting.

EDGAR: You go in; I'll stay here and wait.

MARGO: I couldn't do that to you. We could sit on the aisle, in the back row. That way, we'd be sure to see them when they come in.

EDGAR: I really hadn't planned ...

MARGO: (*Hearing the movie, rises*) It's *him*.

EDGAR: One of us on each side of the aisle, that should do it.

MARGO: You mean, with an aisle between us?

EDGAR: Sure. Just until they get here.

MARGO: *If* they get here. (*Pause*) I really have to see that movie. That's what counts, I suppose.

EDGAR: (*As they exit*) A two dollar investment, after all.

MARGO: You'd think they would have the common courtesy to tell a friend, a best friend.

EDGAR: (*Offstage*) Ex-best friend.

MARGO: (*Offstage*) What do they think they're doing? (*Long pause*) Take some popcorn.

(*Lights fade out*)

Scene Two:

Spotlight—Edgar strides across the darkened stage with a telephone in hand.

EDGAR: Phil? You're still there—yeh—Correcting papers for Prof Graham?—yeh. (*Pause*) "Oh, how are you Ed"—I'm mad, that's how! I get invited to a Lana Turner movie, I'm waiting there, a person shows up—not you, not Sally—just What's-Her-Face Feld shows up. (*Pause*) No, sure, so you blind date me with this Margo person ... (*Pause*) Bad? ... Phil, I got her to sit in the back row, on the other side of the aisle, to wait for you! Fellow grad, my best friend, I never expected ... It was your wife, right ... who put you up to this. Of course it was her, Phil, you don't need to tell me, I should have known. She meant well, sure—in your position how can you say different? Well, you can tell Sally for me: it won't work, Sally! (*Pause*) She did? (*Short pause*) Margo Feld called just to say that? O.K., you're sorry, I accept. It's just I can do my own dating ... O.K.? ... Sally has no need. So this Feld woman, I'm just curious, what else did she say?

(*Spotlight, further upstage and center. Margo sits on a bed beside which is an endtable with pastel telephone. The receiver is already to her ear*)

MARGO: Sally? (*Short pause*) You're home. Yes, it's Margo, that former best friend you embarrassed last night.

Yes, embarrassed. I'm invited to a Garfield movie, which you know I can't resist—I'm there, John Garfield's there, and Edgar What's-His-Name.

EDGAR: You're making all this up.

"Usher this week at the film club," "usher next week," "do a service"—funny the same fella happens to always be assigned with me.

It wasn't me, it was the movie ... or the candy bar; she liked the candy bar I split with her, a lot.

I can find my own men, Sally. I don't need donations. (*Short pause*) Don't "I'm sorry" me, tell it to poor Edgar.

(*He shrugs*) Well, yes, I walked her home. It was late, after all, I had to.

It was Phil's idea, wasn't it. Of course as a wife you can't admit it. But I know a man thinks like that: Put two people together in a dark place ...

O.K., so she's an interesting person, sure, about films and books and that. She's also fat.

"She's cute" maybe, got "personality," sure, under a dozen pounds of zoftig. Not that I'm a prize package myself—isn't that what you were thinking? The Lana Turners are not standing in line for a homely part-time grad student with temp typing jobs and loads of self-pity. Do him a favor, you were thinking, unload this cute personality on him!

He did? Edgar actually called and said that? Well he was ... nice. The movie's what he liked. You know and I know, a movie's always better when you're sitting ... nearby somebody.

No, Phil, I'm not mad at you; I'm mad at *me*. Go back to correcting your papers, not your friends. Goodbye.

You really think so? He did seem to appreciate my popcorn, that I shared with him.

(*Edgar has stopped pacing downstage right. He stares down at the telephone, lifts the receiver to his ear, is about to dial, and stops.*

He slowly places the re- ceiver back, only to lift it abruptly and dial)

You're making all that up.

Well, he did split a Snickers bar with me. I mean, I for one liked his company.

Information? Yes, Feld, Margo. F-E-L-D as in "drowning." Northwest, I guess, somewhere on 17th.

He walked me home, sure.
Very polite about it, not one forward move. Men have always
been awfully polite with me.

... 3472. Thank you.

He talked, that's what, about
the film and his lit classes.
Sally, he's nearly bald. Looks
aren't everything, sure, well his
conversation was so-so and
he's closer to welfare than rich.
(*Pause*) I'm not holding out for
some impossible ideal! Not forever. I'm almost thirty, after all.
I'll never be your gorgeous type.
I'll never be noticed in that way
by some cute stud, after all.
(*Pause*) Schuster with a "c"?
Did you hear me ask for his last
name? And ... (*Scribbling it
down*) telephone number? I'm
not interested, Sally; goodbye,
Sally.

(*Margo hangs up. Edgar is pacing again. They're both staring at their phones. He stops. He rapidly dials again. Her
phone rings once, a mere moment's dazed hesitation, before
she picks it up*)

MARGO: Yes? (*But at that, he fearfully hangs up, very
quietly*) Hello? (*Pause*) Anybody? (*It's she who dials now.
His phone rings, startling him: one, two—but he's afraid it
might be her—three, four ... She lowers her phone. The ringing
stops. For some moments, neither moves. As she rises to exit,
he takes a deep breath and dials once again. Her phone rings.
She reappears on the run, under the spotlight, only to interrupt
her reaching for the phone: it rings a second time, third ...
before she picks it up with an impressive casualness*) Yes?

EDGAR: Margo?

MARGO: Yes.

EDGAR: Edgar, you know, Schuster.

MARGO: Yes. (*Silence*) You called about something? Last night, I mean, thanks for walking me all the way home.

EDGAR: We could have split a taxi, I suppose.

MARGO: No, not at all; I could use the exercise.

EDGAR: Right. Anyway, the whole mix-up was Phil and Sally's fault.

MARGO: I know. Still, it wasn't a total loss: the movie was good.

EDGAR: Right. When he's there for the first time and that lipstick case rolls across the floor and Lana Turner's there—doorway, medium shot—and he sees her—close-up, music rises—and she's stiff and snooty because she's really afraid but drawn to him in a sexual way, wearing those white shorts and high heels and that white turban, and she's blonde and slim ...

MARGO: He made her interest easy to believe, in a sexual way, skinny as she was. Like a little boy, that's him, strong and tough outside but underneath he's shy, and with that beautiful face and that curly hair ...

(*Silence*)

EDGAR: Well, I just thought I'd call.

MARGO: Sure. There doesn't need to be any particular reason to telephone a person.

EDGAR: About last night, I suppose you told off Phil.

MARGO: No, I ... Didn't you call up Sally?

EDGAR: Well, no.

EDGAR/MARGO: (*Simultaneously*) He/She told me ...

EDGAR: Damn!

MARGO: Edgar? Don't hang up.

EDGAR: I'm sorry. You know what they're trying to do.

MARGO: I really resent it.

EDGAR: That's just what I told Phil. It has nothing to do with you, Margo. I didn't mean to imply ...

MARGO: I did appreciate your company, I want you to know that.

EDGAR: Well. It was the least I could do, you know, under the circumstances. A situation like that, that could have been embarrassing, you made a lot nicer for me.

MARGO: I did?

EDGAR: Sure.

MARGO: Well, it was the two of us together, actually, that made the most of a ... difficult situation.

EDGAR: You could see it that way.

MARGO: Well, if you see it like that ...

(*But the phrase hangs in silence*)

EDGAR: Margo? Are you still there? I did something wrong; is that what you were going to say?

MARGO: No, I mean, Edgar, my department's having its spring barbeque this Saturday, you know, at Rock Creek Park, on Saturday, you know, nothing special really, only ... the thing is ... to go at all I need a kind of escort.

EDGAR: To go with you?

MARGO: Escort me. There's the outdoors, interesting people, lots of food and free beer.

EDGAR: Free?

MARGO: You'd be doing me a great favor, just to bring me there.

EDGAR: Like an escort.

MARGO: Well? (*After pause*) One-thirty? The Metro—Dupont Circle.

EDGAR: I might have to leave early.

MARGO: Sure.

EDGAR: Well ... I guess I'd be glad to, Margo.

MARGO: At one-thirty.

EDGAR: Uh-huh.

(*She hangs up. Then, as he's hanging up, she quickly lifts the phone*)

MARGO: Goodbye! ... (*She hears only the buzz*) ... Edgar.

(*She hangs up once more. A moment later she rises, to walk into the darkness beyond the spotlight*)

Scene Three:

Lights rise, placing the bed and endtable and telephone in Margo's efficiency apartment: upstage, its brass bed, pastel quilted cover, an old doll on its rolled pillows; behind it, a draped exit onto a foot-deep railed balcony; downstage from it, a small white round table and a bookshelf and dainty wastebasket; to stage left, a door to the unseen kitchenette,

on which hangs the before-seen The Postman Always Rings Twice *poster. Stage right, another door, to the bathroom.*
  The table is cluttered with emptied dinner dishes. From stage right, Edgar skitters in barefooted, wearing slacks and a T-shirt on the front of which is a John Garfield photoprint.

EDGAR: My pants are dry but not the shirts or the socks. (*At the balcony*) It's almost stopped raining.
MARGO: (*Offstage*) I'm sorry. It wasn't much of a Saturday afternoon for you.
EDGAR: For anybody. No fault of yours.
MARGO: (*Offstage*) It was fate, all this. (*Margo, robed, enters to place on the table two stemmed glasses and a bottle of white wine*) I mean, I no sooner took a paper plate and the wind kicked up and before I had it filled ...
EDGAR: No fault of yours.
MARGO: It's fate, that's what. (*Offering wine*) I just happened to find this. (*As he takes it and sips approvingly*) Those pants aren't really dry.
EDGAR: I felt funny in here without them.
MARGO: I'm sorry about the salad and the stroganoff. If I'd known you didn't like mushrooms ...
EDGAR: How could you expect to know anything like that about me?
MARGO: I do now.
EDGAR: I liked the sour cream.
(*She gulps down her wine, pours another*)
MARGO: And I know that now, about you.
EDGAR: The wine's very good.
(*She eagerly pours him another glassful*)
MARGO: I bought it. For myself. For my birthday. I was thirty years old yesterday.
EDGAR: I thought you said ... oh. For your birthday. Congratulations.
MARGO: For what?—another signpost in the desert?
EDGAR: (*Rising, to move away from her*) You keep a nice little apartment here.

MARGO: You're the first man to be inside it since my telephone was installed. It's not much, really, it's just me. (*He's at the bookshelf*) I only keep my Book-of-the-Month Club books.

EDGAR: Updike.

MARGO: You remember. Nothing ever did happen (*flipping through its pages*) after all that. None of them really truly wants to risk something happening, that's why. Which is O.K. on page one, even page fifty, but then ... (*She tosses it into the wastebasket. He turns to the balcony, where he opens the drapes*) It used to be a panoramic view to the Washington Monument. (*Closing the drapes*) I'm sorry. Now it's a bird's-eye view of the new Saville Arms.

EDGAR: I should be going.

MARGO: Why? (*Pouring it*) Have another glass of wine. You just said it's good. And once a bottle—anything like that's—opened ...

EDGAR: (*As he puts down the full glass, moves to the bathroom door*) My shirt and socks must be dry by now.

MARGO: They're not, I'm positive. (*She reaches him, her hand on his arm, at the door*) No, please, don't go.

EDGAR: They're sure to be dry in another few minutes.

MARGO: Another few minutes, and the storm might be over. (*She plunks herself on the bed to gulp down another glassful of wine. He empties his own glass with equally desperate gusto while carefully making his way back across the room from her to the tiny table and his chair*) It fits you.

EDGAR: What.

MARGO: The T-shirt.

EDGAR: I'm no John Garfield.

MARGO: I'm no Lana Turner.

EDGAR: No.

MARGO: Well, but who is?

EDGAR: (*Shrugs*) Somebody must be.

MARGO: You think so?

EDGAR: I'd like to think so.

MARGO: Me, too. I mean, that there must be somebody like Garfield. Even Garfield. But, well, I don't know now.

EDGAR: Anyway, they made a good movie, the two of them together.

MARGO: He died five years later; he was thirty-eight, heart attack, late one night at a friend's house, a woman friend.

EDGAR: He was just like his movies, then.

MARGO: Sure. He was a romantic, I guess you'd say, strong but he tried to be gentle, tried to smile behind those sad eyes. And he was so beautiful. (*Pause*) You don't want to hear all this.

EDGAR: We all need our dreams, to look up to, hope for.

MARGO: Except yours is blonde, slim, and gorgeous.

EDGAR: What's wrong with that? (*Margo shrugs into her wine glass*) This wine is great.

MARGO: You said "what's wrong with that." Actually, his name was Jules Garfinkle. And he died from too much smoking and drinking. His wife was divorcing him. His friends laughed at the way he tried to act educated. And that beautiful face of his had a nose job.

EDGAR: I suppose the real Lana Turner had her faults.

MARGO: Her hair was bleached, her legs sweat, her gigolos were Mafia gangsters ...

EDGAR: Did I ask?! I don't need to know. It's not meant to be real.

MARGO: That's all I mean, that they're not meant to be real.

EDGAR: All I meant was, well, you only hurt yourself, putting down your ideal.

MARGO: I suppose.

EDGAR: It's harmless enough, after all, a little fantasy to lift us from this everyday life.

MARGO: Harmless, maybe, but it doesn't seem to do any good, not for me. But that's not your fault. I'm sorry.

EDGAR: You say that too much.

MARGO: I mean it.

EDGAR: ... Too much. Sorry for what? You invite me here to this nice place, cook me a very nice dinner ...

MARGO: Except for all those mushrooms.

EDGAR: A nice dinner.

MARGO: I had my reason.

EDGAR: I'll have some more of that wine.

(*He gets up to take the bottle from her, and pours himself a glassful of wine*)

MARGO: Come to bed with me. (*A stunned paralyzed moment. Bottle in hand, a bit wobbly on his feet, he takes it to the table across the room from her*) You're thinking of how to say "no".

EDGAR: I'm not.

MARGO: Then turn out the light.

EDGAR: It's the wine. You drank too much wine. That happened before, and I took advantage of her, and it really wasn't very good.

MARGO: You wouldn't be taking advantage, not of me.

EDGAR: You're sure?

MARGO: It's me who's taking advantage.

EDGAR: No, really, you don't need to feel like that.

MARGO: I won't, if you'll turn out the light.

(*He gulps down his glassful of wine; offers the bottle to Margo, who shakes her head. He pours the last glassful for himself*)

EDGAR: I can't promise anything ... fancy.

MARGO: Me neither

(*He flicks off the light. Darkness*)

Scene Four:

A few minutes later. Lying under the blankets of the bed is Edgar, still T-shirted. He leans to look towards the bathroom door. He settles back restlessly, only to hastily light a cigarette. He stares straight ahead. Suddenly, he grins obscenely, slapping his free hand into the bed.

EDGAR: (*Under his breath*) You did it!! (*Pause; his grin abruptly disappears*) Oh, my God.

(*Margo enters from the bathroom, stage right, pulling her robe around herself*)

MARGO: (*Holding them out to him*) Your shirts are dry.

(*She sits across from him, at the table, to watch him take off the Garfield T-shirt for his own. He hands the T-shirt back to her*)

EDGAR: Thanks, Margo.

MARGO: You needed something, while you waited for your own.

EDGAR: That's right.

MARGO: Well, I'm sorry, that's all.

EDGAR: No, Margo, now don't say that ...

MARGO: Well, you were being so ... careful, and I couldn't respond much, and then it was over.

EDGAR: (*After pause*) You mean you're apologizing for *you?*

MARGO: I just laid there, didn't I, waiting for it to happen to me.

EDGAR: It was only your second time, you said.

MARGO: But I just don't seem to feel ... thrilled.

EDGAR: It could have been me.

MARGO: Oh, no. It could have been John Garfield himself and been the same.

EDGAR: Don't think that. I was awfully nervous, and drinking all that wine so fast ...

MARGO: Sure, drinking all that wine, because I'm not blonde, beautiful, and slim—is that *your* fault?

EDGAR: Well, it's not *yours.*

MARGO: No, sure—it's the fault of Margo's Mouth, a very busy acquaintance.

EDGAR: For me it was ... nice.

MARGO: "Nice" as in "rotten."

EDGAR: Nice meaning "very nice." It's not some kind of test score, Margo; it's two people, trying hard to be close for a little while.

MARGO: I was trying.

EDGAR: This was our first time; we weren't perfect, neither one of us.

MARGO: You're being polite.

EDGAR: It's just that there's nobody to blame. It's a mutual sort of thing, Margo, two people being very together.

MARGO: Being very together. (*Pause*) Like you say, this was only our first time ...

EDGAR: Right.

MARGO: ... Not our last.

(*Edgar grabs his pants off the floor. Holding them, he's about to step out of bed when, eyes on her, he hesitates.*

Then, Margo, stumbling into the breach) I could get us some ice cream.

EDGAR: From the kitchen.

MARGO: (*As she exits into the kitchen*) Right.

EDGAR: But not much, not for me. (*He leaps out of the bed and into his pants, then his shirt*)

MARGO: (*Offstage*) It's Jamoca Almond Fudge—is that all right? (*Pause*) Edgar? It's difficult, like you said, being with someone, without any idea ... It was all so here and now and feeling scared ... that I'd spoil everything and you'd hate me and I'd hate me. You know?

EDGAR: Jamaica Fudge!—is great!

MARGO: (*Offstage*) And now, well, now I'm just so ... relieved.

(*She reenters to the table with large bowls of the ice cream as he's snapping on and examining his watch*)

EDGAR: It stopped. There goes another broken watch. Twelve ninety-five.

MARGO: Maybe if you wouldn't tamper with it. You're too rough without realizing. (*Bending over it*) When what it needs is ... a ... touch.

EDGAR: It's working.

MARGO: Nine ... forty-five.

EDGAR: That late? Oh, Margo, really, thanks for everything. My socks—where are they?—and my shoes.

MARGO: You need to have them right now?

EDGAR: To know they're dry, anyway, just in case. It's been long enough—don't you think?

MARGO: You could stay here, if you want to, for tonight.

EDGAR: I don't think I'd better, for tonight.

MARGO: Just to sleep—as a convenience.

EDGAR: Oh, no, it's just that I'm not used to another person, you know, with me. Anyway, looks like there's no reason, the storm's over now.

MARGO: I'll get your shoes and socks. (*She exits into bathroom, stage right. He just begins to quickly consume his ice cream when she reenters to put the shoes and socks on the floor beside him. He sits with purposeful casualness, eating the dessert with studied leisureliness. But she's seen his haste. She begins her own. Silence. Margo stops*) I shouldn't be eating this. (*She waits for his response: silence. She drops her spoon. Then with her eyes on her bowl*) We could go back to bed, you know, right now, for awhile.

EDGAR: No. I'm afraid ... your ice cream would melt. (*Short pause*) You really want to?

MARGO: Now that we know so much more about each other.

EDGAR: (*Glancing towards the bed*) We do know a little more.

MARGO: You said you liked it.

(*He walks away, to put on his shoes and socks*)

EDGAR: Maybe some time ... in the future.

MARGO: To see you again ... like this?

EDGAR: I don't know. I need a while to think.

MARGO: I want to. It was like fate—that movie and the rainstorm and this. Like what I've always dreamed, that's what. You're just like him: passionate, but you tried to be gentle. And underneath you're shy, that's what, a romantic.

EDGAR: I'm not all that. (*Pause*) You really think so?

MARGO: Sure.

EDGAR: I can't promise anything definite, you know, not yet. (*Margo's hands frame his face. They kiss ... until he stops her*) Margo. All you said—"fate" and romance—that was make-believe. This is not. It was you, all this, what you wanted from the start: at the movie ...

MARGO: But we were tricked ...

EDGAR: ... And the picnic ...

MARGO: But when it rained ...

EDGAR: And the dinner. And after.

MARGO: I suppose you had nothing to do with it!

EDGAR: Well, but your "dreams" and "romance" had nothing to do with it! It's wrong for you to see me like that. I'm not your own personal John Garfield. I wish I *was* him, could even come close. But I have to be honest with you. I won't be used that way, like it's not me who's here.

MARGO: And not me who's here? Would that be so bad? Margo Feld is nobody special to hold onto.

EDGAR: Yes, you are.

MARGO: Then be with me again.

EDGAR: You need to be with just somebody—even Phil and Sally could see that—and it was me who happened along.

MARGO: Because I'm that desperate!?

EDGAR: I didn't mean ... That's not what I said. I'm sorry. I'd better just go.

MARGO: Sure, I'm so "special," now you want to leave. (*He stops*) You're right, sure, I'm desperate, because you're also right, that you are nothing like John Garfield: you're practically bald, after all, you're not pretty or talented or rich. And sometimes when you talk to me, you're boring and not too smart.

EDGAR: Well, there you are—isn't that what I've been telling you?—that's me, nobody's ideal, not even close. So you had to say it, so I hope you feel better!

MARGO: No.

EDGAR: Me neither!

MARGO: But I also want to say you really can be strong and passionate; you really were gentle. That's you, too. And you are a deep-inside-yourself romantic. About the breath-taking blonde with a soft spot in her heart for you, somewhere someday.

EDGAR: That's right.

MARGO: I wonder if it is right. Maybe for me there is no John Garfield.

EDGAR: I don't know about you. I'm still a student, still deciding a future for myself. And I'll set my sights high, in everything.

MARGO: Sure, your sights high, like on some Lana Turner? So tell me, I want to know: who was the last one of your Lana Turner types to give you a second look?

EDGAR: I've had ... friends.

MARGO: I've had friends, me too, handsome men friends who confide in me—I'm nice and cute and I'll listen to their every word, about their terrible emotional problems and their terrible women problems—'til four in the morning, talk and nothing more. Like handsome hunk Phil Cafritz who's so sweet to me and palsy-walsy sincere, along with his slim, pretty, blonde wife Sally.

EDGAR: Yeah. She's ... friendly, in that way.

(*Silence*)

MARGO: I hate them. They don't know anything about us.

EDGAR: (*After pause*) I know.

MARGO: A dream like that, my own John Garfield, isn't much to hold onto.

EDGAR: It's all there is. Because with anybody else I'll always think I'm settling for less, I settled for second best.

MARGO: Not less, maybe different, maybe right, for me, for us.

EDGAR: No.

MARGO: Are you sure?

EDGAR: You must think, for a person like me to hope for my own Lana Turner is awfully silly.

MARGO: No, I don't think that, Edgar, I never meant that.

EDGAR: Maybe it's silly, but to put down a person's dream is to put down that person. I have to look in the mirror everyday. And you stand here and tell me, "Hey, look, that's all there is."

MARGO: I'm looking, at what's here, Edgar, and telling you I like it.

EDGAR: Don't kid yourself. That's not enough, not for out there, it plain stinks, out there. The world's not (*Sweeping the room*) here, or inside here—it's out there. And I can't give up my one hope that one little part of out there's going to change and come my way.

MARGO: For a person like you, I guess there's every reason to keep hoping. If that's what you need.

EDGAR: And you? (*She does not respond*) Then I guess we understand each other.

MARGO: But there's "meantime." Like, meantime it wouldn't prevent us seeing each other ... like this.

EDGAR: If there wouldn't have to be anything final about it. Nothing exclusive.

MARGO: Sure.

EDGAR: A kind of between-times for the both of us.

MARGO: Like tomorrow?

EDGAR: Wait, no, I can't, so fast ...

MARGO: Next week.

EDGAR: Yeah.

MARGO: I'll call Friday.

EDGAR: Sure, just in case one of us finds, you know, that particular someone.

MARGO: Bring something. Like wine. An inexpensive wine. Or, well, a fruit. For our dinner together.

EDGAR: Oh, that, right.

MARGO: For me, a very low-cal dinner. And for you, no mushrooms. (*Showing him to the door*) Next week, then.

EDGAR: You'll call, you know, just in case.

(*He kisses her awkwardly on the lips. And leaves.*

Alone now, Margo takes down the Postman Always Rings Twice *poster, tears it, drops it into the wastebasket. She takes the John Garfield T-shirt, drops it into the wastebasket. She takes the doll off the bookshelf, lays it on its back in the still-mussed bed. She sits now, at the table, surveys the room, then the doll in her bed, only to finally be staring at the still-left ice cream. Finally, she dumps what was Edgar's bowl into her own, and is consuming it with avid compulsion*)

The End

Ernest Ferlita

THE MASK OF HIROSHIMA

> I have travelled, sinned, and
> suffered by the name of Hiroshima.
> Strindberg, *The Great Highway*

> Those eighteen upon whom the
> tower in Siloam fell and killed them,
> do you think that they were worse
> sinners than all the others who
> dwelt in Jerusalem?
> *Luke 13:4*

Ernest Ferlita

Ernest Ferlita completed his Doctor of Fine Arts degree in playwriting and dramatic literature at the Yale School of Drama in 1969. While completing his studies, his first full-length play, *The Ballad of John Ogilvie,* was produced off-Broadway.

Dr. Ferlita's play, *Black Medea,* was the only American play featured in the first Spoleto Festival U.S.A., and the Actor's Outlet production of *Black Medea* in 1987 took four awards at the 5th Annual Black Theatre Festival in New York City. Two other Ferlita plays have been seen in New York—*The Obelisk,* at Fordham's Lincoln Center Theatre, and *The Mask of Hiroshima,* at the national convention of the Association for Theatre in Higher Education and at the Actor's Outlet. Adapted for radio, *The Mask of Hiroshima* won the 1985 American Radio Theatre Script Writing Competition (under the title *The City of Seven Rivers.*) *The Mask of Hiroshima* is published here for the first time. Another play, *The Truth of the Matter*, won the Miller Award in the 1986 Deep South Writers Conference.

Dr. Ferlita has authored three books, including *The Theatre of Pilgrimage*, and he co-authored three other books, notably *Film Odyssey.* Currently he is Professor of Drama at Loyola University in New Orleans and is a member of the Dramatists Guild.

Dr. Ferlita dedicates his play: "To Masayuki Sano, who gave me the plot and characters."

Characters:

CHORUS, *dressed in black*
OKUMA, *a small man of sixty, in a kimono*
SHINJI ISHIKAWA, *a young man of twenty-nine, in Western dress*
HISA ISHIKAWA, *a young woman of twenty-five, in a kimono*
A WOMAN, *forty-three, in a kimono*
A DOCTOR, *thirty-nine, dressed in white*

Setting:

The action of the play takes place in Hiroshima, seven years after the bomb.
A bare platform stage center. A sliding screen hides a more intimate acting area, slightly raised, to the rear of the platform. A "flower-walk" leads to the platform from upstage right. In front of the platform is the acting area of dream and memory.
At the start of the play all the characters sit in full view of the audience. Chorus, sitting somewhat apart from the others, comes forward.

CHORUS:
Here we are in the city of seven rivers.
Seven years have passed, seven years
since that drift of elemental power
unleashed its light across our sky
to dim the rising sun.
(*Okuma rises*)
The man of many moons is Mister Okuma.
He is a tailor by trade.
His daughter Hisa is in bed with a fever,
and here he waits,
in the Hospital of the Red Cross.
(*Shinji rises and paces. He walks with a slight limp*)

Waiting with Okuma is Shinji Ishikawa.
Shinji is his son-in-law.
He is a teacher.
He remembers the last time his wife was sick.
But now there is more to fear,
for now she is with child.
> OKUMA:

I hope it is a boy.
> SHINJI:

I know that's what Hisa wants.
> OKUMA:

Everybody wants a boy. Some day
it may be possible to decide ahead of time.
Then they will have to pass a law against boys.
> (*Quickly*)

But I'll have you know I was very glad
when my little Hisa was born.
Yes, yes, that was a day
oversprinkled with flowers.
> (*There is a rumble of thunder*)

It is going to rain.
> (*Shinji moves a couple of paces to see if the doctor is on his*
> *way, limping slightly. Okuma watches him*)
> OKUMA:

I am ashamed.
> SHINJI:

Why?
> OKUMA:

I am ashamed that I alone, of all my family,
passed through that day unhurt.
On you, on Hisa, I see its marks so clearly;
on my wife it was the mark of death.
Why was I spared?
What god made me go alone the night before
to see my mother in Mukaihara?
"Come with me," I said to my wife.
"No," she said, "they will blow up the train."
And she begged me not to go.
When I got back and found her body,
the dark flowers of her kimono

had sucked-in the sun
and left their shapes upon her skin.
> *(Shinji turns his face away. A clock strikes seven)*
> OKUMA: *(After the first stroke)*

Seven o'clock. Seven is a good number. Nothing bad ever
happens at seven.
> *(A silence. He looks at Shinji)*

Shinji.
> SHINJI:

Yes, father.
> OKUMA:

Shinji!
> *(Shinji looks at him)*
> I'm afraid for Hisa!

She was never very strong, Shinji.
And now the child in her womb
unravels her strength,
now when she most needs it.
> SHINJI:

What is it you want?
> *(No answer)*

Do you want her to give up the child?
> *(Okuma tenses)*

But isn't that what you're saying?
> OKUMA: *(With great force)*
> Yes! While there is still time.

To save her, Shinji! With the child,
the risk is too great.
> SHINJI:

I don't want to talk about it.
> OKUMA:

What!
> SHINJI:

Not until the doctor comes.
> OKUMA:

Will things look different then?
Do you think you can tear away in seven minutes
the mask we have worn for seven years?
It will not come off, you fool!
It is fixed on the face of the earth!

(*Okuma's face freezes into a mask*)
CHORUS: (*Speaking the word simultaneously*)
Earth!
"The Song of August the Sixth"
In the silence of the melted syllable
I saw the mask of Hiroshima
Molded to the features of her face,
The convolutions of her brain.

"Oh well. That's war. Too bad."
But in her day she was a bright flower
With blue brows and topaz hair
And seven ribbons streaming.

Now there is ash upon her head,
A drift of ash on her shoulder,
Her eyes the color of mist,
Dull moons that shun the light.
    SHINJI:
That's all behind us now.
    OKUMA:
It is still with us!
    SHINJI: (*With fierce articulation, as if to convince himself*)
With us, yes, but behind us! Like sin.
And so we suffer it with faith.
    OKUMA: (*Snorts*)
Faith. You know the saying: "Faith
is like a wild deer on the mountain.
It will not come when you call it."
    SHINJI:
I will hound it until it does.
    OKUMA:
Does Hisa feel as you do?
    SHINJI:
We go up the mountain hand in hand.
Sometimes it's me that lags behind,
sometimes it's Hisa.
    OKUMA:
I am too old to follow.
And yet I would be where Hisa is.

She's all I have, Shinji.
We mustn't risk losing her
for a child that may not even live.
Have you considered that?
(*Shinji makes no answer*)
I met a little girl on the porch today.
She was making paper cranes.
"By the time I make a thousand," she said,
"I'll be well again."
Poor child! She still had hundreds to go.
And already, like a cloth of feathers,
the cloud had begun to cover her.
    SHINJI:
What do you mean?
    OKUMA:
The cloud, the cloud will claim her too,
fire and ice mixing in the blood.
    SHINJI:
For you, then, no one escapes.
    OKUMA:
That is for sure.
It is all a matter of time and place.
And for Hisa it will be here and now,
unless we do what we must to save her.
    SHINJI:
Please ...
    OKUMA:
I must say what I think!
    SHINJI:
Think of something else then.
    OKUMA:
Don't you care if Hisa dies?
Don't you love her any more?
What is it? Can't you bring
yourself to touch her any more?
    SHINJI:
You're talking wild.
    OKUMA:
Once, when she was a child,
I made her a red kimono

with a black and silver sash.
As I fitted it to her body,
I saw for the first time
how her skin gave light
like the plum flower.
But now the light is gone.
Only the scars remain—
a cloud of thick scars
around her neck, her arms,
her shoulders.
            SHINJI:
I see the light in her still.
It's a light that comes from depths
that no mask of scars can ever hide.
For me, she has not changed.
            CHORUS:
And the young man remembers:
            HISA'S VOICE:
Changed? How have I changed?
            (*Hisa enters the area of dream and memory. Okuma remains
            dimly in the background, as Shinji joins Hisa. They stand
            apart from one another in separate spots till the end of the
            scene*)
            SHINJI:
When I try to walk beside you,
you flow past as cool as a river.
When I try to hold you,
you turn away from me.
When at last you let me look at you,
your eyes cloud over like a day in August.
            HISA:
Why can't you leave me alone?
            SHINJI:
You admit it then; you've changed.
            HISA:
Everything changes if you look long enough!
And you have looked at me longer than I like.
            SHINJI: (*After a pause*)
Do you want me to go?

HISA:
You can do whatever you want.
SHINJI:
I want to marry you.
HISA:
What a fool you are!
Can you still say that to me?
Do you think we can still
look down from the moon-bridge
and see the same reflection?
SHINJI: (*After a pause*)
Listen.
HISA:
What?
SHINJI:
Can you hear the pine trees?
They sound the same to me.
Here outside the city,
they even smell the same.
HISA: (*Slowly shaking her head*)
Everything is stale now.
SHINJI: (*Floating out of his memory*)
"But I make all things new."
HISA:
What?
SHINJI:
Sunday's scripture.
It stayed with me.
HISA:
You can't make all things new.
What you make new is soon burnt up.
In one second all flesh is grass.
SHINJI: (*Reaching out to her*)
Hisa ...
HISA: (*Violently*)
Don't touch me!
(*A stunned silence*)
I don't want anyone ever to touch me again.
(*Shinji looks at her long and hard*)

SHINJI: (*Suddenly, with a clap of his hands*)
Watch me, Hisa!
(*Does a kind of grasshopper dance*)
When I try to walk fast,
I look just like grasshopper.
HISA:
Stop that, stop making a fool of yourself.
SHINJI:
Poor little grasshopper!
Who would want to marry him?
(*Hisa turns away, buries her face in her hands. He looks at her*)
I didn't ask you to marry me
because I felt sorry for you,
or because I felt I had to
out of some sense of honor ...
HISA:
Go away!
SHINJI:
Hisa, remember how those crazy flowers
bloomed right after the bomb?
Out of the bones and ashes
they popped up all over the city.
Everywhere there were day lilies
and bluets and morning glories.
But it was horrible to see
because it was all such a lie,
nothing but a frenzied push
to be free of the poisoned earth.
And then winter came,
and they all fell away.
And people said nothing would grow
in these parts for seventy years.
But they were wrong.
(*Goes down on his haunches*)
The other day
I saw a morning glory still half asleep.
It looked very shy in the shade,
as if it'd rather not be noticed.
But then the sun came poking around,

and before I knew it
that little bit of a blossom
was looking up at me wide awake.
And do you know what it said to me?
It said, "I did not forget to bloom."
"People," I said, "will not forget to build,
to build houses and cities,
to build lives again."
    (*Rises*)
Hisa, let me touch you.
    (*They come together briefly*)
    CHORUS:
Now there is meeting between them, two hearts
Gone astray in the dark of yesterday's snow:
A dream-bridge daring the thaw and the flood,
Braving the swirl of the shadows below.
    (*The lights take Hisa away. Shinji joins Mr. Okuma on the
    platform*)
    SHINJI:
When I lean on her,
I am no longer lame.
When she leans on me,
her flesh is whole again.
    OKUMA: (*Nods slowly*)
I know how much you mean to Hisa,
and I thank you for it, Shinji.
Did I ever tell you that before?
Yes, I thank you for teaching her
how to smile again.
    SHINJI: (*Wondering aloud*)
Is the smile that is taught
ever more than a mask?
    OKUMA:
Perhaps in the beginning one wears it
like a mask. But to put it on
is a sign of life, and in the end
the smile itself becomes the sign.
    SHINJI: (*Looks at him*)
I hope so.

OKUMA:

Why won't you listen to me then?

(*Shinji turns away*)

I must speak my mind, Shinji.

You don't know what it is to lose your wife.

Have you ever seen a turtle try to swim on land

thinking he had reached the sea?

Where did I hear that?

Yes, it was on Bikini, I'm told,

when they first dropped the bomb.

He got all turned around, that turtle did.

So with a man without his wife.

SHINJI:

There are things that you don't know.

OKUMA:

What things?

(*A Woman enters, stops when she sees Shinji. Neither he nor his father-in-law take note of her*)

SHINJI:

Never mind, father;

this is a matter between me and Hisa.

OKUMA:

And me! And me!

SHINJI:

No ...

OKUMA:

What are you keeping from me?

I have a right to know.

CHORUS:

But the young man sees the woman. She is

the mother of a little girl he used to teach.

(*Shinji looks up in consternation*)

WOMAN:

The last time I saw you,

you looked at me and walked away.

SHINJI:

Did I? When was that?

WOMAN:

They make me come here every three months.

Are you sick too?

SHINJI:
Yes—I mean—it's my wife.
WOMAN:
I happened to pass by the school the other day.
There was a little girl playing on the swing,
climbing the wind like a wild duck.
For a minute I thought it was Michi.
SHINJI:
I think of her often.
WOMAN:
Thinking is all there is.
(*Looks at him sharply*)
But I'm not blaming you.
Who can say where the blame lies?
SHINJI:
Believe me, I tried to save her.
But there was no time, no time.
WOMAN:
You told me you didn't even see her.
What do you mean, you tried to save her?
(*Shinji starts to answer, but stops in confusion*)
WOMAN:
Did you see her or didn't you?
SHINJI:
I saw her, yes.
WOMAN:
Why did you lie to me before?
(*Shinji bows his head*)
WOMAN:
Tell me what you know!
SHINJI:
You must try to understand—
WOMAN:
Tell me!
SHINJI:
Everything was in confusion:
ceilings dropping on top of us
and some of the walls collapsing.
Windows blew in,
and the glass went slashing by.

Most of the children were dead,
but others ran about screaming
through a maze of overturned desks
or lay with bones breaking under debris,
all their breath consumed in crying.

WOMAN:
Michi? Where was Michi?

SHINJI:
When I tried to get up,
I saw that my leg was badly torn.
With the weight of it dragging behind me,
I crawled over the wreckage,
digging holes where the crying stopped me.

WOMAN:
Michi?

SHINJI:
I found her pinned under a heavy beam.
But then the fires started,
and the room was filling with smoke.
I tried desperately to free her,
I did everything I could,
but in the end I had to leave her.

WOMAN:
What? You left her trapped there in the wreckage?

SHINJI:
The room was filling with smoke!

WOMAN:
You ran away!

SHINJI:
I didn't ...

WOMAN:
You ran away and left her there to die!

SHINJI:
I did everything I could!

WOMAN:
I don't believe you.
You lied to me before.
You lied because you ran away.

SHINJI:
That may be so.

Perhaps if I had struggled
one more minute,
put my shoulder to the beam ...
WOMAN:
Michi, where are you?

(*Goes out*)
CHORUS:
"The Song of the Burning Child"
Mantled with feathers of fire,
I fell beneath the crossbeam
And lay in a table of flames
As thick as twigs in a duck's nest.

When I looked for help, I saw
Eyes of fire mocking me,
In a mask of yellow smoke,
And a multiplication of tongues.

My heart like a bird ensnared,
I cried blindly: "Teacher, teacher!"
But the fire ate up all my tears,
And the yellow smoke my cries.
OKUMA:
The children, so many children.
Don't misunderstand me, Shinji.
A grandson would be as sweet
to me as a cup of moonlight—
SHINJI:
I know, I know—
OKUMA:
But a man has to prepare himself,
free himself from desire
before desire is denied.
SHINJI:
Set me an example then.
OKUMA:
What?
SHINJI:
Nothing.

OKUMA:
You do see what I mean, don't you?
Only if you prepare yourself
to give up the child—
SHINJI:
I don't see that at all!
OKUMA:
What is this blindness of yours?
Of course, it is natural for you
to want a son, but—
SHINJI:
Has it ever occurred to you that Hisa
may not want to give it up?
OKUMA:
What do you know what Hisa wants?
You haven't talked to her yet.
SHINJI:
I have talked to her.
OKUMA:
About giving up the child?
SHINJI:
About having it.
OKUMA:
But things have changed!
SHINJI:
But not her reason for wanting it.
OKUMA:
What are you trying to tell me?
What is her reason?
SHINJI:
I'm going to die, old man.
I'm going to die before you.
CHORUS:
And the young man remembers:
HISA'S VOICE:
Shinji! Where are you?
(*Shinji joins her as she moves into the area of dream and memory, again each standing in separate spot till the end of the scene*)

HISA:
Come see: the river is red with leaves
where it bends around the maples.

SHINJI:
I'm coming.

HISA:
Look how thick they are!

SHINJI:
Yes. So thick, so thick
I can't even see my face in the water.
It's as if I didn't exist.

HISA: (*Looks up at him sharply*)
Why do you say that?
What is it, Shinji?

SHINJI:
I lied to you last night.

HISA:
About what?

SHINJI:
About what the doctor said.

HISA:
What did he say?

SHINJI:
He said I haven't long to live.

HISA:
How long?

SHINJI:
A year, maybe two.

HISA:
He could be wrong!

SHINJI:
I'm only telling you what he said.

HISA:
I had dared to hope that by now
we could be clear of the past.

SHINJI:
The past is in our blood.
Fire and ice, your father says,
mixing in the blood.

HISA:
"I make all things new."
Houses and cities,
everything except ourselves.
SHINJI:
Seven years, Hisa,
we were given seven years together.
HISA:
How shall I live all alone
on the edge of a pit?
Why did I ever crawl out of it?
You should have left me there to die,
there in that pit in Asano Park.
I wish you had never found me!
SHINJI:
No, Hisa! The years we've had ...
HISA:
What do they mean now?
There's nothing left.
SHINJI:
There's still whatever time is given us.
HISA:
One year!
SHINJI:
Suppose it were three, or another seven?
Is it the *length* of life that gives meaning?
HISA:
If there's no other meaning,
the length of it is everything.
SHINJI:
Or nothing at all.
HISA:
Everything! If you can spend it
with someone you love.
SHINJI:
Then its meaning begins there,
with someone you love.
HISA:
And it ends when he goes.

SHINJI:
No, Hisa.

HISA:
I can't see beyond you!

SHINJI:
O God, Hisa, if only I could,
I'd give you all that you ever wanted!

HISA:
I want you!
I want to be your wife.
I want to bear your children.
(*With sudden decision, a decision made in all defiance of the
past*)
Shinji, I want a child!

SHINJI:
Hisa ...

HISA:
Your child.

SHINJI:
But the risk ...

HISA:
I don't care about the risk.

SHINJI:
You're asking me to kill you.

HISA:
No!

SHINJI:
What about the risk to the child?

HISA:
O God, the child! I knew a girl
who strangled hers with her own hands.
It wasn't made to live, she said.
But that child was in the womb when the bomb fell.
A child conceived seven years later
wouldn't run the same risk.

SHINJI:
I don't know what to tell you.

HISA:
You said you'd give me anything I wanted.

SHINJI:
If only I could!

HISA:
Give me this reason for living then.

(Shinji and Hisa join their crossed hands and move as if around the axle of a wheel)

CHORUS: *(From "Awoi No Uye" by Ujinobu)*
"Man's life is a wheel on the axle,
there is no turn whereby to escape.
His hold is light as dew on the Basho leaf.

(They let go, and Hisa drifts away as Shinji moves back to the platform, his hands still reaching for her)

It seems that last spring's blossoms
are only a dream in the mind."

OKUMA:
Shall I outlive you both?
Shall I live to drench your graves
with the dew of my shame?

CHORUS:
Then at last the doctor comes.

(Shinji and Okuma turn to him anxiously)

DOCTOR:
She's resting better now.
But the old sickness
smolders in her blood.

SHINJI:
What of the child then?

DOCTOR:
She cannot carry him and live.

OKUMA:
What? What did he say?

SHINJI:
He said she must give up the child.

OKUMA:
So now the hour is upon us.

SHINJI: *(Bitterly)*
A thousand children
quenched by a single blast.
What's so terrible
about not saving one?

DOCTOR:
I'm sorry.
SHINJI:
Have you told my wife?
DOCTOR:
No, it is for you to tell her.
SHINJI:
But are you sure ...
OKUMA:
Come, Shinji.
SHINJI:
Hisa was right:
I should've left her
to die in Asano Park.
OKUMA:
What are you saying?
SHINJI:
Left her to die in the pit.
(*Okuma follows the Doctor out. Shinji remains in place*)
CHORUS:
"The Song of Asano Park"
Dressed in precise patterns,
I recline by pools that mirror me,
Perfumed with pine. But in my hair
Settles an electric smell.

They lie on the green of my lap,
The dead entwined with the living.
The river heaves at my side
Like a dragon with seven heads.

Fire-flakes floating on the wind,
A face with melting eyes,
A swirl of blood on the moon-bridge,
And the rain on the dragon's back.
(*Hisa slides open the screen of the inner room and kneels, sitting back on her heels. Shinji goes up to her and kneels behind her to one side*)

CHORUS: (*From "Genjo" by Kongo*)
"Slowly the night draws on
And the dew on the grasses deepens.
Long after man's heart is at rest
Clouds trouble the moon's face—
    through the long night till dawn."
SHINJI:
Are you cold?
HISA:
No.
SHINJI:
I thought I felt you shiver.
HISA:
I was thinking of the night.
SHINJI:
So was I.
HISA:
I don't see the moon. Do you?
SHINJI:
Behind the clouds.
It leaves us both in deep shadow.
HISA:
There are three of us, Shinji.
SHINJI:
Three of us, yes,
and the child lies in deepest shadow.
HISA:
I know.
SHINJI:
Do you really?
HISA:
What did the doctor tell you?
SHINJI:
Don't risk it, he says.
HISA:
We knew about the risk.
SHINJI:
But now, he says, you risk everything.

HISA:
What do you want me to do?
SHINJI:
I want you to go on living.
HISA:
Is it so certain that I will die
if we let the child live?
SHINJI:
I have told you all I know.
HISA:
Shinji, what *is* this child?
Is he nothing apart from you and me?
I wanted him to love when I no longer had you,
and you wanted him out of love for me.
But is that love enough for him now?
SHINJI:
No one would blame you, Hisa,
if you let him go.
HISA:
That's not for me to decide.
SHINJI:
What?
HISA:
You are the father: you must decide with me.
SHINJI:
Was I trying to run away again?
I have seen so much life
slip through my hands!
Hisa, how can I let you go?
What if I say to him *live!*
and then he dies in spite of me?
What if you both die?
HISA:
That would be a hard mystery.
Could you face it more easily
than the certainty of having killed him?
SHINJI:
Could you?
HISA:
It is for you to answer.

SHINJI:
Hisa, Hisa!
HISA:
Shinji, remember the day I let you touch me
standing on the moon-bridge in the park?
SHINJI:
I remember.
HISA:
You told me about a flower you had seen,
a morning glory, still half asleep
in the shade. Even so, you said,
it did not forget to bloom.
SHINJI: (*Lifts his eyes to hers*)
Let it bloom, then;
O God, let it bloom!
CHORUS:
"The Song of the Morning Glory"
A medley of remembered flowers:
The bluets and the yellow lilies,
And the little trumpets of the dawn.
Will they ever blow again?

They broke like a cry from the ground,
Blared in the city's wounds,
Flared and flaunted for a time.
Will such a time come again?

The winter moonlight weaves
A thick brocade of frost.
A flute inquires of the night:
Will morning's glory come?
(*The lights change*)
Seven months have passed, seven moons.
Seven moons have come and gone.
The spring mist is already abroad,
and the time of the child is come.
(*Okuma appears, removes his shoes, and bows low, as in a
Buddhist temple. Kneeling, he plucks a taper out of the air
and lights a candle*)
O heart, in your anxious watching

you beat the silks of foreboding.
No one listens, the old man thinks.
Seven months ago, if only they had listened,
we might have opened to the wind
one more fold in the cloth of fear.
Now the time of the child is come.
And my heart—oh, my heart
is like an old rooster
afraid to bring on the dawn.
> (*Hands joined before his face, Okuma bows till his head
> touches the ground: then he rises, bows as before, and goes
> to his position on the platform*)

Seven months, seven moons.
The wind searches in the cloth of fear.
The folds lift and fall, lift and fall.
> (*Shinji appears, bows low as in a church, and kneels down.
> He plucks a taper out of the air and lights a candle*)

But the young man remembers:
We have passed our nights
in a tangle of passion and pain.
> (*Based on lines from Nishikigi*)

Will some vision issue from the night,
some pattern emerge from the tangle?
If not, what are these signs of spring to us?
This thinking of someone
who has no thought of you,
is it only an illusion?
And yet surely it is the natural way of love.
> (*Shinji makes the sign of the cross, then joins his hands
> before his face; he rises, bows as before, and goes to his
> position on the platform*)

Seven turns of time,
and the child stirs in the womb.
What are these signs in the sun and moon?
> (*The Doctor approaches*)

OKUMA:
The doctor, Shinji!

DOCTOR:
Your wife has given birth to a boy.
> (*Shinji stares at him*)

Did you hear me?
> SHINJI:

Yes; yes, I heard you. And my wife—?
> DOCTOR:

She's resting now.
> OKUMA:

Ah!
> SHINJI:

A boy, did you say?
> DOCTOR:

Yes.

(*They go out*)
> CHORUS:

"The Song of the Firstborn"
Like a branching tree in April
And the bright unmindful grass,
I do not forget my time:
I pluck on the strings of the air.

The blue air turns red and gold.
Fireflies jewel my window,
Echoing light like little
Drumbeats, then flying and flying.

A face in the morning moonlight,
A kiss as light as dew
On the Kaji leaf; and two sleeves
Scattering flute-notes in the air.
> (*Shinji joins Hisa in the inner room*)
> SHINJI:

Hisa.
> HISA:

Did you see him?
> SHINJI:

Yes.
> HISA:

Do you like him?
> SHINJI:

There was once a wild and beautiful crane
who loved another crane.

And they came together crying in the night.
She wanted to give him something
that would make them one forever.
So she made him a cloth woven of feathers
taken from her own body.
And she was very tired at the end.
When she gave him the gift
she asked him if he liked it.
He did not know what to say.
So he did a dance for her.
I'd dance for you too, Hisa,
except that I dance like a grasshopper—
remember?
(*Laughs*)
What shall we name him?

HISA:
We'll name him after you, of course.
Oh, Shinji,
if only to keep you here at my side
it were enough to speak your name!

SHINJI:
When you speak it over the child,
it will be like the sound of water.

HISA:
Live for the child, Shinji!

SHINJI:
All my desire is before you.
Can I say more than that?

HISA:
I feel myself again on the edge of the pit.

SHINJI:
No, Hisa, all the passion and pain ...

HISA: (*Eyes wide with terror*)
Shinji!

SHINJI:
What is it, Hisa?

HISA:
I see—I—see—

SHINJI:
What?

(*Following her gaze*)
What is it you see?
(*Turning back to her*)
Hisa, why are you staring like that?
        HISA:
It comes again!
        CHORUS:
I see a dragon rising from sleep!
I see him come in pursuit of the woman
intent upon the child,
and his brushing wings are a storm.
        SHINJI:
Hisa!
        CHORUS:
I see fire and black rain
crouching in the clouds,
and a great surge of blood
rising up to meet it.
And in that sea of blood and fire
I see a red beast—
        HISA:
The beast, the beast!
        CHORUS:
And the dragon giving him power.
And I hear someone say,
"It is not over. It comes again."
        (*Hisa falls back upon the mat with a cry*)
        SHINJI:
Hisa! O God! Doctor, doctor!
        CHORUS:
"The Song of the Beast"
I sit on the dragon's throne,
And his mark is on my thigh.
Seven times seventy thousand
Cry, "Who is like the Beast?"

From the rising of the sun to its setting
I shadow the world with my power.
And I know how to strike out life
Like firefly's flash in the dark.

The wild monkeys cry out in alarm.
The owl mourns from the pine
With eyes melting in a mask of moss.
Woe to the bird without wings!
    SHINJI:
Hisa! Hisa ...
    CHORUS: (*Based on lines from the psalms*)
What gain, I said, what gain would there be
from her lifeblood,
from her going down into the grave?
Can dust utter thanks
through the tangles of grass?
But like a weaver who severs the last thread
you have folded up her life.
    DOCTOR:
I did everything I could.
    SHINJI:
Of course. I do not blame you.
If anyone is to blame, it's me.
    DOCTOR:
If I were looking for someone to blame,
I would go further back than you.
    OKUMA:
To whom shall we go?
Death comes.
We are punished for living.
And there's an end of it.
    (*The Doctor goes out; then Okuma*)
    CHORUS:
Death is both a mask and a sign.
It tells us and does not tell us
that the only punishment God sends
is not to send his Spirit.
    (*Shinji looks up*)
And the young man remembers:
    SHINJI:
I ... make ... all things ... new.

CHORUS:
"The Song of the Apocalypse"
All at once,
In a trance,
Behind a mask of rain,
I saw the city in a jasper sea
Fed by seven rivers.
I looked down, and remembered the dew on the Kaji leaf.
I looked up, and beheld a man with a silver flask,
The river-waves dancing on his sleeve.
He bent down by the Kaji leaf and treasured up the dew.

The End

Ethan Phillips

PENGUIN BLUES

Ethan Phillips

Ethan Phillips's first play, *Penguin Blues*, selected here for first-time publication, was a hit in the 1987 Philadelphia Festival of New Plays. Reviewer William B. Collins describes the play in *The Philadelphia Inquirer*: "*Penguin Blues* is a funny and touching struggle for understanding between two very different people in a rehabilitation home for alcoholics. The characters are a guilt-stricken nun and a young man who does voice-over readings on commercials and looks properly dismayed by his invisibility." And reviewer Michael Caruso in the *News of Delaware County* raves, "Phillips convincingly brings the two together in one of the loveliest moments of emotional revelation I've seen in the theatre in more than 11 years of reviewing. In writing that is crisp and concise, yet flowing with sentiment (but not sentimentality), Phillips lays to rest a horrible past and looks out onto the future with hope."

Mr. Phillips received a Master of Fine Arts degree from Cornell University in 1976. As an actor, he has performed Off-Broadway in the premieres of Dennis McIntyre's *Modigliani* at the Astor Place theatre and Christopher Durang's *The Nature and Purpose of the Universe* at the Wonderhorse Theatre. He was in the smash revival of *The Last of the Red Hot Lovers* for the America Jewish Theatre and has also appeared in plays at Playwrights Horizons, the Courtyard Playhouse, and the Direct Theatre. His regional acting credits include performances in the premiere of Kevin Kling's *Lloyd's Prayer* and in Richard Dresser's *Alone at the Beach* for the Actors Theatre of Louisville's Humana Festival. He has played leading roles at Princeton, New Jersey's McCarter Theatre; the Alaska Repertory Theatre; Theatreworks at the Boston Shakespeare Company; the Los Angeles Public Theatre; the Salt Lake Acting Company; and the Westport Country Playhouse. Recent stage performances include roles in *Almost Perfect*, directed by Geraldine Fitzgerald at the Hudson Guild Theatre and in Terrence McNally's *Up in Saratoga* at San Diego's Old Globe Theatre.

As a film actor he appears in *Ragtime, Critters, Burglar, Bloodhounds of Broadway*, and *Lean on Me*. In television Ethan was a regular on ABC's *Benson*, and has guest-starred in a score of other television shows and TV movies. Mr. Phillips is a founding member of First Stage, the Los Angeles-based playwrights' workshop, has been an actor with the Sundance Institute's Playwrights' Conference in Utah for the past five summers, and is a member of the Dramatists Guild.

Penguin Blues, developed in part with the support of the Sundance Institute, was produced by the Philadelphia Festival Theatre in 1987, directed by Gloria Muzio, and starred Helen-Jean Arthur and Peter Zapp. The author dedicates this play to Peter Hay and to David Kranes.

Author's Note:

If the central nervous system becomes addicted to alcohol, feelings get stuffed, unarticulated, buried, boiling underneath. When the substance is withdrawn, feelings will rush to the surface, pushed to an extreme by the chemical dependency.

Denial is the backbone of addiction. The disease does not allow one to see that s/he is addicted. However, denial can be broken. Sometimes life puts you in a situation where you can let go.

Characters:

ANGELITA, *fifty-five.* *She wears a polyester smock, plain skirt, black shoes. She is a good woman who has been lonely and cloistered much of her life. She is frightened and very anxious. She needs a drink.*

GORDON, *thirty-five.* *He wears casual but expensive clothes. He is balding. He is a jester and has a difficult time with silence. He is nervous. He is angry, but the key word is likeable. He tries to be nice. The attacks come almost in spite of himself. He needs a drink.*

Setting:

A room somewhere in the midwest. A bed. Two chairs. A small desk. A window. There is a crucifix on the wall.

Time:

It is summer, it is early evening.
Lights come up on Angelita, alone.

ANGELITA:
God is our refuge and strength
A very present help in trouble.
Therefore we will not fear though the
Earth should change
Though the mountains shake in the
Heart of the sea;
Though its water roar and foam,
Though the mountains tremble with
Its tumult.
God is our refuge and strength.
(*Lights come down. In a moment lights come up on Angelita and Gordon, sitting. There is a long uncomfortable pause*)

GORDON: Nice room.

ANGELITA: Thank you.

GORDON: Same as mine.

ANGELITA: Yes. Of course.

(*Pause*)

GORDON: My bed's too soft.

ANGELITA: Oh.

GORDON: Yep. (*Pause*) My bed is too soft. (*Pause*) Huh. So.

(*Pause*)

ANGELITA: Where are you from?

GORDON: Los Angeles. Now. I was born in New Jersey. (*Pause*) Where are you from?

ANGELITA: Wisconsin.

GORDON: Ah! Milk and cheese. Heavy cream always gives me a hard-on. Sorry.

ANGELITA: That's fine, please. Don't worry about me. I know what that is, and it's okay.

GORDON: Well, it's true. It does. It always has. Very rich, on cereal, it's ... I like dairy products. Do you like dairy products?

ANGELITA: I'm not allowed any.

GORDON: I do. They're good. I like dairy products. (*Pause*) So, how about those Mets!?

ANGELITA: Is Los Angeles nice?

GORDON: I like cities with green air, but you may not.

ANGELITA: I've never been there.

GORDON: Los Angeles ... is ... like ... if you have this date with this gorgeous girl ... I mean she's ... she's the girl of your dreams ... you can't believe you're going out with her ... and you're real excited and you go over to her house to pick her up and when you get there she's dead. So-o-o ... you do some cocaine, you take her out anyway. (*Pause*) We're talking about a town where you meet people who want to be game show hosts. How long do we have to talk? What did she say, about fifteen minutes?

ANGELITA: I think so, Gordon.

GORDON: Don't call me Gordon, okay? I know that's my name, but for some reason I hate it when you say it.

ANGELITA: Don't I say it right?

GORDON: I don't think you can.

(*Pause*)

ANGELITA: Well, thank you for making the time.

GORDON: Well, I've been lax. Supposed to do this with all the new people, I just haven't.

ANGELITA: How long have you been here?

GORDON: Oh-h, I'm an old-timer now. Twelve days. I'm gonna smoke, okay?

ANGELITA: (*Disconcerted, there is no ash tray*) Please.

GORDON: (*He lights cigarette and makes an ash tray from the match box he carries. He may continue to smoke throughout the play*) Huh. I never used to ask that. I guess I'm getting better. I had a sign on the wall in my apartment that said, "Thank you for smoking." (*Pause*) Not that you *had* to smoke if you were visiting me, my point was ... uh, fuck it. Whoops, shit. Sorry! God, I got a foul mouth.

ANGELITA: That's all right, really.

GORDON: I'm just aware of you.

ANGELITA: Don't let it bother you.

GORDON: Don't let it bother me. Okay. (*He laughs*) What's black-and-white and can't turn around in an elevator? (*Pause*) A nun with a spear through her head. (*Pause*) Wisconsin, huh?

ANGELITA: Yes.

GORDON: That was one of those states when I was a kid, like Montana, I thought was weird, you know? Wisconsin ... Montana ... North Dakota ... lies made up by the government to explain vast tracts of land ... I never drank in Wisconsin. I've never been to Wisconsin. I've always wanted to visit it to see if it really existed.

ANGELITA: It does.

GORDON: I know that now. Do you know Wisconsin consumes more brandy than any state in the union?

ANGELITA: Brandy?

GORDON: Yeah.

ANGELITA: Hmm.

GORDON: Yeah, brandy.

(*Pause*)

ANGELITA: How are you getting on here?

GORDON: It's tough. You kind of get used to it. I think it's good sometimes.

ANGELITA: I just got here.

GORDON: Well, you're fixing up your room nice. Nice crucifix.

(*Pause*)

ANGELITA: You seem worried.

GORDON: I'm losing all my hair. Rip-off. I was going to this woman in L.A. ... uhh ... who's supposed to make it grow again. Jesus Christ. Dumb treatment. She's got this dumb treatment thing she does, it costs like sixty bucks a shot, she squeezes this lemon citrus solution on the scalp, and then rubs it in really hard, and it stings, she's this French woman, and it really stings like it's on fire, and then she puts "special mud" on it, which kind of cools it off a little, and you sit there with this mud on your head for twenty minutes and there's all these other women in the room, you know, her other clients, getting their eyelashes dyed or something, and talking about shoes and stuff and you feel like an idiot sitting there. And then finally she washes it off, and then she takes this electronic comb, it has this, umm ... have you ever seen those electronic fly catchers, those electric grill-like boxes with a zappy blue light that kills flies? When they fly into it?

(*Pause*)

ANGELITA: No.

GORDON: This comb, it's the same kind of thing, this static blue light ... uhh, electricity that kind of pops when she scrapes it across your scalp, and she just rakes this comb over your head and it really hurts, you feel like punching her, and then she takes a regular comb and combs around your hair and she always goes, "Ooh ... I see all these little bébé hairs coming up," but it's all bullshit 'cause I'm still losing my hair and I'm out three thousand bucks from seeing this woman, the only thing is I don't have any flies on my scalp, bit fat deal.

(*Pause*)

ANGELITA: My brother is going bald.

GORDON: That makes me feel a lot better. Brother's bald. Got a balding brother, huh? (*Pause*) What's your family? Who's in your family?

ANGELITA: I have five brothers and three sisters.

GORDON: Big family. Are you the only one who became a bride of Christ?

ANGELITA: Yes.

GORDON: Where do you fit in?

ANGELITA: I'm the oldest.

GORDON: Are your parents alive?

ANGELITA: My father is. He's almost eighty.

GORDON: Does he drink?

ANGELITA: He still likes his beer.

GORDON: Huh. (*Pause*) A lot?

ANGELITA: What?

GORDON: Does he like his beer a lot?

ANGELITA: It keeps him from scowling.

GORDON: Yea, it has that effect on some people.

ANGELITA: Do you have a big family?

GORDON: Lots of sisters. Does your family know you're here yet?

ANGELITA: No, they don't.

GORDON: When are you gonna tell them?

ANGELITA: They're scattered in all different places.

GORDON: So are you gonna tell some of them you're here?

ANGELITA: I don't think I have to.

GORDON: You don't have to. But Grace is gonna ask you to notify them.

ANGELITA: Well, I won't worry them.

GORDON: She's gonna insist that you tell them.

ANGELITA: I don't think so.

(*Pause*)

GORDON: Did you check yourself in?

ANGELITA: No.

GORDON: Interesting.

ANGELITA: I was ... sent here.

GORDON: By who?

ANGELITA: "By whom."

GORDON: Thank you. Thank you. I needed that. By whom were you sent here?

ANGELITA: I was sent here by the Sister Superior.

GORDON: Had a problem, huh?

ANGELITA: I came because apparently I might have a problem.

GORDON: You don't think you have a problem?

ANGELITA: I was sent here.

GORDON: (*To himself*) I wonder if the pig from hell drank.

ANGELITA: Pardon?

GORDON: (*Crossing to window*) What? Ohh, ... this, this, this, this, lady I, you know, these grounds are nice here, though, huh? Do you think the grounds are nice?

ANGELITA: No. I don't think they're all that special. They seem institutional. They gave me a pass and I went on a walk before dinner.

GORDON: Dinner? You call that dinner? Please. I've had bad food before, and I even like bad food—hospital food, plane food, I like that, but I wouldn't feed this slop to a dog. I had some rice pudding last night, the raisins walked out. (*Pause*) A lot of people think I'm funny.

ANGELITA: I'm sorry, I don't know what you mean?

GORDON: The "raisins walked out"—of the rice pudding. (*Pause*) The rice pudding was so bad, that the raisins, who were in the rice pudding, even they couldn't take it there, they had to leave the rice pudding, that's how bad the pudding was.

ANGELITA: (*She gets the joke half-way through his explanation and attempts a laugh*) Oh. Yes. I see.

(*Pause*)

GORDON: The food is bad. You better watch out: they put this brown gravy on everything. I woke up this morning, it was on my sheets! (*Pause*) This is fun for me.

ANGELITA: Did someone send you here?

GORDON: I checked myself in. I don't have any doubts. I'm a drunk. It's hard talking to you.

ANGELITA: I guess we don't have much in common.

GORDON: Except booze. And the mother church.

ANGELITA: Were you raised a Catholic?

GORDON: I was lowered a Catholic.

ANGELITA: I mean were you brought up a Catholic?

GORDON: I was brought down a Catholic.

ANGELITA: Are you Catholic, Gordon?

GORDON: (*Mimics someone in electric shock. Then:*) I was.

ANGELITA: You aren't in the church now?

GORDON: No, they binded with briars my joys and desires.

ANGELITA: William Blake.

GORDON: No, the church. Blake just hit the nail on the head.

(*Pause*)

ANGELITA: Jesus said His teachings would be misinterpreted. Jesus said that.

GORDON: He did?

ANGELITA: Well, I wasn't there when He said it.

GORDON: (*Laughing*) That's good! That's a joke!

ANGELITA: Yes. Thank you. And the God that was preached to me as a little girl was vindictive. He was a vindictive God. But I knew ... I know He's a loving God.

GORDON: Well, they fooled me.

(*Pause*)

ANGELITA: I assume ... Catholic schools?

GORDON: School of the Immaculate Conception. My formative years. Immaculate Conception. Only the Catholics would name a school after a sex act. In this case, an asexual act, but still ... Sodomy High?

ANGELITA: I certainly am getting an education here so far.

GORDON: Huh.

ANGELITA: Some things ... that young man in group today, with that problem?

GORDON: Leo, yeah. The cross-dresser.

ANGELITA: Now, I'm not sure ... what that means. At first I thought it might mean he wears a crucifix, but I know it's not that.

GORDON: You don't know what it means?

ANGELITA: No. I don't know what it means.

GORDON: Where are you from? Wisconsin?

ANGELITA: Yes.

GORDON: What, some little town in the middle of nowhere?

ANGELITA: Yes.

GORDON: You must have been pretty confused then.

ANGELITA: What?

GORDON: About Leo.

ANGELITA: Oh, yes ... he seemed ashamed.

GORDON: I thought it was pretty brave of him to bring it up in front of everyone.

ANGELITA: It was difficult for him. (*Pause*) And it means?

GORDON: He likes to dress up in women's clothing.

(*Pause*)

ANGELITA: Oh, I see.

(*Pause*)

GORDON: So, you're not gonna tell your family?

ANGELITA: I don't really see why I should do that, it would just upset them unnecessarily.

GORDON: You're not going to tell them.

ANGELITA: I believe I've answered that question now.

GORDON: Kind of.

(*Pause*)

ANGELITA: Have you told your family?

GORDON: Nope.

ANGELITA: You haven't?

GORDON: Nope.

ANGELITA: Are you afraid to?

GORDON: No ... I haven't lived at home in fifteen years, they don't have the slightest idea I've got any kind of problem. I'm not gonna call them up and say, "Hi Mom, hi Dad, guess what? I'm chemically dependent? What's new with you?" They're too old. They don't care. They'd probably get real mad.

ANGELITA: They couldn't support your being here?

GORDON: They think I'm a well-adjusted success, Sister Angelita, so why should I upset them unnecessarily?

ANGELITA: They have a right to know.

GORDON: And yours doesn't?

ANGELITA: I'm here because I may have a problem.

GORDON: That's good, be firm. Hey! What do you drink?

ANGELITA: Oh, very little.

GORDON: No, no, not how much. What did you drink?

ANGELITA: I drank some beer.

GORDON: Beer? You liked beer?

ANGELITA: You don't like beer?

GORDON: I love beer. Do you *love* beer?

ANGELITA: I like the taste. It was refreshing.

GORDON: It is. It was. It was. It was. (*Pause*) You know, I was thinking this morning of all the places I never got to drink. I mean, I never had a beer in Manitoba ... or a bottle of bourbon in ... Baja ... all the places I didn't get to drink.

ANGELITA: I used to enjoy sharing a beer with my father.

GORDON: Yeah?

ANGELITA: Out on the porch. When I would visit him.

GORDON: What'd'ja talk about?

ANGELITA: We didn't talk. He doesn't talk much, and I'm not a talker.

GORDON: So, what was so enjoyable about it? (*Pause*) The beer, huh? Let's talk quantity. How much did you drink?

ANGELITA: Oh, I didn't drink much.

GORDON: Angelita, you're here. Social drinkers don't end up here.

ANGELITA: I have no social life. I couldn't very well be a social drinker.

GORDON: How much do you drink? It's a very simple question.

ANGELITA: I drank about a twelve-pack every two days, I suppose. Yes.

GORDON: That's a six-pack a day. You're not a big woman. Twelve ounce? Twelve ounce cans?

ANGELITA: The ones that were a little bigger?

GORDON: Sixteen ounce.

ANGELITA: They were sixteen ounce?

GORDON: Yeah, I'm an expert. That's ninety-six ounces of beer a day, there's an ounce of alcohol in every twelve ounces of beer, twelve goes into ninety-six eight times, you were drinking eight ounces of alcohol a day, that's four doubles, or like a half a pint of scotch a day. Where'd you drink? You were in a convent?

ANGELITA: I live in a convent.

GORDON: Where do you drink in a convent?

ANGELITA: We have our own rooms.

GORDON: I thought you were going to say we have our own bar. You know, a place to unwind at the end of the day, after the rigors of teaching catechism.

ANGELITA: You don't know anything about me.

GORDON: Okay. Okay. (*Pause*) I was in a convent once. I think it was fourth grade. It smelled like wax. Me and Dick Kolb had to take a crate of orange juice ...

ANGELITA: Dick and I.

GORDON: Me and Dick. (*In a parody of a TV ad voice*) "That's right! Confront your addition *and* brush up on your grammar." You know, I was reading something recently about how they think now there is actually a nice nun somewhere, but they just haven't been able to locate her yet.

ANGELITA: (*Rising*) Grace said we had to talk and we have talked, so if you would be so kind as to leave now, I will see you in the morning.

GORDON: Come on, let's hang out a little. I'll go and get us some beer. I'm kidding.

ANGELITA: I don't like this.

GORDON: It's important for us to talk. Isn't it?

ANGELITA: Grace said yes ...

GORDON: Screw Grace ...

ANGELITA: ... for a short time, outside group, one-to-one conversation with other members ...

GORDON: Besides that.

ANGELITA: ... of the group are important, but I am very uncomfortable with you.

GORDON: So am I. With myself. I'm not very comfortable with myself at all. I've got the serenity of a subway.

ANGELITA: You confuse me. And I am already confused.

GORDON: I can't go yet, I'm sorry. Please? (*Gordon crosses and lies down on the bed. Pause*) What did you do with the cans?

ANGELITA: I ... left early in the morning with them. Before prayers. There was a garbage container down the block behind the A&P.

GORDON: Sneaky.

ANGELITA: And someone caught me at it. Father Lahey caught me at it. He'd been watching me for several days. He confronted me. He was concerned, he said. I was standing there by the dumpster with a bag of empty beer cans. The sun was coming up. He said that I could get help. But this seems so extreme ... I liked the taste.

GORDON: Yeah. The taste. The touch. The tickle.

ANGELITA: Sneaky me. (*Pause*) And what did you drink?

GORDON: What have you got? Bourbon for a long time, I drank. But the last year or so I was drinking Popov vodka with a splash of Shasta diet cream soda on the rocks. Ahh! I wasn't really drinking anymore, though, when I came in here. I wasn't drinking any less either ... the last binge I went on was so long my bonds matured ... I woke up, I felt like Ireland—really ... I drank so much I put it on my résumé ... hell, I was even abusing placebos ... my liver looked like Beirut ... shh, don't, don't laugh so loud, you might disturb, uhh ...

ANGELITA: I'm sorry. I don't laugh much.

GORDON: I was a lot funnier when I was drinking.

ANGELITA: No, you're funny, it's me. (*Pause*) What do you do? For your work?

GORDON: I invented alcohol, I'm living off the royalties. (*Angelita laughs. In TV announcer voice*) Thank you! Thank you! "We'll be right back!"

ANGELITA: What do you do?

GORDON: I'm a voice-over artist.

ANGELITA: A voice-over artist?

GORDON: "If you could go for another Schaeffer, but don't want to *go* for another Schaeffer, next time get *two* six packs of Schaeffer, and don't get caught short."

ANGELITA: What are you telling me to do?

GORDON: No, that's what I do. Listen: "If you think you're better off with a less acid coffee, this will interest you. Here we have Kava, Sanka here. This is baking soda. It foams when it finds acid. Watch. Heavy foam shows acid here, there's almost no foam on Kava. Clear proof Kava is a less acid coffee. Put less acid in your cup with Kava: You'll enjoy it all the way down."

ANGELITA: (*Understanding now*) That's what you do?

GORDON: Yeah, they're radio ads. Ever listen to a radio?

ANGELITA: Yes. I see. I know what you mean.

GORDON: The first one I ever got was for Wrangler jeans. There were three of us in front of the mike and it went, "The new captain of the football team is Hal Smith." And then you hear another voice go, "Hunh?!!?" And then the third voice says, "Gee, he's not even on the team." And the first guy, the coach, says, "He is now, ever since he started wearing Wranglers." I was the guy who said, "Hunh?!!?" That's all I did. "Hunh?!!?" I got thirteen hundred dollars. It took fifteen minutes. "Hunh?!!?" Thirteen hundred dollars for simulating surprise. I said I think I'll do this for a living. Lots of free time, you don't have to look your best, hairline doesn't matter.

ANGELITA: What a peculiar job.

GORDON: It's a lot like being a nun.

ANGELITA: Why is that?

GORDON: It's a dirty job but somebody's got to do it.

ANGELITA: Being a nun is not a job.

GORDON: They did a job on me.

ANGELITA: You have a versatile voice. Do you sing?

GORDON: In third grade we were singing Christmas carols and Sister Venatia told me to shut up because I had a monotone. I've kind of had a block since then.

ANGELITA: I'll bet you could sing.

(*Pause*)

GORDON: What do you do? I mean, as a nun?

ANGELITA: I'm a teacher. I teach.

GORDON: You're an educator! What grades?

ANGELITA: Oh, Lord, I've had all of them ... from first through eighth.

GORDON: What was your favorite?

ANGELITA: I liked the little children the best.

GORDON: Get 'em early, huh?

ANGELITA: They're so willing then. So sweet and simple. Little faces. Later they become ... they're not so sweet and simple, later.

GORDON: (*To himself*) Yes, they are. Yes, they are.

ANGELITA: (*She looks at him*) When I was a little girl once I ... danced. I was alone, and I was dancing. I was just dancing. By myself. I was having a good time. But my father saw me. He was frowning. And I stopped.

(*Pause*)

GORDON: I don't dance.

ANGELITA: You could dance.

GORDON: So could you.

ANGELITA: No. But you could.

GORDON: Forget it. No ... maybe sometime ... I could dance, I could sing ... I could dance ... I don't know how ... I am so ... an ocean of beer, right now! This place drives you crazy ... all they talk about is alcohol ... everywhere you turn, they're handing you stuff to read about "the disease," so much to read, I got the pamphlet the other day, "Alcohol and Your Laundry." (*He laughs*) I'm only kidding. I think I'll go get some fruit. Nice crucifix. Good talking to you. (*He goes to leave*)

ANGELITA: They did a job on you.

GORDON: What?

ANGELITA: The nuns. (*Pause*) They did a job on you.

GORDON: I'm a big boy now, they can't touch me, so fuck 'em. And I don't even care. What makes me so ... ? It's so immature ... I'm so ... this is all really ... "What are you feeling, Gordy?"

ANGELITA: Is that why you drink?

GORDON: God, you're naive! They didn't ... I may have been a sensitive kid, but they weren't that powerful.

ANGELITA: Please keep your voice down.

GORDON: Listen: I drank because it was the first goddamn thing in my life that made me feel good. Right from the bottle, baby, eyeballs burning, sucking in that beautiful booze ... and I miss the good old days, of which I'm reminded of by everything I look at, the sun, the moon, the *TV Guide*, oh it's Thursday I think I'll have a (*Rapidly*) drink, drink, drink, drink, drink—hey, but you know? You're here, what, two days?

ANGELITA: Yes.

GORDON: I spent my first week here desperately trying to prove I was not an alcoholic so that I could go out and drink! Are you a drunk, Angelita?

ANGELITA: Please don't call me ...

GORDON: Why are you here?

ANGELITA: A sign of God is being lead where we didn't plan on going.

GORDON: That's very cute. Are you an alcoholic?

ANGELITA: I'm a sister.

GORDON: That excludes you? You're immune? I read a history of the papacy. It's a list of screwballs and freaks. Damascus I was a pimp. Clement X was a wino. I'd tell you what Benedict XV was, but I doubt you'd know what it means.

ANGELITA: You're being cruel.

GORDON: Just beer?

ANGELITA: What?

GORDON: Just beer? Maybe a little wine? Come on ... we lie like rugs. All of us do. Didn't the nuns clean the sacristy? Dust up after the priest? After he cracked the bones of Christ and washed it down with His blood, there was always a little left over, I was an altar boy, I used to help myself, how about you?

ANGELITA: I have done nothing to you!

GORDON: Oh! You want to see the claw marks? The school sisters of Notre Dame. These women were trained by the SS, they slapped the shit out of me daily, I got their fingerprints on my soul.

ANGELITA: That wasn't ...

GORDON: Sister St. John the Baptist, she'd put a thimble on her pinky, her own little form of brass knuckles, it gave a slap a little extra ping, she'd run down the aisles with her arms spread out hitting everyone along the way, she'd get to me, I'd duck. Charley Welch sitting right behind me got it twice as hard, today he can't come unless he's in a confessional booth!

ANGELITA: That was her, Gordon, not me.

GORDON: She grabbed Rick Shea's head like a hardball and pounded it into the blackboard to make a point about sentence declension, only there was a nail there and it went into his skull. She made her point. They took her away. Finally, they took her away. But ole lucky me, I got the psychotic little bitch for three grades.

ANGELITA: But that's not me, Gordon.

GORDON: "Let's play Nancy Drew," she'd say, "Let's play Nancy Drew today." And then she'd—and I hate all this hate that I got—she'd become this sick little detective and pin these imaginary crimes on me. She told me she had pictures of me growing drugs in my basement! This is 1959! I was a little boy!

ANGELITA: Don't you see? She was sick, Gordon.

(*Gordon looks at Angelita*)

GORDON: She ... I was staying after school one day ... in eighth grade ... I was being punished for something ... I can't remember what. And she told me to go down to the principal's office to get something or deliver something or something ... and I was running down the hallway, feeling pretty good, believe it or not, and I tripped—my sneaker had a hole in it—and I tripped and hurt my knee when I fell—and I got real mad 'cause I was in a football game the next day and now my knee hurt, so I tore off the sneaker and started to rip it apart, I was really mad, and I said, "Shit. Fuck." And there, standing over me were these two nuns, and they heard me say, "shit, fuck" and they just looked at me and then they walked away, but I knew by the way they looked at me they were gonna tell Sister John and the next day was Saturday and football went okay and on Sunday I went

to the children's mass and I'd been scared all weekend, but
when I saw the look on Sister John's face at that mass, I was
terrified. On Monday I was an angel all morning. I wasn't
taking any chances. And then standing in line to go to lunch, in
front of me was my best friend, Howie Jackson, and we used to
do this thing —it was a silly little thing—I'd blow on the back of
his neck and he'd kind of slap it, like that.

(*Gordon slaps his neck, lightly*)

I don't know where we got it from, but we used to do it all
the time and it always made us smile, and I smiled and she saw
me and that was all she needed ... and this pig from hell came
over and slapped me very hard, but she kept slapping me ... in
front of everyone ... she just kept slapping me ... and slapping
me ... and slapping me ... she wouldn't stop ... and I was just a
little boy.

ANGELITA: I'm sorry.

GORDON: I was just a little boy. And I couldn't hit back.
That was a sacrilege, even to think it. Burn in hell forever. And
I couldn't tell my mom and dad because I was afraid of them, too
... I was just ... afraid ... all the time.

ANGELITA: She was sick, Gordon. She was a sick woman.

GORDON: She was sick.

ANGELITA: I'm not going to hit you.

GORDON: No.

ANGELITA: She hurt you. And I know you're in pain.

GORDON: She hurt me.

ANGELITA: But let her go, Gordon. Let her free.

GORDON: Maybe she was ...

ANGELITA: (*She touches her heart with her first*) ...
hurting ...

GORDON: ... too ...

ANGELITA: (*Pause*) I saw what went on. There was
cruelty. There was terror. (*Pause*) I taught fifty girls and boys
eight different subjects. Fifty girls and boys. Seven hours a day.
Do you know I had third grade and eighth grade simultaneously?
In one classroom. For thirty minutes the third grade for their
arithmetic, the eighth grade had to wait, and then I'd give the
eighth grade their geography while the third grade sat and
waited. And they waited with all the patience of children. It
was crowded. And dull. And then we got all the discipline

problems, they didn't give them to the public school, they gave them to us. Because we were allowed to handle them. And so I was strict. I had to be strict ... but I never hit anyone.

GORDON: Huh.

ANGELITA: I never hit anyone, I understand that that happened and I know women, good women, who come to their wit's end ... simply couldn't take it ... couldn't take any of it. And they left, some women left, weren't strong enough ... have enough faith ... It was trying ... trying ... trying to be obedient, trying to please Christ ...

GORDON: Angelita.

ANGELITA: Oh, you don't know. Up at 5:00 a.m. for prayers, then mass, and yes, I cleaned the sacristy, at one time that was one of my chores. They celebrated mass, we cleaned up after them, and that is hard: I see now. You know we aren't permitted to perform in the liturgy, any layman can ... but we women, second class citizens of the church ...

GORDON: Hey, Angelita?

ANGELITA: Isn't it valuable? Being of service? Who thanked us? Who ever thanked me? For what I did? I put aside everything, everything and we're freaks. We are freaks.

GORDON: No. No, no, no, wait. The beer.

ANGELITA: Oh, look at me. We don't wear habits anymore. I'm so exposed.

GORDON: The beer, Angelita, the beer!

ANGELITA: Gordon, do you know what it's like to believe in a God that's only in your mind? I am a child of God ... I am a bride of Jesus ... and it is so lonely to be God's lover ... it is so lonely.

GORDON: Angelita, listen to me. The beer, the dumpster ...

ANGELITA: I am a sister! And I am so ashamed ... to be here...

GORDON: (*Smiling*) Yeah.

ANGELITA: I am so ashamed that I am a ... that I am a ...

GORDON: Angelita. (*He is able to go over to her now and embrace her*) My God.

(*Lights down*)

The End

Katherine Snodgrass

HAIKU

Katherine Snodgrass

Haiku is the first play written by Katherine Snodgrass. It won the 1987–88 Heideman Award presented by the Actors Theatre of Louisville and appears here in print for the first time. The play is a sensitive character study focusing on a mother who is going blind and her exceptional younger daughter who has provided the poetic inspiration for the haiku published under her mother's name. The older daughter questions her sister's ability to have written the poems and doubts the credibility of her mother's report.

Katherine Snodgrass was born in Wichita, Kansas, and received a B.A. in English Literature from the University of Kansas and a B.A. in Speech and Drama from Wichita State University. She studied acting at the London Academy of Music and Dramatic Art and in New York City with disciples of Sanford Meisner and Michael Chekhov. She has worked in New York City as an actress and as a director. She taught English composition at Wichita State University where she attended the Master of Fine Arts Program in Creative Writing and where she was awarded the Creative Writing Fellowship in Fiction in 1987. She received an M.A. in Creative Writing (fiction and playwriting) at Boston University in 1988, where she teaches creative writing with an emphasis on playwriting.

She is also a member of Actors Equity Association; the film actors union, A.F.T.R.A.; and the Dramatists Guild. She is currently at work on another one-act play and a full-length play.

NELL: You were born in early winter. John and I planned it
that way. I couldn't imagine having a baby in the summertime.
It gets so sticky in August, humid. A breech baby. You tried to
back into the world. I remember, the doctor had to pull you out.
It was night when they finally brought you to me.
LOUISE: November evening.
Blackbirds scull across the moon.
My breath warms my hands.

(*Nell writes haiku, then checks what she has written, holding the paper two inches from her eyes*)

NELL: John said you were too beautiful to live. It was true. You and Bebe together, you were like china dolls. Delicate, perfect. And then ... I sensed it that day when I saw you through the window. Billie was on the swingset, and you were there. Outside. She was in red, and you had on that blue jumpsuit, the corduroy one with the zipper. The ball lay beside you and that Mama doll that winked. You were so quiet. You'd stared before, of course, when something fascinated you, as all children do when they ... as all children do. But this time, you were ... different. I called for you to come inside. *Lulu, come inside and have some lunch!* But you didn't hear me. *Bebe, bring Lulu and come inside!* I went out then. I had to get down on my knees beside you. I touched your hair and then your face. I held up that Mama-doll, but you stared through it in a way that ... Funny, I don't remember being afraid. I remember the look on Bebe's face.

LOUISE:
Chainmetal swings clanging
In the empty schoolyard.
Silent summer rain.

(*Nell writes haiku. She goes through same process as before*)

NELL: Do you know, I used to cry when school ended? It's true! I used to cry on the last day of school every year. My mother thought I was crazy. I'd come dragging my book bag over the fields, my face all wet. And my momma! ... Nellie, she'd say ...

LOUISE: Nellie, she'd say ... (*Nell looks sharply at Louise*) You're the strangest girl I ever did see!

NELL: Yes, that's what she said. Are you tired?

LOUISE: No, no. Tell me again about John.

NELL: You look tired.

LOUISE: Please. You haven't talked about John in a long time.

NELL: John. All right then. John was tall and thin like Icabod Crane, only not so scared.

LOUISE: John wasn't scared of anything.

NELL: He wasn't scared of anything, not John. He had a big, strong jaw and a tuft of yellow hair that stood up on his head, as yellow ...

LOUISE: ... as Mr. Turner's daffodils.

NELL: At least. And he would take you on his knee. Do you remember the song he used to sing? (*Nell clears her throat and sings*) "*Here come a Lulu! Here come a Lulu to the Indian dance.*" (*Louise joins in*) "*All of them Indians, all of them Indians dance around Lulu's tent.*" (*Like a drum*) "*Here come a Lulu! Here come a Lulu! Here come a Lulu!*"

(*They laugh, remembering*)

LOUISE:

Icy branches bend,

Breaking over stones.

I hear my dead father laugh.

(*Nell writes haiku, same process as before*) Wasn't there a story about a fox? Who had a bushy tail?

NELL: You remember that?

LOUISE: And John would rub Bebe's back until she went to sleep. He smelled of soap and something ... sweet?

NELL: (*Drily*) Sweet! Cigars. From Havana.

LOUISE: (*Repeated with Nell's exact inflection*) Cigars. From Havana.

NELL: (*Looks at her sharply*) Let's stop now.

LOUISE: No!

NELL: I think I should give you your medicine.

LOUISE: No, no, I want to do more.

NELL: Louise.

LOUISE: I'm not ready to go back. Please, not yet.

NELL: We've got to be careful.

LOUISE: But I can do it! I promise. Give me a chance. Please, Momma, I get so little time as it is, and I hate to go back. It's like being smothered.

NELL: I know ...

LOUISE: Everything is so dim, and I can't hear you properly. Or see you or touch you or ... (*Louise sees the bruise on Nell's arm*) Did I do that?

NELL: It's not bad. (*Nell touches Louise's bandage*) Does this still hurt?

LOUISE: It's almost healed. Please, Momma? That was before, before I knew what to do. I can stop it, I know I can. I need to practice, you said so yourself.

NELL: Yes, I know what I said, but ...

LOUISE: If you don't let me practice, I'll never learn what to do.

NELL: I think it would be better ...

LOUISE: Let me see Bebe first. Then I can stand it.

NELL: Billie! My God, what time is it?

LOUISE: (*Repeating*) My God, what time is it?

(*During this next exchange, Nell removes football helmet from Louise's head and hides it. She then fishes in her pocket for a bottle of pills and brings it to Louise. There is an urgency*)

NELL: She'll be here any minute. Sit quietly.

LOUISE: Why is she coming?

NELL: I don't want to wait too long. You know we can't wait too long.

LOUISE: But I'll be good, I can control it.

NELL: You said that last week. We can't wait too long. You'll hurt yourself.

LOUISE: You'll hurt yourself. I mean no, I won't and you promised I could talk to Bebe. You said I *had* to talk to her this time. That we could show her.

NELL: We will, we will. But she'll be here any moment. (*Holding out pills*) I want you to take this now.

LOUISE: You promised I could wait for Bebe.

NELL: I know, but right now it's more important that you take ...

LOUISE: I need some water. I can't swallow.

NELL: Louise.

LOUISE: I can't swallow. My throat is dry.

NELL: Yes, yes, all right. Just a minute. (*Nell exits*)

LOUISE: Just a minute. Just a minute.

(*Billie is heard offstage. Abruptly lights change as Billie enters hurriedly with overnight case*)

BILLIE: Mother? Did you get my telegram? Where are you?

(*Billie glances at Louise, but does not greet her. She puts down her bag and exits again. She re-enters with another suitcase. Nell enters with glass of water. They face each other. There is an awkwardness in this exchange. Billie tries to hug Nell, but Nell has her hands full. Billie does not try again)*

BILLIE: Whew, I made it. How are you? You look exhausted. The traffic is worse than ever. I mean, the noise level, how do you stand it?

NELL: You're here. *(Nell sets down glass of water and pill)*

BILLIE: I knew you'd be surprised. It's not often I show up uninvited, is it? But I couldn't resist. I was so close on this buying trip.

NELL: Did Michael come with you? Your telegram didn't ...

BILLIE: No. No, he didn't. *(Quickly)* I'll just camp out in my old room. I didn't think you'd mind.

NELL: No, of course not, but is that all?

BILLIE: Oh, and look what I found in a little shop in Boston. They had all three of your books, is that unbelievable? And get this, they actually had them in the poetry section. I get so tired of searching through the books on Japanese culture. Do you need them or can I keep them? You know, I really love the cover on this last one.

NELL: You should have waited. I was going to send you a copy, but ...

BILLIE: They're finally getting the hang of it at that place. It took them long enough. Black and white photography is much closer to what you wanted all along, isn't it?

NELL: I've been so busy lately. I don't know how I could have forgotten ...

BILLIE: Of course, I had to see that lovely dedication. I'm such a pushover, I know, but it always gives me a little thrill to see my name in print. Even after the fact.

NELL: Let me get ...

BILLIE: I was just so surprised to run across them, and I was really impressed with this new cover. Where did they find the photographer?

NELL: Let me give you your copy now.

BILLIE: No, really, this one's fine. Well, Mother, it's not as if I can't afford it. At least it's not one of those dry biographies you usually write, the lives of saints or some such thing. Maybe you could sign it ... God, it never fails. Somehow with you I always feel like a groupie at the stage door. "Please, ma'am, it's a first edition and would you sign it, please?"

(*Billie holds out book for Nell to sign, but Nell is hesitant*)

NELL: I've already signed your copy of the new one. It's in the other room. But if you want me to sign this, too ... Why don't I do it later, all right? Let me do it later when Lulu's asleep. That way we ...

BILLIE: Fine, sure. Later is fine, whatever. Oh, I forgot. I brought something for Lulu, too.

(*Billie brings out package from her large bag and hands it to Nell. It is wrapped in very shiny wrapping paper with a bright ribbon*)

NELL: You did? Why, that was thoughtful. What is it?

BILLIE: Open it. Oh hell, it's another music box.

NELL: It's wrapped so prettily, why don't you let Lulu open it?

BILLIE: (*Laughing nervously*) Do we have time before dinner?

NELL: Billie.

BILLIE: I'm sorry. It's just that she'll like the wrapping paper better than the music box.

NELL: That's not true.

LOUISE: That's not true.

NELL: Lulu loves presents.

LOUISE: Lulu loves presents.

BILLIE: Yes, well ...

NELL: Here, you take it to her.

BILLIE: (*Sighing*) All right then.

(*Billie crosses to Louise. Lights fade to flashback colors on Louise and Billie. Throughout this sequence, Louise mimics Billie. They are children. Dolls must be mimed*)

Now see the dolly? This is the baby doll, and this is the mama doll. Now you take the baby doll and rock her to sleep like this. (*Singing*) "*Rockabye baby in the treetop. When the wind blows, the cradle will rock,*" that's right. You be the babysitter. And now the mama comes to play with the baby. Hello, baby.

LOUISE: Hello, baby.

BILLIE: My, you are sleeping so soundly I don't want to wake you up. How did my baby do today, Mrs. Lippoman? Was she a good baby?

LOUISE: Was she a good baby?

BILLIE: Let me see her. Isn't she the most beautiful baby in the whole ... No, give it back. No, you can't have the mama doll, you have the baby doll.

LOUISE: You have the baby doll.

BILLIE: No, let go. Let go!

LOUISE: Let go!

BILLIE: Give it back, you can't have both of them.

LOUISE: Both of them.

BILLIE: All right, then give me the baby doll.

LOUISE: Give me the baby doll.

BILLIE: Give it to me. It's my mama doll, and it's my baby doll. Let go, let go ... !

LOUISE: Let go, let go!

(*Baby doll breaks*)

BILLIE: Oh! That was my baby doll, it was mine, and I'm going to tell on you, you ...! I didn't want to play with you anyway. You're stupid, stupid!

LOUISE: Stupid, stupid!

BILLIE: I'm going to tell, and then I'll never have to play with you again. Not ever!

LOUISE: Not ever!

(*Lights come back to normal*)

BILLIE: My God, what happened to her forehead? Is she banging her head again?

NELL: No, no, of course not. We just had a little accident.

BILLIE: Isn't the medicine working?

NELL: Of course, yes. She fell down, that's all. She fell in the kitchen when I was making dinner.

BILLIE: Let's look at it. (*Billie moves to remove bandage, but Nell stops her*)

NELL: No, it's perfectly fine now. Almost healed.

BILLIE: Did you get that bruise at the same time?

NELL: (*Lying*) Oh, this? This is nothing. I don't even remember where I got it.

(*Louise holds up her hands for a hug*)

LOUISE: Bebe.

BILLIE: Good lord. Lulu, my love, you amaze me.

(*Louise and Billie hug*)

NELL: That's new, isn't it?

BILLIE: What?

NELL: She's different than when you saw her last, isn't she?

BILLIE: Because she hugged me? We all know how much that means.

NELL: Billie, what will we do with you?

BILLIE: Well, they're supposed to get more affectionate as they get older. I might as well be a rag doll that she's fond of. But if that's what you mean, that she's more ... responsive, then yes, we can thank whatever gods there be that she's not gone the other way. At least the medicine is doing that for her.

NELL: The medicine.

BILLIE: Yes. (*Touching Louise's bandage*)

NELL: But don't you think she's really getting better though? Honestly, look at her. Isn't she more alert?

BILLIE: Alert.

NELL: She knew you, Billie. She wanted to touch you.

BILLIE: Of course she knows me. I'm her sister. She's wanted to get her hands around my neck for years.

LOUISE: For years.

BILLIE: (*Laughing*) There, you see? All right, all right, let's try this. (*Billie takes wrapped music box and places it before Louise*) Ah, it's a lovely bow, isn't it? And look at that shiny wrapping paper. You love that, don't you? Look at her. I tell you, Nell, I wasted my money on the music box. This wrapping paper's going to be enough.

NELL: Let's just take this bow off. Here.

BILLIE: No fair, no fair helping.

NELL: Now this paper comes off. (*Louise suddenly tears the paper off the music box. She opens the box slowly as it tinkles out a song. She is enthralled*) There, now. There. Why that's beautiful, isn't it, Lulu? That's beautiful. See, see how she loves it?

BILLIE: Yes.

NELL: But look, look at her. She unwrapped it herself. She

...

BILLIE: Mother.

NELL: She knew exactly ...

BILLIE: No!

NELL: ... what to do. Don't you see the difference in her?

(*During next speech Billie closes music box and hands the shiny paper back to Louise*)

BILLIE: You never change, do you? No, I don't see any difference, no, she's not more alert, and no, she's not getting any better. All right, all right, maybe she's a little more affectionate. Maybe. But that's natural. Most of them become more affectionate. They learn to feed themselves and to go to the bathroom and to hug their sisters when they come home to visit.

NELL: You don't understand. You can't possibly know, you don't see her every day.

BILLIE: Yes, and you do, and you take every wink, every gaze out the window and rationalize it into some sort of normal reaction.

NELL: I don't rationalize. I don't need to. I see real change for the better.

(*Lights switch to flashback colors*)

BILLIE: Better bring her inside, Mamma. She's staring at the sun again. Maaa-maaa! (*There is no answer, so Billie takes a shiny prism from a chain around her own neck and shines it in front of Louise. Louise's eyes follow the prism. They are children again*)

BILLIE: (*Singing*) "Twinkle, twinkle, little star, how I wonder who you are." Oooo, pretty twinkle, pretty twinkle.
      Where is Lulu? Where is Lulu?
      Here I am, here I am.
      How are you this morning?
      Very well, I thank you.
(*Billie pulls Louise to her feet*)
      Please stand up. Please sit down.
(*Billie pulls Louise back down*)
      Where is Booboo? Where is Booboo?
      Here you are, here you are.
      How are you this morning?
      Very well, I thank you.
(*Billie pulls Louise to her feet*)
      Please stand up. Please sit down.
(*Billie pulls Louise back down. Billie begins to substitute Louise's name for different sounds. Louise imitates, repeating the last words*)

BILLIE:
> Where is Poopoo? Where is Poopoo?

LOUISE:
> Poopoo.

BILLIE:
> Where is Bongbong? Where is Bongbong?

LOUISE:
> Bongbong

(Billie gives up on the song and does the sounds rhythmically and playfully as Louise follows, repeating after each set of sounds. Facial expressions are imitated also)

BILLIE: *(And Louise after)*
> Grunt-grunt.
> Blah-blah.
> Heh-Heh.
> Oink-oink.
> Snort-snort.
> Snort-snort.
> Snort-snort.

(As the sounds become funny to her, Billie laughs and Louise imitates Billie. Billie realizes that Louise does not really understand so she holds up prism again. Louise follows it and Billie finally gives it to her, disappointed)

> Pretty twinkle, pretty twinkle.

(Lights go to present)

NELL: I know you've never been able to understand. You were too young, I suppose. It was asking too much of you.

BILLIE: Was it? Why have you never dedicated one of your books to Lulu?

NELL: What?

BILLIE: I've always wondered. When the first one came out, I felt so proud, so ... It seemed to make up for the times that you ... But then the second one ... and now this last. I'm wondering why. Why not for Lulu? Is it because she can't understand?

NELL: Can't ... ? No, no. That's not it at all. I'm glad you're here, Billie. I'm glad you came. I've been wanting to talk to you, but I haven't had the courage until now.

BILLIE: *(Waiting)* Yes.

(Silence)

NELL: *(Frustrated)* It's my eyes.

BILLIE: Yes. That's why I'm here.

NELL: Yes. You knew?

BILLIE: Doctor Dave called me. Don't look so horrified. What did you expect him to do? Ignore it?

NELL: I expect him to allow me to tell my family in my own good time.

BILLIE: And when would you have told me?

NELL: I was going to tell you today.

BILLIE: And what if I hadn't come today?

NELL: I would have told you.

BILLIE: I don't believe you.

LOUISE: I don't believe you.

(*Silence*)

BILLIE: Can you see me?

NELL: I can make out your shape. But it'll get worse.

LOUISE: But it'll get worse.

BILLIE: What are we going to do? Will Daddy's trust fund cover a nurse for Lulu?

NELL: No, and even if it would, I don't want some stranger in my house caring for Lulu. I'll do it myself.

BILLIE: How? How will you measure her medicine?

NELL: I'll manage. I've done it up until now.

BILLIE: What if she dirties her clothes? What if she has a reaction to the medicine? What if you were to fall, what would happen to Lulu? She couldn't help you. She wouldn't know what to do. Why, she wouldn't even understand that anything was wrong.

NELL: I do not have to have someone here. I've managed this long. Besides ...

BILLIE: Yes?

NELL: Lulu understands more than you know.

BILLIE: Lulu understands only what *you want* her to understand. Momma, you can't ignore your blindness like you do Lulu's illness. If you do, you'll only jeopardize your health and Lulu's.

NELL: I would never do that.

BILLIE: What would happen if she were to start one of her scenes? Could you help her alone? Mother, put her in a hospital where she can be taken care of properly. No, listen to me. I can help you. Michael and I have talked it over, and ... we'd be happy if you'd come live with us. Really, you can visit her every day. You can sit with her. Please. It's not as if she's going to know where she is.

NELL: Of course she knows where she is! What are you talking about? You haven't heard what I've been trying to say.

BILLIE: What haven't I heard?

NELL: That she's different. She's changed.

BILLIE: Changed how? And if you say that she's more affectionate ...

NELL: It's not just that. It's more. Much more. I haven't told you before this because I knew you wouldn't believe me. But you don't live with her, Billie, you don't see. (*Pause*) You asked why I dedicated the haiku to you and never to Louise. It's because I don't write the haiku.

(*Silence*)

BILLIE: What are you saying?

NELL: It's Louise.

(*Silence*)

BILLIE: No.

NELL: It's true.

BILLIE: That's impossible.

NELL: No, I swear it.

LOUISE: I swear it.

BILLIE: Momma.

NELL: It started two years ago, right after we changed to that new medication.

BILLIE: What are you saying? That the medicine changed her or that ... ?

NELL: I was reading a book. Very absorbed. Lulu was sitting, as she always does, next to the window. I don't know what made me remember because she hadn't made a sound. But suddenly I realized that I had forgotten to give her the afternoon pill. I glanced up and noticed she was sitting forward in her chair, leaning on the sill. (*Louise does this as Nell speaks*) It was odd. I knew she wouldn't notice me, but I said her name anyway. *Lulu?* And she turned to me and looked at me. Really looked at me. For the first time.

(*Lights change to flashback colors. Nell and Louise stare at each other*)

Louise?

LOUISE: Momma?

NELL: Baby.

LOUISE: Do you forgive me? (*Nell can't answer*) I don't mean to hurt you, but I feel so strange, as if ... I get trapped, Momma. It's as if I'm in a maze and everything's all white, like cotton, or clouds, or ... and I get trapped and can't get out. Everything looks the same. I try and try, but I'm moving so slowly. And sounds, they ... distract me. Sounds. They pull me away, and I can't concentrate. I can't get out. I can't ... tell you ... I can't tell ... I can't ... I can't ... can't ... can't ... (*etc. Louise begins a rocking motion with these words that builds with sound, so that we see she is becoming more and more excited. She would become out of control and hurt herself if Nell does not say her next lines. As Nell speaks, the lights switch back to normal*)

NELL: I had to get her medicine then. But, you see, she'd been there. *Louise* had been there. Once I'd seen, once I knew that she was there, how could I abandon her? She was so frightened. So I waited, and I watched and talked until I was hoarse. But she didn't come again. Not that day, nor all the the next. I tried to talk to her, to bring her back to me, but nothing worked. Then I remembered.

BILLIE: The medicine.

NELL: Yes. On that day it was late. So on the third day, again I held back her afternoon pill. And again, she was Louise.

BILLIE: I can't believe it.

NELL: I know, I couldn't either.

BILLIE: Dear God.

NELL: Yes.

BILLIE: If she can be normal for a few moments, she can be normal ... I've read about dramatic changes. They know so little, but this is ... !

NELL: Yes.

BILLIE: ... incredible. When did this happen—two years ago? Why didn't you tell me?

NELL: I couldn't yet. I didn't dare believe it myself. Then when we started working, we decided it was better if no one knew for the time being.

BILLIE: But why, why?

NELL: It was so fragile, don't you see. So delicate. It seemed to happen only at certain times. Yes, when her medicine was late. But even then, not every day. And when it happened, she only stayed for a little. It's gotten longer and longer since we began working, but even now, it seems such a short time ...

BILLIE: And the poetry?

NELL: Yes, yes. She began that on her own.

BILLIE: By herself?

NELL: We were at the window. This was weeks and weeks after we began to meet. I was trying to build her concentration because we had so little time before she had to go. Billie, it's like she's being pulled back, back inside herself. It's like those flowers the magicians use that appear and disappear at a flick of the wrist. But let me tell you. We were at the window. It was October and just about dusk. Mr. Turner was burning leaves and branches in his incinerator out back. I said to her, "Concentrate, Lulu. You can stay if you want to. Look how beautiful the colors are. Autumn evening," and she said ... (*Nell prompts Louise to finish*) Autumn evening ...

LOUISE: ... autumn evening.

NELL: Wood smoke ...

LOUISE: ... wood smoke.

NELL: Curling upward ...

LOUISE: ... curling upward.

NELL: Swallows circle ...

LOUISE: ... swallows circle.

NELL: Overhead.

LOUISE: ... overhead.

NELL: It took me a moment to realize what she had done. It was an accident. I was only saying words, but she had finished it for me, you see. Just like that. By concentrating on what we could see through the window, we had made a haiku together. (*Nell and Louise meet each others eyes and hold. Billie looks down*) After that, it got so Lulu would begin making them up on her own, without my help. We'd opened a floodgate, and they came pouring out, two, three at once sometimes. The days we sat at that window, watching, pointing. Then the window became ... extraneous. Now I simply sit and talk, and she creates.

Billie, it's as if she sees my thoughts, my innermost feelings, and then she translates them into images.

BILLIE: I see. What do you talk about?

NELL: Nothing important. Memories. The past. What happened yesterday in the news. But she'll take the most ordinary event and make it so personal somehow. Well, you know. You've read them.

BILLIE: Yes. I thought they were yours.

NELL: I know you did. But no, I'm only the catalyst.

BILLIE: Catalyst. Is this every day?

NELL: No, I told you.

BILLIE: How long does it last?

NELL: Not long.

BILLIE: *How* long?

NELL: Half an hour at the most. But she's trying very hard. She wants to practice. She wants to be ...

BILLIE: ... Normal?

NELL: No. More than that. She wants to be extraordinary. And she is.

BILLIE: Mother, if this is true, ...

NELL: If ... ?

BILLIE: I mean, *when* this happens ... Why haven't you told Dr. Dave about it?

NELL: No doctors and no more hospitals. They brought on this problem in the first place. If I hadn't rushed her to the doctors so quickly, maybe she would have come out of it. If they didn't have her taking all these drugs ... No! We don't know! Nobody knows what might have happened!

BILLIE: If you mean that, then take her off the drugs entirely.

NELL: We can't do that.

BILLIE: Why not? If that's what you believe, take her off the drugs. We could put her in the hospital and have the drug levels monitored.

NELL: No. I told you, no hospitals.

BILLIE: But they could wean her off the drugs slowly, and then we could ...

NELL: No!

BILLIE: Why not? *Why not?*

NELL: She needs the drugs. She's not herself yet, so she needs them to ... to protect her until ... It's a question of will power.

BILLIE: Whose, yours? What do you mean, protect her from what?

NELL: I told her you wouldn't understand. I warned her, but she wanted me to tell you. She said we *had* to tell you.

BILLIE: *She* said that?

NELL: She loves you, Bebe. What you saw today was only a tiny indication of that.

BILLIE: Why do you tell me, why now?

NELL: Can't you guess?

BILLIE: I don't believe any of this.

NELL: Because I'm losing my sight. (*Pause*) I can barely see to write them down anymore. Do you understand?

BILLIE: I'm sorry, but I don't.

NELL: I need your help, Bebe. *We* need you.

(*Flashback colors switch on. Billie is teaching Louise about makeup. The lipstick, mirror, et al., is mimed*)

BILLIE: (*To imaginary mirror*) Now then, we need this, and this, and this. Okay, now, you take the lipstick and you put it on like ... that. See? Okay. Pucker up. (*Billie puckers and Louise imitates her as Billie applies lipstick to Louise's mouth, then to her own*) M-m-m-m, luscious pink! Now then, you take this pencil. And *don't* put it in your eye!

LOUISE: *Don't* put it in your eye!

BILLIE: (*To mirror, applying makeup to herself*) You draw around the eye ... underneath ... above ... but not too much. There. See?

LOUISE: *Don't* put it in your eye!

BILLIE: Right. And now for the shadow. What color shall we use? Let's use turquoise, or what about this purple? Yeah, let's use the purple.

LOUISE: Yeah, let's use the purple!

(*Billie puts it on for the mirror while Louise picks up turquoise and draws circles over her face, over her cheeks, and above her eyes*)

BILLIE: And we put it above the crease of the eye, not just on the lid. Then we take this black pencil and we draw in the crease, just like Elizabeth Taylor, and draw it out like she did in "Cleopatra." Now, then, what's next?

LOUISE: Now, then, what's next?

(*Billie looks at Louise, whose face is covered with makeup. Billie reacts as Nell enters*)

BILLIE: Oh, you ... !

NELL: Billie, how could you!

LOUISE: Billie, you could you!

(*Nell crosses to Louise and begins wiping off makeup*)

NELL: I thought you knew better than this. What were you thinking of? Oh, Lulu, such a mess. Get me the cold cream off the dresser and a wet washcloth. (*Nell wipes at Louise's face. Billie mimes cold cream*) Her face is as red as a fire engine. And this turquoise! It'll take days for these colors to wear off. Why on earth ... ? (*As Nell wipes her face, Louise begins slapping her legs rhythmically. Nell stops her immediately, but Louise continues to struggle lightly*) Now you've done it! Here, hold her hands while I clean off this mess. This is not the first time this has happened, but by God it will be the last. For the final time, do not take it upon yourself to teach her. You leave that to me, or you can leave this house. Do you understand? (*Billie lets go of Louise's hands and rushes out of the light as Nell finishes*) I have no time to clean up after the both of you. Look at this, just look at it! I've got this all over me. Lulu, *be still*. (*Louise stops suddenly. Nell drops her head*) Billie.

(*Lights switch back to normal*)

BILLIE: What do you want me to do?

NELL: I want for you, I *need* for you to write down the poems. To listen to her and believe in her so that she can be ... who she is. The doctors don't understand. The illness is still in control, so it's only sheer will power that allows her to get out at all. If you don't believe me, let me show you.

BILLIE: Show me?

NELL: Yes, you can talk to her. She wants to talk to you, Billie. She needs you to believe in her, just as I do. If we believe, she can get well. We can help her, I know it. Come. Louise? (*There is no sign from Louise*) Louise. (*Louise does not respond*) Louise, Billie's come.

BILLIE: She doesn't hear you.

NELL: Billie's here, and you wanted to talk to her. Remember? *(Nell turns Louise's head toward Billie)* You see? There. Now, Bebe, say something to her. Go on.

BILLIE: *(Hesitantly)* Lulu. It's Billie.

LOUISE: Bebe.

BILLIE: Yes. Is it really you?

LOUISE: Is it really you?

BILLIE: I mean, is it true?

LOUISE: True?

(Billie looks back at Nell for encouragement)

BILLIE: *(Trying again)* It's been a long time since I've seen you, Lulu. It's been months and months, I think. How ... how are you?

LOUISE: How are you?

BILLIE: I've been fine, but how are you?

LOUISE: I've been fine.

BILLIE: *(Giving up)* She's just repeating, Mother.

NELL: She's tired. We were writing right before you got here. It's hard, but she can do it. Concentrate, Lulu. This is important. It's Billie.

BILLIE: I've read your poems. They're lovely.

(Louise laughs very becomingly as if at a compliment)

LOUISE: We were writing right before you got here.

NELL: You see?

BILLIE: Momma told me. I want so much to believe it's true. Are you really there?

LOUISE: Believe it's true.

BILLIE: No, no, say something else. Say anything else. Make up a poem. Will she do that? Will she make up a poem? Can you do that for me, Lulu? Make up a poem. Please do that.

LOUISE: Make up a poem?

BILLIE: Yes, yes, please. *(To Nell)* What if I point out the window, will that help? *(To Louise)* Look, look out there. Winter's nearly over. Mr. Turner's daffodils are in bloom, see? And the hydrangea bushes we planted that year Daddy died. Remember? They're big now. Why, they cover the whole corner of the porch. Momma's already put out that old birdfeeder ... No, I can't do this.

NELL: Keep going, she's listening.

BILLIE: Is she? Is she, well then ... It's almost sunset. The sky is red.

NELL: Red sky at dusk.

LOUISE: Red sky at dusk.

BILLIE: One gray cloud lies just ... over the trees across the southwest.

LOUISE: Over the trees one gray cloud lies ...

BILLIE: She's mimicking me.

LOUISE: ... in my sister's eyes.

NELL: There! Bravo, Lulu! Good girl! (*Nell and Louise laugh. Nell turns to Billie and sees her face*) What.

BILLIE: She's repeating.

NELL: No.

LOUISE: No.

BILLIE: She says nursery rhymes with the same rhythm.

NELL: No. Louise? Help me now.

BILLIE: She's repeating what I say and what you say.

NELL: We've got to make Bebe understand.

BILLIE: Please don't try anymore.

NELL: Louise?

BILLIE: I don't think I can bear it.

LOUISE: I don't think I can bear it.

NELL: Try just a little harder, baby.

BILLIE: Mother!

NELL: Try a little harder. Concentrate now.

BILLIE: Please, please don't!

NELL: Just a little longer now.

BILLIE: I'm asking you to stop.

NELL: Louise, answer me. Look at me and answer.

BILLIE: *Mother, stop!*

(*Louise is startled by the shout and begins screaming, accompanied by the banging of her head against her chair. Both Nell and Billie break into action and shout over the screaming. Nell gets the football helmet but can't get it on while Louise is screaming. Nell hurts her bruised hand*)

NELL: The helmet, the helmet. Lulu, Lulu, there.

BILLIE: Where is her medicine?

NELL: Oh, my hand! On the desk. Get the water. (*Billie instead crosses to where she has put the music box and opens it for Louise to see. Louise immediately stops the banging and screaming and focuses on the music. Nell puts the helmet back on Louise. Billie brings the pill and water glass to Nell)* Now take this, Lulu. There.

(*Louise takes the pill calmly, all the while fascinated with the music box. Billie and Nell recover quietly*)

BILLIE: Will she be all right now?

NELL: Yes.

BILLIE: Is this what always happens?

NELL: No, but sometimes we wait too long ... I hate so to see her leave. (*Billie touches the bruise on Nell's arm*) I know what you're going to say. But every word I've told you is true. You heard it, but you didn't want to believe.

BILLIE: That's not true, I want to believe. Just don't ask me to see something that isn't there.

NELL: Then let us prove it to you. We'll try again tomorrow.

BILLIE: No, no, I don't want to try anymore. Momma, I'm sorry, but I've tried before. I can't keep trying and have it not be ... not be true.

NELL: It doesn't always happen, so I'm not promising anything.

BILLIE: No.

NELL: Bebe.

BILLIE: No, it hurts too much. You talk to her as if ...

NELL: ... as if she's real, as if she's a person. And she is.

BILLIE: Yes. Yes.

NELL: She is. Let me try tomor— ...

BILLIE: No.

NELL: I'm not asking you to believe it.

BILLIE: Aren't you?

NELL: I'm only asking you to let me try. Wait and see.

BILLIE: Wait and see.

NELL: You'll do that, won't you? Just that? For me?

(*Silence. Louise closes the music box*)

BILLIE: Yes, Momma.

NELL: You'll wait?

BILLIE: I think I can do that.

NELL: That's my Bebe. You can stay as long as you like, you know. As long as you need to.

(*Lights slowly begin fading from normal back to the first setting with which we began the play. The fade finishes before Louise's last words. Billie crosses to window and stands, looking out. She is framed by the light from the window, separate from Louise and Nell)*

BILLIE: It's almost spring.

NELL: I remember when I was a girl, we had a cherry tree in the backyard. It was just big enough for me to sit in. The thickest branch was my backrest. It was curved, like a hammock, and I could lean back into that tree and rest my legs on either side of the trunk. In the spring, I took books out there and devoured them along with the cherries. The Brontes, Alexander Dumas. Jane Austen and I were surrounded by flowers. The perfume.

BILLIE: I was never very literary. I can't even make a good rhyme.

NELL: You're your father all over again.

BILLIE: He wasn't scared, not John. But I am, Momma.

NELL: No, John wasn't scared of anything.

BILLIE: I wish Daddy could be here.

(Pause)

LOUISE:
Walking in his garden,
Suddenly in the twilight,
White hydrangea.

(We hear the autoharp strummed up the scale slowly. Fade to blackout)

The End

Andrew Foster

CHEMICAL REACTIONS

Andrew Foster

Chemical Reactions was developed at the New York StageWorks and premiered in a revised version in the 11th annual Humana Festival of New American Plays produced by the Actors Theatre of Louisville. The play was also presented at the West Bank Theatre in New York City. It appears here in print for the first time.

Mr. Foster's first play, *Reunion*, was presented Off-Broadway at the New York StageWorks. The play won *The Villager* Award for Distinguished Playwriting in the 1979–80 season. A second play, *Options*, was produced by StageWorks in 1980. In 1982, a revised version received a staged reading in Chicago at the Victory Gardens Theater, followed by productions at Los Angeles's Theatre 40 and a return engagement in New York. *American Abroad* received several staged readings in regional theatres and a staged reading followed by a workshop production at Manhattan Theatre Club. The Actors Theatre of Louisville commissioned a short comic play, *Poor Reception*, in 1987. Mr. Foster's newest full-length play, *Lies*, received staged readings in 1987 at Playwrights Horizons and the Manhattan Punch Line theatre; the play also had a workshop production in the spring of 1988 at New Jersey's George Street Playhouse.

Mr. Foster's most recent plays are the one-acts, *Civil Rites* and *Talking Dirty*, paired under the collective title *Political Dreams*. In addition to his plays, Mr. Foster has recently completed a novel entitled *Snow Fall*. His non-fiction credits include "Predator and Prey," published in the *Los Angeles Times Magazine,* and an article entitled "In the Cellar."

During the past five years Mr. Foster has spent part of his time in the development and administration of non-profit programs for the theatre, notably with the FDG/CBS New Plays Program and The Stage Two Awards.

Author's Production Note:

The characters in *Chemical Reactions* can be New Yorkized or Chicagoized or St. Louisized in accent—there is no necessary location although the inspiration is in New Jersey's eastern marshland dumpsites and New York's much publicized Mafia pizza takeovers.

The "special effects" of falling barrels can be handled just offstage by having Ike roll Lom away during his fight with Bern. That allows a couple of visible barrels to topple, with flash powder and a fire extinguisher to handle the rest. Lom's barrel should be thoroughly cleaned and have interior handles as well as padding for the occupant. The barrel should also have bullet holes and slashes to allow good air movement.

Characters:

BERN, *early twenties, sizeable, not smart but not uncurious about his surroundings. An unconsciously funny person with quite sensational timing.*

IKE, *late twenties, harder and more complex—a short prison background, a lackey in the crime world, there only for the occasional and unthreatening easy buck. He still has a conscience simmering away. Lean and wiry.*

LOM, *late thirties, he sounds like a large man. He is a laid-back and humorous man, but the kind that is very protective of family and friends. His humor in this case is born of desperation as he tries to shield himself from the situation.*

The sound of a truck engine revving, slowing, and shut off. The ticking of the hot engine. One door opening and closing. Lights up on the truck, halfway through a sagging gate into a fenced-off section of a dump. Its back is facing us. The bed is filled with industrial barrels. On one side of the dump there is a pyramid of weathered barrels similar to the ones in the truck. Pieces of old crumbled iron scatter the grounds. There is an array of warning signs on barrel and fence. The light is pre-dawn, cold and misty.

BERN: Sheez. This is a dump.
(*Bern walks from the truck into the dump. He is about to put non-dairy creamer into his cup of coffee. His footsteps slop in the mud, a sucking kind of noise. A background static of someone looking for something and clattering things around in his efforts*)
IKE: (*From the truck*) Damn.
BERN: (*Leaning against a barrel, looking at the creamer label*) Disodium glutamate. Polysorbate. Soybean protein. Soy extract. Two percent carbonate bisulfate ...

IKE: (*Calling from the truck*) Bern! Would you give me a hand? Ahh! Never mind. Damn!

BERN: Emulsifiers, artificial flavorings and colorings ...

(*Another door slams and footsteps approach*)

IKE: We must of left the gloves at the warehouse. Careful you don't get no goop on your hands. Next time say something when I call, huh?

BERN: Cremona.

IKE: What?

BERN: Cremona. They don't give you milk no more, they give you Cremona.

IKE: Cremola, Bern, it's Cremola. Cremona sounds ... filthy.

BERN: It's what my gal calls it. Cremona. She says I ought to sell the stuff, I drink so much.

IKE: It's 5:30 in the A.M. Would you cap your mouth?

BERN: Guess I'm just a morning person.

(*He slurps his coffee*)

IKE: You are a morning fruitcake is what you are!

(*Bern gets excited by the sunrise, which is beginning to lighten and redden the dump*)

BERN: Hey! Hey! Hey! Red sky in morning, sailors take warning. No fishin' today. We should 'a' been out there last night ...

IKE: Tonight's another day.

BERN: ... pullin' in them blues, snappin' and twistin'. Oh yeah, better than this.

IKE: Easy money here, kid. Don't forget that. You do this one, you get time to spend it.

BERN: I don't want to sound ungrateful, Ike. Thanks for callin' me in.

IKE: Would I call anybody else? Huh?

BERN: Nah. Not since you go out with my sister.

IKE: Drink your coffee. There's work to do.

BERN: I don't care you're goin' out. Don't get me wrong, I ain't one of those jealous brother types, one of those guys can't imagine his sister havin' fun, goin' places, seein' people ...

IKE: That's real of you, trustin' the two of us like that.

BERN: Just so you stay off her. (*Bern finds this very funny*) Otherwise I have to box those big ears you got. Huh? Huh? (*Bern is up and dancing, right, left, right, shadow boxing. He exhales puffs as he punches and jabs*) Whooo! Whuff! Hunh! (*Bern spills coffee from the cup he is still holding. A splash lands on Ike*)

IKE: Hey! No, look at this stain!

BERN: It's not like it's Sunday dress, man. It's not your disco drawers.

IKE: Aww, Bern! Damn it! You always have five cups of coffee and I get one all over me. Would you finish so we can get a move on?

BERN: All right, I'm sorry, I am sorry. I am your slave! (*Sound of the coffee cup as he crumples and drops it*) Let's get to work! (*Pause. Ike is watching Bern, shaking his head*) What're you looking at?

IKE: Anybody ever teach you to pick up after yourself?

BERN: Hey, all right, this is a dump already. You want maybe I should sweep up? Jesus, we have a truck loaded with these big cans of friggin' Comet cleanser or whatever, we bringin' it to some garbage place with, I mean, look at that thing of barrels ...

IKE: What thing?

BERN: You know, it's what those Egyptians called it, pyramid! I mean all these barrels, all this old junk, and you're flappin' about some cup! Some rubber cup!

IKE: Foam.

BERN: Foam rubber.

IKE: It's styrofoam. Foam rubber they use for other things, like those false titties. Does the cup feel like false titties?

BERN: (*Disdainful*) I wouldn't know.

IKE: (*Cracking up*) All right ... Let's get a move. We got to be out of here before they open this dive.

BERN: You see me disagreein'? So what's the deal, we just gonna' jam these cans up against them others? (*He whacks the side of a barrel. A dull, full "thunk"*)

IKE: Hey! We do not whack, we do not jam. These things is loaded with some kind of sludge, we jam them, they probably glom up in our faces.

BERN: They're not gonna' glom, it's in a steel can.

IKE: We ease 'em on over, okay? We do not jam.

BERN: Okay.

IKE: You want to jam, let me get out of the way.

BERN: I'm just sayin' if we ease, let's ease at high speed, 'cause this is a dump!

IKE: Come on, let's go.

BERN: Know what I mean, Jesus, it is ugly. Looks like crucifixion day, hey, you know that film? You know that story about John Wayne, the Duke? This guy told me. The Duke is playin' this dude who is casin' Christ on the cross?

IKE: I don't know the story, let's get goin'.

BERN: He's sayin', "He must 'a' been the son a' God." (*Bern does a good John Wayne imitation*) Some clown comes up to the Duke, says, put a little respect, a little "awe" into your line, champ. Duke nods and comes out with ... "Awwwww, He must 'a' been the son a' God."

(*Ike is not impressed*)

IKE: I don't get religion stories, you know? Grab a hand.

BERN: All right, yeah, anyway, like I said, this is a dump.

IKE: Bern. Just take it easy, all right? You're not spendin' your vacation here. We get this done, d-o-n-e, then we go get paid, p-a-i-d. Leave with some bucks, have a good time.

BERN: All right, Ike, I am not remedial, okay? You sure they're gonna' p-a-y?

IKE: Johnny Olander does not dog out on his debts, he's got an organization. Now give me a hand.

BERN: Look, I'm sorry to be a little, you know, a little, I don't know, like nervous. I was seein' this movie about stuff like this, you know, where these two chemicals meet up and start doin' a real number on each other.

(*They start to pick up a barrel*)

IKE: One, two, three. (*Exhalations as they pick up the barrel*) Got it, let's go.

BERN: (*Talks with effort as they carry the barrel*) So in this movie, it's like a warehouse, but it feels like this dump, big barrels, spooky lighting, and these two chemicals just snake out from these two cans, man they just flow on over to each other like with these fingers, Ike, and when they fix on each other, you get this blob and it kind of pulses its way into a real ugly mess.

IKE: It kind of glommed up, huh?

BERN: How do you mean?

IKE: Like I told you earlier, it glommed up, like in our faces, which is why we're easin' these barrels, not jammin', right?

BERN: I'm easin', I'm easin'.

IKE: Down right here. Careful. (*Grunts as the barrel is put down*) Let's go. Number two.

BERN: I was just trying to tell you why I feel a little freaky.

IKE: Freaky?

BERN: That's what my mom says when she's a little off and that's exactly how I feel today.

IKE: You gonna feel freaky when we get paid? 'Cause if you feel freaky in front of Johnny Olander, I don't want to be there, right? One, two, three.

(*More groans of effort as they lift a second barrel*)

BERN: I'm just tryin to tell you this is a lousy place.

IKE: I know that for Christ's sake, it's a dump.

BERN: That's exactly my point.

IKE: You're actin' like it's some kind a mausoleum.

BERN: There is no such word.

IKE: You'd know, right? Watch your hand.

BERN: You're a real fool sometimes. There's nausea ...

IKE: Will you watch your hand? There's goop ...

BERN: And there's like, hell, I don't know, auditorium, but there's no nausoreum.

IKE: ... It's suckin' out of that barrel, just like you ...

BERN: And if there was, you'd still be a jerk to say it.

IKE: Crusty, real crusty goop, right on your old paw right about ... now.

BERN: Hey! Hey! What is this crap?

IKE: Somethin' just dying to bust its way through your skin and join up with some good eatin'!

BERN: Ahhhh! Dammit! Ahhh! Help me, help my hand!

(*Bern reacts in panic. The barrel drops, a solid "thunk"! The sound of the barrel dropping and Ike's protest as he pulls away just in time*)

IKE: Bern! Don't drop no barrel on me, my finger was in there!

BERN: Damn! Look at this stuff. What is it? (*Bern tries to clean his hand off*)

IKE: Wipe it with a rag. Phewww! What a lousy day.

(*A strange sound*)

LOM: Ohhhh.

(*Bern looks around wildly. Ike doesn't notice anything*)

BERN: Did you hear something, man?

LOM: Ahhh. Ohhh.

IKE: Quiet, Bern. Your hand's all right.

BERN: Can't you hear that? That's not me! (*There is a metallic thump. Ike is startled. Both start backing off and looking around*) It's some kind a' blob, some kind a' weird thing!

IKE: Would you shut up?

LOM: Ahhhh. Acchhhh.

(*Another thump sends Ike tripping backward*)

BERN: I never should a' come to this dump.

IKE: It's just some kind a' noise, Bern, it's all right.

(*The barrel begins rolling and creaking. The noises are coming from inside and have that metallic echo. The noises move from awakening to surprise, to panic, to anger, as Lombardi comes to*)

LOM: Ohhh. Rrrrrrr. Yaahhh.

BERN: Jesus, let me run! Let me run!

LOM: Yahhh! Yahhh!

(*The barrel is rocking and creaking violently*)

IKE: Let's get out of here! (*He starts for the truck*) Bern! Come on!

(*Bern is rooted to the spot*)

BERN: I can't move! I can't run! Jesus help me!

(*The barrel stops rocking. From inside, the sound of tears. Ike and Bern are both silent and still*)

LOM: Damn. Damn.

(*More crying*)

BERN: What kind of blob is this?

LOM: (*Finally reacting to the voices*) Hey. Hey! Hey! Hello?

IKE: There's some guy in that barrel.

LOM: Binxie! I'm over here, I'm okay. Gator!

BERN: Who's he talkin' to?

IKE: I don't know.

LOM: Binxie! Over here! (*Ike and Bern look around, still scared and unsure*) Hello? Gator? Is anybody out there? Is anybody there?

(*A long pause*)

BERN: (*A sigh of tension*) Yeah.

LOM: Oh, people! Oh, yeah, people! I am so glad to hear people!

BERN: (*As if to an alien*) What did you expect to hear?

LOM: Who are you guys? (*Pause, then with an edge of desperation*) Hello? You still there?

BERN: Yeah.

LOM: Good. Who are you?

IKE: Ike.

BERN: Bern.

LOM: Ike and Bern. Hi. Hi. Hi. Can you let me out?

IKE: Who are you?

LOM: Lombardi. Would you let me out?

BERN: Lombardi who?

LOM: Just call me Lom, Ike, but get me out of here.

BERN: That was Bern speaking.

LOM: I don't care if you're Frank frigging Sinatra, let me out!

IKE: Take it easy.

LOM: Take it easy? Get me out! Get me out!

(*The barrel starts rocking and creaking again. It begins rolling towards the large pile of old cans. Bern and Ike move to it and try to hold it steady*)

BERN: Mister! Calm down, come on, you're gonna knock this whole place to hell.

IKE: You want us to get you out? Calm down! (*Pause. The barrel stops. We can hear Lom breathing heavily. Bern and Ike take a closer look at the barrel. Ike whistles*) You been welded.

LOM: What?

IKE: You been welded in. Good job. You're lucky there's holes in the barrel.

LOM: I feel lucky. I feel real lucky.

BERN: (*Fingering the seams*) Wow. Looks like somethin' from a' auto shop.

IKE: So what are you doin' in there?

LOM: Where?

IKE: In the barrel.

LOM: What do you mean, what am I doin'? Let me out!

BERN: He's stuck in there, Ike!

IKE: No, I mean, is it some kind a' prank or what?

BERN: That's a filthy joke to pull.

LOM: Hey! Binxie! Jumbo!

(*Pause as Ike and Bern again look around*)

IKE: Nobody here, man.

LOM: Nobody else?

BERN: Just us.

LOM: Great. The Ike and Bern show. Where the hell is here?

IKE: In a dump.

LOM: I am in a dump?

IKE: Yeah.

BERN: We was droppin' off these barrels of chemicals ...

LOM: (*Desperate cry*) Binxie! Shhhooo, no Binxie ... oh, God.

BERN: You want to listen?

LOM: Do I have a choice?

IKE: Hey, who is this Binxie?

LOM: My slice man.

BERN: (*Faintly alarmed*) He carries a knife?

LOM: He sells slices, you know? Slices. (*Bern and Ike look at each other. Both shake their heads silently*) You seen him around?

BERN: Nobody's here. We're in a dump.

LOM: Yeah, well, I live in a dump, I work in a dump, it'd be a miracle if I wasn't in a dump right now. (*Lom finds this almost funny*) Kind of a joke on me, huh?

BERN: Sort of like what Bette Davis would have said.

LOM: You know her personal?

BERN: Yeah, I seen her movies. This is like a movie, you know? It's like a movie.

LOM: Got you, sport. Listen, you guys figuring how to crack this thing? I tell you, I don't feel so good.

BERN: I told you, it's like movie, we'll get you out.

IKE: I don't know why you're in there, mister.

LOM: The point is I am.

IKE: It's a pretty heavy thing to do. I mean, somebody must be carrying the axe for you. Some kind of contract. How come you didn't say nothing all the way here?

LOM: All the way where?

IKE: In the truck when we was bringing you here.

LOM: You brought me here? You guys brought me here? Did you put me in here? Did you?

BERN: Hey, no, we thought you was chemicals.

LOM: Chemicals?

BERN: Yeah, you know, chemicals nobody wants.

LOM: Do I sound like chemicals?

BERN: Well, you got warnings like chemicals ...

LOM: Do I sound like chemicals you have known?

BERN: No.

IKE: He thought you were a blob.

LOM: A what?

IKE: You know, like a blob.

LOM: Like a dead guy?

IKE: Like a live guy made out of chemicals.

LOM: I am a normal guy. I am not a blob, I'm just a normal guy.

IKE: Why didn't you say something?

LOM: Are you kidding? I was out!

IKE: Out drinkin'? Out takin' a walk?

LOM: Like knocked out. And I got stuff all over me, I don't know, I think it's blood, maybe it's sauce.

IKE: Sauce?

LOM: Tomato sauce, what's wrong with you?

BERN: (*Puzzled by this sauce thing*) You feelin' all right?

LOM: Oh, I can't complain. How about yourself.

BERN: Fine, thank you.

IKE: That's good, Bern, that's really good. You want to maybe pass the guy in there a copy of your last physical, really make his day?

LOM: (*Banging on the barrel*) You guys gettin' me out? I don't hear nothing happening!

IKE: (*Exasperated*) Where did you come from?

LOM: You brought me here, you tell me!

BERN: (*Matter of fact*) From Johnny Olander.

LOM: Johnny Olander?

IKE: Bern you shut your mouth!

LOM: That jerkface? That asshole?

IKE: You know Johnny Olander?

LOM: That's my goddamn partner.

BERN: He's your partner, and he put you in the barrel? That is bad.

LOM: I didn't know he was my partner. He walks into my joint one day and he wants a slice, so Binxie cuts one up for him, slides it right over. This clown says "glad we have you on board, kid, you got a nimble blade there." Ruffles his hair. "Nimble blade," little faggot gangster. Binxie looks all puzzled like a dog, which is how I felt. And I said, "on board what?" He says "Lombardi! I'm your partner, you got a faulty connection or what?" Things went down the chute from there.

IKE: He was takin' over your joint, a pizza joint, huh?

LOM: Says I can stay but he gets half. Bull! I'm not takin' that!

IKE: So you end up in a barrel.

(*Pause*)

LOM: I thought he was jokin'. It's dark in here. There's these little slits in the barrel, little slices of light. Hey! Give me the whole pie!

BERN: (*Looks around*) What pie?

LOM: Sun out?

BERN: It's real foggy. (*He shivers*) It's like a movie.

IKE: We know.

LOM: This blob wants out!

BERN: Okay. (*Bern starts looking over the barrel*) Don't move, I'm like looking for a weak spot.

IKE: You're stupid, man. Why didn't you let him have half your joint?

LOM: I'm not dancing to that tune.

IKE: He's getting the whole place now!

LOM: I'll put him in jail. Him and his insects. He says to me "you gonna wind up dead." Hey, I say what you gonna kill me for? My Neapolitan or my Sicilian? Please tell me, my customers argue this all day! (*Lom laughs*)

IKE: You got bravado, man.

LOM: You know what he gives me for half? A bunch of chemicals! He says he got some supply house. I said I don't need chemicals. He gets this leer and says, "without chemicals life would be impossible." I say maybe life, but not good pizza.

IKE: I bet you had him rollin' in the aisle.

LOM: Then Binxie pulls his roto-rooter on the guy.

BERN: His what? He's got a what?

LOM: What he calls his blade. God, let me out. I can't joke on you, boys, I want some air, I'm feelin' mushed. Air!

(*Bern shrugs at Ike, no luck on welds*)

IKE: You are really sealed in, man. Olander didn't intend you to get out. I don't know what we can do.

LOM: Can you sit me up? I can't think lyin' down.

IKE: I really don't know what to do.

BERN: What do you mean? We get him out, guy's in a barrel, we let him out.

LOM: I give you free pizza.

BERN: You don't have to do that.

LOM: For the rest of your lives, no joke.

IKE: Great, we get pizza for two maybe three weeks.

BERN: Ike ...

IKE: We let him out, we won't be eating pizza, we'll be on the pizza. Olander ...

BERN: We don't know what's goin' down, we just let some dude out of some barrel.

IKE: Don't talk to me Bern, this is serious.

LOM: I see what you mean. How about sittin' me up so I can think?

(*Ike kicks the barrel viciously*)

IKE: Just knock it off, cut the cute jokes!

LOM: I'm tired of bein' on my back! Is that all right? I just feel like sittin' up. You don't want my pizza for life deal, that's your choice. I just feel like change of scene, nothin' major, I want to sit up!

BERN: Let's sit the man up!

IKE: This is not the time for one of your acts of generosity.

LOM: For god's sake, I'm goin' crazy lying down in this barrel!

(*The barrel begins creaking and rolling*)

BERN: Calm down. I'll get you out. (*The barrel slows*) How long you been in there?

LOM: I don't know. Long enough, if you know what I mean. (*A sob*)

BERN: Hey, guy ...

LOM: It's okay, it was worse at night. I woke up somewhere at night. I knew I died. I knew it. And, ohhh, I don't know, it was dying and finding there was nothing, you know, no silver, no light, no nobody at all, dark, nothing and you were, you know, gonna be awake for all of it! This is better than that.

(*Pause*)

IKE: All right, Lom. We'll set you up.

LOM: Thanks. Thanks.

IKE: Bern, grab hold.

(*They lift the barrel and set it upright*)

LOM: (*Groans and then a sigh*) Don't mean to be such a burden. Mom was right. She always said I spent too much time in the can.

(*Ike looks at his hand. There is blood on it. He smells it*)

IKE: Not pizza sauce.

LOM: My old momma. Hey, is it still light out?

BERN: Yeah.

LOM: I thought so. How come? Is it daytime?

IKE: What do you think?

LOM: Might be lights or somethin'.

BERN: It's morning.

LOM: Nice day?

IKE: It's foggy. And it stinks in this dump.

LOM: Stinks in this dump too.

IKE: Shut up and let me think.

LOM: Guys, let me say something here. You want my half the pizza joint, I ain't against talkin', but let's make an agreement here pretty soon. Okay?

BERN: Half your joint?

LOM: Would you like that?

BERN: What joint is it?

LOM: The Vesuvius on Central.

BERN: You're kiddin'!

LOM: That's the place.

BERN: I had a slice on Central. Is it the place with that mural?

LOM: The dancing girls of Pompeii. Yeah.

BERN: That is a great mural.

LOM: You been there?

BERN: I been there, I wanted a copy of that mural. Guy told me there was just one in the whole world. That is amazin'.

LOM: What you look like?

BERN: Me?

IKE: He looks like a jerk. Bern, we got to take a walk and talk this out.

(*There is severe coughing from inside the barrel. Ike and Bern stare at the ground. Bern leans down, touches and stands, his finger dappled with blood*)

LOM: (*Weakly*) Guys? (*Bern and Ike are lost in thought*) Hey! Guys? Guys! Anybody there? Oh God, oh Jesus, don't let them leave, don't go away! Please! Guys!

BERN: We're here.

IKE: We're here, Mr. Lombardi.

LOM: You want the whole joint. Is that it?

IKE: We didn't know you were in the barrel. We didn't know there was anything wrong at all.

LOM: Yeah, yeah, I believe that.

IKE: We was hired to dump chemicals. You was just in one of the barrels.

LOM: I understand, I know.

IKE: Olander is a powerful man, our employer ... I don't know what to ...

LOM: We nail him.

IKE: I got a bit of a record, Mr. Lombardi, you know parole ...

BERN: This is bullshit, I'm getting a crowbar.

IKE: Bern!

BERN: Cut it, Ike, I don't like it when you get all polite and weasely.

IKE: You be in trouble you get him out.

BERN: I can't worry about that.

IKE: You don't know how to worry, you don't know the word, you don't know think, worry, plan, you don't know jack!

BERN: (*Disagreeing*) I know!

IKE: Yeah, you think you can walk into something like this and come out ahead? Isn't that your plan, to come out ahead? My man, you are not thinking straight. Arrow, remember? Arrow-straight! Nothing in your way but air. You do this, this is in your way. I double guarantee it.

BERN: What are you talkin'?

IKE: I am talking what you gonna' do? You want to be a hero, you want to tell the police?

BERN: You're afraid of the cops, you little pisser!

IKE: You want to walk in with a gangland killing, no witnesses, just us? You want go against Olander?

LOM: Listen boys, I'm hearing you. I agree, see? Maybe I just go back, get Lucie and Binxie and disappear.

IKE: Disappear? Now that is rich. Guy's in a barrel he's worried about disappearin'.

BERN: I'm getting a crowbar.

IKE: Think it out!

BERN: I can't let this guy die, I ate his pizza.

IKE: You clown, you joker, he is dyin'! You saw the blood, you saw the bullet holes in the can! He is gonna pass on and leave us to sing the songs. You want to go against Olander for a dead man because of pizza?

BERN: Don't mess with my head!

IKE: You are an idiot! An idiot!

(*Bern goes to the truck*)

LOM: Listen guys, tell me something, tell me you're letting me out.

IKE: There's only one guy here and I can't say that, Mr. Lombardi.

LOM: I'm in a barrel, you let me out! What kind of place are we talkin' about, leavin' me stuck in a barrel?

IKE: This place, man, a dump, so shut up!

LOM: You lyin' to me!

IKE: You are in a dump, clown! You hear somebody sayin' it's Times Square? (*Bern reenters with a crowbar. He goes to the can and tries to jam the tip of the crowbar in the edge of the can. Then, to Bern*) Listen to me, I try to tell you things about the world, the real world.

LOM: Get me out!

BERN: I'm letting him out.

IKE: Look at you, you need a blow torch. You gonna hurt yourself, then I say I told you so.

BERN: I'm getting him out.

IKE: Bern, we have to split and split now. The dudes come and this place opens and we are stuck to the fucking wall!

BERN: Shut up!

(*Bern is jamming at the can. Ike comes and tries to grab the crowbar. The bar hits the can with a "clang!"*)

LOM: AHHH!

BERN: No!

IKE: Damn it, get away from the can!

(*The barrel rocks as Lom panics. Bern and Ike fall back against it, and it rolls against the pyramid of barrels. A massive creaking like a piece of crumbling glacial wall as the pile totters*)

IKE: Watch out!

(*The pile gives way, burying Lom's barrel. A hissing of liquid and smoke. Bern and Ike, exhausted, hyperventilate, stare at the smoking wreckage. Pause*)

BERN: Lom? Mr. Lombardi? (*Pause*) Lombardi? (*He bangs lightly on a barrel. A hiss of smoke. He coughs*) Oh no. No.

(*Pause*)

IKE: I didn't knock those barrels over. I didn't mean it.

BERN: Lom! Hey, Lom!

IKE: I wanted him out as much as you did.

BERN: Lombardi!

IKE: I just needed to think it through.

BERN: We have to move all these barrels. Come on, he's at the bottom.

(*They roll away one barrel*)

IKE: Watch the goop. (*They both cough*) Just ease 'em off, don't crack 'em.

BERN: Oh shit, oh man.

(*More hissing*)

IKE: Bern, I'm sorry.

BERN: Lombardi! (*He reaches under another barrel. A hiss and flash of light and he yells in pain*) AHH! Oh, damn! My hand!

IKE: Get it out! Get it away!

(*Bern gets the hand free, holding it by the wrist*)

BERN: Oh God, oh God!

IKE: Give it to me, man, let me see it. (*More smoke as Ike grabs the hand and checks it out. A growing noise of chemical combinations. Bern is in pain, torn between the pain and the search*) Let me wrap it, here, hold still. (*He rips his shirt*) Jesus, whole place is leakin' ...

BERN: Ahh. Got to find him.

IKE: Damn barrels could blow ... they could burn.

BERN: Don't scare me.

(Fear is exactly what Ike is looking for)

IKE: Glom, that's what's happening. Probably already got him ... *(He can feel Bern's sudden response)*

BERN: What are you sayin'?

IKE: Place is glommin' up. Look, Bern, over there, those chemicals, they're snaking man, they're snaking around like fingers.

BERN: You are cold, man, really cold.

IKE: They're doin' a dance, they're flaggin' a ride on over to each other, they're gonna' glom!

BERN: They are?

IKE: They're gonna' pulse into a real blob.

BERN: Like in the movie, in the warehouse ...

IKE: It's almost too late, it may be too late ...

BERN: We gotta get ... we gotta ...

IKE: Its gonna' slide right out and suck us dry!

BERN: Go. We gotta go! *(Bern begins to cry)*

IKE: Good, good buddy. Everything be all right, we do that, right now. *(He turns with Bern and comes face to face with the truck)* Oh, no.

BERN: What?

IKE: Ohhh. Oohhh man. We can't leave yet.

BERN: What do you mean we can't leave?

IKE: We have barrels to unload.

BERN: It's glommin up. You said. You said we could leave, we gotta go!

IKE: We can't be tied to the barrels, we gotta get them off the truck.

BERN: You should a' thought of that before you tried to make me pee my pants. You're a mutt! A mutt! A sucker, an asshole, a fucking weenie! Why did you get me into this?

IKE: Get you in ... ? Did I call you, as a favor, did I ask you, as a friend? You have to say yes? Din't you want to come?

BERN: I'm not going to be seeing any more of you. I'm not.

IKE: Don't act like I set this up, I'm a sucker? Fine. I am, look at this! I am. God, God I am! *(Ike is nearly collapsing)* So fine, we do what you want to do, you call the shot, you think I know what this is all about? Go on, Bern, you tell me, what do we do?

BERN: Me?

IKE: I don't know what to do, Bern, what do we do?

BERN: Oh. Ohhh. We ... we ... (*Pause. A discovery—Bern thinks something through*) We get the barrels off the truck. (*Pause. Ike nods. They turn to the truck. Ike waits for Bern's orders. Bern looks confused*) We ease it, okay? Ease it on over.

IKE: Sure, Bern.

(*They pick up a barrel and start to heave it along*)

BARREL: Ohhhh. Ohhhh.

(*It's the barrel they are carrying. They panic*)

IKE: Gahhh!

BERN: Ahh!

(*They get off the truck and away from the barrel*)

IKE: No, not another, I don't believe it!

(*Bern looks at his hand in horror*)

BERN: Oh God, ahhh ...

IKE: What is it, man, more goop, some chemical?

(*Ike wordlessly wipes his hand across the t-shirt. A bright red slash of a stain. It's blood*)

BERN: (*Looking at the blood*) Ohh, God.

(*Another noise, from the side. They look, backing towards each other*)

BARREL #2: Ohhh.

(*Then another groan from one of the pyramids. They both look front, trying to place it*)

BARREL #3: Ohhhh.

IKE: The barrels are alive.

BERN: The whole place is alive.

IKE: Can't we even ... leave?

(*Pause*)

BERN: Ike, I know this place, like I recognize it, it's like I'm awake but not really, like you know, like I'm watchin some kind of ...

IKE: Movie ...

BERN: Yeah. Like a movie, that I've never seen.

(*More groans. Ike and Bern stare at each other as the lights fade*)

The End

Edward Allan Baker

DOLORES

Edward Allan Baker

Edward Allan Baker is a self-taught playwright from Providence, Rhode Island. He was inspired to pursue a career in playwriting sixteen years ago by the Trinity Square Repertory Company, and studied theatre at the University of Rhode Island where his first plays were produced and where his best known full-length play, *Prairie Avenue,* was developed and staged. *Prairie Avenue* was then optioned and showcased by the Ensemble Studio Theatre in Manhattan and received many laudatory reviews, typified by Brendan Gill's observations in the *New Yorker* magazine: "Edward Allan Baker has written a play that deserves to be called an authentic work of art. Mr. Baker is a master of verisimilitude ... He has an admirable ear. I found it exhilarating."

Under the auspices of the Rhode Island Council on the Arts, Mr. Baker was an "Artist in Residence," teaching theatre in prisons, halfway houses, and on the reservation of the Narragansett Indians, where he worked with emotionally disturbed teenagers.

Other nationally produced plays by Mr. Baker include: *Lady of Fadima, Public Street Marriage*, and *The Buffer.* An earlier one-act play, *North of Providence*, starred Tony winner Joan Allen and Jan Leslie Harding in the Ensemble Studio Theatre's Marathon '85, a play cited by Mel Gussow as "an exemplar of the one-act art ... a one-act play of emotional depth and conviction."

Mr. Baker has also written three screenplays for Bianchi Films of New York, who will produce the film adaptation of his *Prairie Avenue* starring Ed Harris. Professional memberships held by Mr. Baker include membership in the Playwrights's Unit of the Ensemble Studio Theatre and the Dramatists Guild.

Dolores, published here for the first time, employs a black comedy genre approach to the serious problem of spouse abuse. It was first presented as one of the hits in Marathon '86, produced by the Ensemble Studio Theatre, Curt Dempster, Artistic Director; Erik Murkoff, Managing Director. The author dedicates this play: "To Dylan Edward Baker."

Characters:

SANDRA, *twenty-eight*
DOLORES, *thirty*

Place:

Providence.

Time:

Winter. 1985. Early Sunday afternoon.

Setting:

> *A kitchen that is "spic and span" clean. A round table and four chairs are center stage. A long counter is against the backstage wall and a stove and sink are built right in and cabinets are above and below the counter, a window above the sink. Among other things visible on the counter are tin canisters, a Dustbuster, spice rack and an automatic coffee maker.*
>
> *A child's highchair with a laundry basket of clothing is aside the refrigerator, and next to the refrigerator is a wall phone. Children's toys are scattered about the floor along with a child's small tricycle.*
>
> *A small tape recorder is on the table. A door to the outside is stage right, and the entrance to the other rooms within the house is stage left. Before the play begins, there are songs by female vocalists from the '60s and '70s.*
>
> *At Curtain:*
>
> *After a beat in the darkness the song "Will You Love Me Tomorrow?" by the Shirelles begins and after a couple of more beats, lights come up on the kitchen. Sandra is dancing and singing to the tune while removing items from a shop-*

ping bag atop the table. Among items seen are a bottle of Coke, People magazine, a box of cupcakes and a couple of packs of cigarettes.

Sandra is modestly dressed in faded jeans and a sweatshirt. She is pretty with short brown hair, big brown eyes. She folds up the bag and dances over to the kitchen counter, putting the bag away. She proceeds to the wall phone and pulls out the cord happily. The song has taken her over and Sandra is at the stage, physically and facially that one only has when one is alone with a song one loves.

After a pause, the door to the outside opens. Enter Dolores. She closes the door and watches Sandra for a moment. Dolores has light brown hair, is a bit on the chubby side and wears sunglasses and a long winter coat. Her cheeks are red from the cold. Sandra is still dancing and singing, unaware of Dolores. Dolores takes a step into the kitchen, wearing half a smile.

DOLORES: Uh ... Sandra?
(*Sandra spins around and sees Dolores, then quickly turns off the music*)
SANDRA: (*Angrily*) NO! OUT!
DOLORES: Please! I gotta stay here!
SANDRA: NO! NOT HERE!
DOLORES: He wants to kill me!
SANDRA: I'm sick a' this shit, Dolores! Out!
DOLORES: He's afta' me!
SANDRA: I don't care!
DOLORES: I'm ya' fucken' sista'!
SANDRA: I don't care!
DOLORES: What is wrong with you?!
SANDRA: Me?! What's wrong with me?!
DOLORES: He wants ta' kill me!
SANDRA: You got alotta' nerve, girl!
DOLORES: You think I'm kiddin'?!
SANDRA: I don't want to get involved!
DOLORES: Oh, bull shit on you!
SANDRA: I swear I'll smack you if you don't leave!
DOLORES: Oh, that's just great!

SANDRA: I mean it! I'm sick a' only seein' you when you got problems!

DOLORES: You ever visit me?! Huh?!

SANDRA: Don't get me started, Dolores!

DOLORES: He's out there! He's been chasin' me since this mornin'!

SANDRA: Then go ta' Kathy's!

DOLORES: I did. Nobody's there.

SANDRA: Oh fuck! Why me?!

DOLORES: Let me stay for a little while till ...

SANDRA: NO! Whenever I help you, it turns into a horror show!

DOLORES: I'm scared, Sandra!

SANDRA: When are you gonna' learn?! Huh? How many more fucked-up guys you goin' ta' marry?!

DOLORES: I ... I ...

SANDRA: An don't pull the tears on me!

DOLORES: I'm not!

SANDRA: This is my only time alone. Sunday aftanoon Vinnie takes the kids to the park, then to his Mother's, an' it's my only time away from all the aggravation, ya' unda'stand?

DOLORES: (*Removes sunglasses, revealing a black eye*) Just for a little while, then I'll go, okay?

(*Sandra looks at black eye*)

SANDRA: What is ya' problem? You're thirty fucken' years old, Dolores! When are you goin' ta' grow up? Everything you do turns stupid!

DOLORES: I don't ... know what happens ... I ... (*She sits at table*)

SANDRA: An' don't get too comfortable 'cause you got like five minutes, Dolores, an' I mean it! I'm not puttin' up with this shit taday!

DOLORES: I woulda' gone to Mary Ann's but she hates me.

SANDRA: You piss everybody off is why!

DOLORES: I don't mean to! Jesus Christ! I don't think about pissin' everybody off!

SANDRA: If Vinnie comes home an' catches you here, my ass is grass!

DOLORES: An' if Jerry catches me out there, he'll kill me, Sandra!

SANDRA: Why? What dumb fucken' thing happened now? Wait ... let me light a cigarette an' sit, 'cause I can't wait ta hear this one! (*She sits at table next to Dolores and lights up cigarette*)

DOLORES: Don't make fun a' me, all right?

SANDRA: C'mon, let's hear it.

DOLORES: I mean ... I try even though you can't believe that. I'm tryin' ta be normal like everybody else. (*Pause*) Can I have a cupcake?

SANDRA: (*Pushes box in front of her*) Eat it fast.

DOLORES: (*Taking out cupcake*) Any coffee on?

SANDRA: (*Rises*) Gotta be this morning's.

DOLORES: That's all I drink.

SANDRA: (*Turning on coffee maker*) Then you gotta go.

DOLORES: You got Cremora?

SANDRA: Do you hear me?

DOLORES: Cremora, I said.

SANDRA: I heard ya'!

DOLORES: Jesus ...

SANDRA: You drink, eat an' go.

DOLORES: I got nowhere's ta go.

SANDRA: (*Looking for cup*) Go ta Ma's!

DOLORES: (*Eating cupcake*) You gotta be kidding!

SANDRA: Even when she's pissed at ya', she lets you in.

DOLORES: Not any more.

SANDRA: Well, you can't stay here.

DOLORES: She's still mad at me 'cause a' all the shit that went down when Dad was dyin'.

SANDRA: Bringin' in a palm reader to intensive care didn't go over too good.

DOLORES: An' my abortions. She's still pissed about them, I guess.

SANDRA: Then when you brought in the ghetto blaster with the tape of the ocean waves for him to listen to ...

DOLORES: He loved the ocean, plus I sat at the beach all night in the cold taping it for him.

SANDRA: But it was Moonstone beach!

DOLORES: So?

SANDRA: It's a fag beach!

DOLORES: He didn't know that!

SANDRA: He knew. (*Sandra places cup of coffee in front of Dolores*) Drink it fast and ... (*Dolores suddenly grabs Sandra around the waist*) Oh Christ, Dolores ...

DOLORES: (*Hugging Sandra, pleadingly*) Please take me in ... oh God, I don't want to go back there ...

SANDRA: (*Trying to get loose*) Stop this shit, will ya? (*A beat*) Dolores!

DOLORES: I don't want to get hit no more or yelled at ... I'm so tired of bein' yelled at an' ...

SANDRA: (*Manages to break free from Dolores*) An' whose fault is it, Dolores? You pick these fucken' nuts ta marry an afta' six months you come runnin' to everybody! We all try to tell you not to marry these douche bags, but you never listened. Then we go to your stupid weddings an' listen to the same song you pick out as you're walkin' down the aisle ... "We've Only Just Begun."

DOLORES: (*Softly, wiping her eyes*) I love that song ...

SANDRA: But we're all laughin'. Don't ya' know that?

DOLORES: I block it out.

SANDRA: That's ya' problem! You block everything out!

DOLORES: Let me stay just for tonight and ...

SANDRA: (*Cuts her off*) No! Vinnie would never have you stay here, an' me an' him been gettin' along pretty good lately an' I don't wanna break it. I don't need 'im seein' you here 'cause he'll turn right around an' split, an' I don't need that shit on top a' everything else! I got my little house with my little kitchen where I feed my little kids an' Vinnie brings home his little paycheck an' if there's a little extra on Fridays we go out to Valle's by the Airport for a little steak an' salad, then to a show. I got three Dustbusters, a coupon drawer an' I'm savin' stamps for a VCR!

DOLORES: (*After a beat*) You're so lucky ...

SANDRA: On Sunday afta'noons ... it's quiet around here so I can read my *People* magazine an' drink my Coke in peace.

DOLORES: Does Vinnie ever hit you?

SANDRA: Of course not. Shove here, a shove there ...

DOLORES: We *all* get shoved, Sandra.

SANDRA: It's when we're foolin' around and ...

DOLORES: I'm talkin' about whacked, kicked, pushed down stairs, hair pulled back, woken up in the middle of the night for hard sex, insulted in a restaurant, pushed outta' a car ...

SANDRA: (*Interested*) This all happened last night?

DOLORES: No. He hit me this mornin' at, uh, breakfast 'cause ... (*A beat*) Well ... he's a bra fanatic and ...

SANDRA: (*Cuts her off*) He wears bras?!

DOLORES: No ... he makes me wear them when we're havin sex and ...

SANDRA: Is that all? Tommy the mailman used to tie you to trees an' took nude pictures a' you which he sold to porno magazines!

DOLORES: (*Slipping off coat*) That was different.

SANDRA: (*Leans back to look at Dolores*) Oh, my God. You're wearin' my mother-in-law's curtains.

DOLORES: You always was jealous a' my clothes.

(*Dolores is wearing a pink pants suit with bright red floral designs*)

SANDRA: (*Laughing*) I'm tellin ya' She has them in her living room!

DOLORES: Tommy *was* a jerk, but Frankie was nice.

SANDRA: Frankie Depetro? The retard whose sista' was a lesbian an' was puttin' the moves on me as we was walkin' down the aisle at ya' first wedding?!

DOLORES: She's in jail now.

SANDRA: I don't care if she's on the moon! Oh god! (*Stands*) Why am I talkin' about this shit? You make me crazy, Dolores, ya' really do ... so drink up cause you gotta go! I mean it ...

DOLORES: What if he's out there waitin' for me?!

SANDRA: I don't know. Talk it out with him. He doesn't seem that bad. Except for his crooked eye, he seems normal so just figure it out for ya'self!

DOLORES: I'm scared. (*A beat*) I shoulda' married Howard Feingold from high school. I hear Jewish men don't hit their women.

SANDRA: Oh stop, will you please! Go to the police!

DOLORES: Forget that cop shit! They don't do nothin'! I been through it before, an' they come an' usually stick up for the guy. Unless there's a knife comin' outta your heart, they don't do shit an' what am I gonna do when they get there? Show them the bite marks on my bra?!

SANDRA: You said you already went to Kathy's?

DOLORES: I pounded an' pounded at the door but no answer.

SANDRA: They saw ya' comin' an hit the floor!

DOLORES: Just as well. Her Beatle wallpaper makes me real sad and I wish I was fifteen again.

SANDRA: Dolores! Ma beat you up twice a day when you was fifteen!

DOLORES: Yeah. As soon as I got tits she went crazy on me.

SANDRA: You were ten, right?

DOLORES: What?

SANDRA: Nothin. I'm just tryin' to ... get all this straight.

(*Pause. Sandra is picking up toys, slowly, and putting them in a toy box*)

DOLORES: You're not really goin' to throw me out there, are you?

SANDRA: (*Back to Dolores*) Dolores ... I got ... I got my own life here, an' stuff you get involved in is so way above my head. I mean ... he hit you an' ... well, you gotta work it out with him an'—an' this bra thing ... I don't know ... we all have to put up with strange things but you do it, an' when you do it enough ... it's not strange anymore. (*A beat*) Vinnie an' I get along fine 'cause most times we walk around here an' we just don't talk. We watch television an' on Fridays he gets what he wants an' we just go on and ...

DOLORES: (*Cuts Sandra off*) I don't want that! I want more than that, for Chrissakes. No talkin' an watchin' TV ... if I wanted that I never woulda' left Frankie!

SANDRA: Oh c'mon ... Frankie ate his spaghetti an' meatballs with his hands an' couldn't talk straight!

DOLORES: (*Looking away from Sandra*) When I first met Jerry ... I was was down in the pits. I felt I had no family, I had no kids, no nothin' an' I was thirty years old. Goin' to the fucken' bars lookin' around at other thirty-year-old women. I couldn't watch TV no more 'cause family scenes made me sob and the music on the radio, especially Carly Simon songs, made me all soft inside ... like I was dyin' for somebody to just touch my fucken' hand! I'd ... I'd look at some guy, you know, an' think to myself, "oh, please let him say something nice to me 'cause I'm the one for him ..." an' I would just pray he could pick it up in my eyes, but too many times nothin' like that ever happened. I'd look in the mirra' an'—an' my face always looked dirty and I would scrub it till it was red, an' sonofabitch, if it still didn't look dirty! Then one night I was at the Four-Dee's downtown feelin' pretty fucken' low an' thinkin' about death more an' more when this voice came outta nowhere "How would you like to see the sunrise in Montreal?" I looked over an' saw Jerry lookin' at me ... well, one eye was anyway, an' the other was pointin' up at the ceiling an' I thought "well, not too bad. I could live with the bum eye" an' I forgot bein' lonely an' the family, an' other women! I forgot about my dry skin an' how I can hold pencils unda' my tits now. I didn't think about my three abortions anymore an' ... (*A beat*) Did you know I'd have an eight-year-old kid ... nine next June if ... and a five-year-old? Shit ... can ya picture me with kids?

SANDRA: (*Sullenly*) Nope.

DOLORES: (*Moves closer to Sandra*) Rememba' when we slept in the same bed an' we used to talk about how many kids we would have an'—an' wondrin' where our husbands-to-be were?

SANDRA: Little did we know all yours were in jail.

DOLORES: Every night we would say the "act of contrition" together in case we died in our sleep. (*A beat*) I still do that.

SANDRA: (*Nervously*) Yeah, well we're goin' to *have* to say it if Vinnie comes home an' catches me with you! Vinnie likes things in a straight line, no waves an' you ... you freak him out with—with your clothes an' perfume an' makeup an' the husbands he never likes an ...

DOLORES: But I'M your sista', goddamn it! Don't you stick up for me?! Or do you hate me, too?

SANDRA: I don't hate you.

DOLORES: Then help me! Help me get through this, Sandra!

SANDRA: (*Snaps at Dolores*) WHAT?! WHAT DO YOU WANT ME TO DO?!

DOLORES: I ... I ...

SANDRA: What?! Put you in the cellar?! Hide you in the closet?!

DOLORES: No ... I ...

SANDRA: You wanna sleep unda' little Vinnie's bed with Bert and Ernie?!

DOLORES: No! (*Sandra looks at Dolores*) Sandra, I ... I ... (*The words won't come out*)

SANDRA: (*Frustratedly*) Shit, girl!

DOLORES: Wasn't it ... when we were kids, wasn't it always you who used to say, "Hey, I got an idea!"

SANDRA: Oh, for Chrissakes ...

DOLORES: Wasn't it you?

SANDRA: I knew you'd try an' pull me in, I knew it!

DOLORES: I need some help, I need support. I'm good, Sandra, an' everybody comes down on me 'cause I don't like gettin' beat up!

SANDRA: Wait a minute, wait a minute ... why ...

DOLORES: (*Screams*) THEN FUCK EVERYBODY! THEN I SHOULD KILL MYSELF!

SANDRA: Will you hold it an' ... you never finished tellin' ...

DOLORES: ASSHOLES! I'm supposed ta put up with it 'cause Ma did?!

SANDRA: Who says that?

DOLORES: (*Angrily*) I mean, okay, Frankie pushed me around, an' I knew we was goin' nowheres, an' Tommy was just a plain out-an-out crook who fucked up my head more than my body, an' Jerry ... Jerry's just mean an' I put up with the beatin's 'cause I ... I knew what all you would say, an' I wanted so much to make this one work no matter what! I had my fucken' face stepped on an' sometimes he would take a coupla' uppers an' go at me for two fucken' days, wavin' his gun in my face, an' I'd like to see you or—or Kathy or fucken' Mary Ann go through that shit! I'm good in here ... (*Pounds her chest*) Right down deep in here! (*A beat*) That time I saw you an' Mary Ann at the Mall? Rememba'? I just wanted to run up an' ... an' hug you both 'cause you're my sista's but ... MAN, OH, MAN, how the vibes came shootin' out for me to keep a distance! You were like two cheerleaders snickering about the Italian girl with the mustache!

SANDRA: I don't remolosemba' that.

DOLORES: The ... funniest part of it all is that I was gettin' Christmas gifts for you an' her!

SANDRA: Last Christmas?

DOLORES: Do you even rememba' what I got you?

SANDRA: This past Christmas?

DOLORES: Yes!

SANDRA: You got me Charlie perfume and glue-on fingernails.

DOLORES: I got 'em at the mall that day! Both a' you was so cold to me!

SANDRA: By the big clock?

DOLORES: In front of Warren Jewelers.

SANDRA: On the second floor?

DOLORES: First floor 'cause I was on my way out.

SANDRA: We was on our way in?

DOLORES: Just comin' outta Filene's.

SANDRA: You were in a hurry, I rememba' now.

DOLORES: I was in a hurry ... (*A beat*) It *looked* like I was in a hurry 'cause I was happy to see you both! (*A beat*) Afta' the quick minute we spent together, I almost brought back the fingernails!

SANDRA: It's always hectic around the mall at Christmas, an' we didn't have much time an' ...

DOLORES: (*Cuts her off*) Oh, fuck off!

SANDRA: Hold it, girl! You don't talk ta me ... hey, wait an' let's back up for a minute here!

DOLORES: We didn't even show any affection durin' Dad's funeral, that's how fucked we are!

SANDRA: STOP!

DOLORES: We just cried to ourselves in our little space with our separate memories of him an' I *knew* everyone was buzzin' about me, but I'm the oldest so I kept together through it an' then at the little party at Aunt Betty's I gave Ma a present an' she flung it across the room at me!

SANDRA: It was that stupid book, an' it was the wrong goddamn time for it! What's the name of that stupid book?

DOLORES: *My Mother, My Self.*

SANDRA: It was dumb, Dolores!

DOLORES: I felt it was time ... with Dad outta the way, that maybe she an' I could patch things up.

SANDRA: With you an' Ma, it's goin' ta take years, an' I don't know why that is but ...

DOLORES: That's not what my shrink told me.

SANDRA: (*Surprised*) *You* see a shrink? Where do you get money to see a shrink?

DOLORES: It's only a buck a week or whatever you can afford, kinda like welfare shrinks in this clinic on Cranston Street. They listen for half an hour an' ya get stuff out, but I don't feel any different. It's like when you're a kid leavin' confession an' ya' feel good for about twenty minutes. I try things this woman says, but I don't know if I really believe in all that shit, so like usual with me ... if my heart ain't into somethin' ...

SANDRA: Why aren't you runnin' to the clinic then?!

DOLORES: She's only there on Tuesdays and Thursdays.

SANDRA: Jerry know you go there?

DOLORES: (*Bitterly*) Fuck him! Fucken prick!

SANDRA: Okay, okay. Does this shrink say anythin' about him an' what you should do about it?

DOLORES: Oh, yeah. That I should ... uh ... confront him more an' make him aware of problems that I have with him. Stuff you read in *Seventeen* magazine, an' I tell her "Yeah, easy for you ta say cause you're not in front of the mean green eye a' his" an' she says "true."

SANDRA: That's it?

DOLORES: Whaddaya want for a buck? It's me an' a lotta colored chicks sittin' in the waitin' room an' all so fucken' sad and bruised. Kids screamin' an' fightin', runnin' around an'...

SANDRA: Hold it. Have you talked ta Jerry like she said you should?

DOLORES: If you got a problem with Vinnie, say he did some disgustin' thing that pissed you off, do you sit down with him to discuss it? Do you say "Gee, Vin ... you look so ugly in ya' boxer shorts an' ya' gettin fat an' I think it's kinda sick you got tits now an' how ya' think I feel bein' on the bottom all the time?"

SANDRA: Wait a ...

DOLORES: (*Continuing*) Or "Gee, Vin ... are you as confused about God as me, an' do you think that we're slowly becomin' the parents we fought with?" You ever see Ma an' Dad talk when we were kids? (*A beat*) What do you do, Sandra, when you got a problem with "The Big Vin?" Huh? What clues do you give 'im that something's wrong? Maybe slide his plate in front of him a little harda' than usual?

SANDRA: We ... just get by it ... and ...

DOLORES: An' it disappears, right?

SANDRA: Look ... we ... I don't have the problems you have, Dolores. The kids take up a lotta time and ...

DOLORES: And not to mention talkin' on the phone with Kathy an' Mary Ann about Dolores!

SANDRA: (*Angrily*) I think you should go now! Really ... put ya' coat on an' leave! Of everybody who deals with you, I am the straightest when it comes to tellin' you stuff!

(*Sandra throws Dolores her coat, moving her to the door*)

DOLORES: (*Holds her hand up to Sandra*) SSSH!

SANDRA: Don't tell me to ...

DOLORES: (*Waves at Sandra*) Be quiet for a ... (*Sandra watches Dolores walk to the door and listen. Sandra reaches for her Dustbuster and holds it like weapon*) You hear something?

SANDRA: (*Close to Dolores*) No ... I ...

DOLORES: SSSH! (*A beat*) There's someone out there ...

SANDRA: (*Half-whisper*) Prob'ly just the cats next door.

DOLORES: (*Turns to Sandra*) I really did hear something.

SANDRA: Like what? Voices? What?

DOLORES: (*Returning to table*) Footsteps. First one ... then another. (*A beat*) Could it be Vinnie?

SANDRA: No way. Vinnie clears out his throat an' his nose, then lets out a lugar the size of a pond, *then* he comes in. (*Sandra looks at Dolores, who has returned to her place at table. Sandra places Dustbuster on counter and turns to Dolores*) Listen to me, Dolores ... I really think you ...

DOLORES: (*Cuts her off*) Would you do my hair for me?

SANDRA: Oh shit, Dolores!

DOLORES: Kinda like the girl on channel six has it.

SANDRA: You come here an' screw up my day, tell me some war stories and even get in a few insults and I'm supposed to fix your hair?

DOLORES: (*Snaps at Sandra*) You told me at Christmas time you'd do something with my hair! You promised me! (*Dolores throws kid's toy at Sandra's back. Sandra spins around and glares at Dolores*) Oh god ... I'm sorry ... (*They face each other*) Do you think it's nut house time?

SANDRA: I ...

DOLORES: I might not have a choice ...

SANDRA: (*Softly*) A nut house might be good.

DOLORES: You think?

SANDRA: Maybe.

DOLORES: People be there to help.

SANDRA: True ...

DOLORES: I wouldn't be buggin' anybody.

SANDRA: Prob'ly make friends.

DOLORES: I make friends fast.

SANDRA: You always did.

DOLORES: On Sunday afta'noons you could come an' sing to me ... (*Sings, softly*) "Will you still love me tomorrow?"

(*A beat*)

SANDRA: (*Crosses in front of Dolores*) Uh ... so listen ... if Vinnie does come home ... I'm goin' to tell him that, uh ... you're here an' that I talked you into gettin' help at a, you know ... a head hospital, all right? If he comes in, all right? That way there'll be no trouble or yellin' an' he'll understand.

DOLORES: Vinnie, Vinnie. Shit ... nobody wants to hear the truth. I mean ... say you know things about somebody that you care for, an'—an' we talk about that something, that fucken' something with everybody *but* the person you supposedly care for.

SANDRA: (*Not listening, flipping through phone book*) What do I look unda'?

DOLORES: That always bugged me an' I guess it's why I don't have any friends left an' my family could care less.

SANDRA: Not nut house, right? They wouldn't do it that way, would they?

DOLORES: I mean my whole life ... flashes ... lots of flashes an' places. Like watchin' a movie in fast motion an' then WHAM! I'm sittin' across from Jerry an' livin' in a duplex in Johnston and I wonder how I got there.

(*Pause. Sandra looks up from phone book and at Dolores who is kneeling on a kitchen chair facing Sandra*)

SANDRA: Uh-huh, right ...

DOLORES: When I was at the clinic last week or maybe it was two weeks ago ... but anyway ... I was readin' this article about you should look back to when you were ... I think it was age nine through twelve 'cause it's the time when you form ideas about ya'self, you know, an' it said that we usually stick with those ... uh ...

SANDRA: Ideas.

DOLORES: Right an' how affected we are by our parents and ... and ... it was interestin'.

SANDRA: I don't really know what you're talkin' about but ...

DOLORES: (*Takes phone book from Sandra and throws it down*) Do you rememba' anythin' about me durin' that time?

SANDRA: Nine through twelve?

DOLORES: Nine through twelve.

(*Sandra goes to the laundry basket and picks it up*)

SANDRA: Uh ... well, you wet the bed, I rememba'. (*She puts laundry basket on table and begins folding clothes*)

DOLORES: Right ...

SANDRA: Seemed like ya' did that for a long time.

DOLORES: I know, I know. What else?

SANDRA: You okay about that now?

DOLORES: YES! (*A beat*) What else?

SANDRA: I don't know! You always had to get in the last word an' ...

DOLORES: That was afta' twelve.

SANDRA: You used ta pass out all the time an' Ma was always throwin' water in ya' face and ...

DOLORES: That was afta' too.

SANDRA: Then I don't know. I wasn't paying attention. I was only seven, an' what did I know?

DOLORES: I think we was livin on Richard Street.

SANDRA: That small yellow house? (*Dolores is helping Sandra fold clothes*) I rememba' that house. Next to the funeral parlor! (*A beat*) We could always hear Ma an' Dad foolin' around in their bedroom and ... (*Sandra starts to laugh*)

DOLORES: (*Looking at Sandra*) What? (*Sandra is laughing harder*) What?

SANDRA: (*Collecting herself*) I was just thinkin' a' that crazy night when Dad busted in on Ma's tuppa'ware party all shitfaced, an' I'm pretty sure that was on Richard Street.

DOLORES: Yes, it was! (*Starts to laugh*) An' he went into the bedroom an' came out with Ma's girdle on and ...

SANDRA: Aunt Betty was throwin' stackin' storage boxes at him and ...

DOLORES: Right, right, while Ma was getting everybody out the back door!

SANDRA: I never seen her so pissed!

DOLORES: An rememba' he couldn't get the girdle off and ...

SANDRA: He *wouldn't* get the girdle off! (*They laugh together*) He was such a ballbuster, an' then when he finally got her quiet, you had to start with scratchin' ya' legs and ...

DOLORES: My dry skin gets bad when it gets cold ...

SANDRA: An' you drove everybody crazy an' we were screamin' for you to stop an' ...

DOLORES: An' you had the biggest mouth!

SANDRA: Get outta here! Mary Ann did, an' you're one to talk ... "MA ... MY LEGS ARE BLEEDIN'!"

DOLORES: Well, they were ...

SANDRA: An' then we heard Ma's door open ... CRASH! An' then she started ... "Goddamn ...

DOLORES and SANDRA: ... Son of a bitchin' girl!"

SANDRA: She came flyin' in with ... whad she have? Shoelaces?

DOLORES: Her old nylons.

SANDRA: Old nylons, an' she tied ya' hands an' legs to the post in about two fucken' minutes and ...

DOLORES: She said she'd gag me if I made one more sound!

SANDRA: It was dark, but I saw your face up to her's sayin' ... "Ma, please don't tie me up, I'll be better."

DOLORES: She never heard me.

SANDRA: "Ma ... please do something ... " (*A beat*) An' then she slams the door, an' Mary Ann said ... (*Laughing*) "Dolores, let us know when you want to sleep on ya' stomach, we'll turn the bed over for you!"

(*They laugh together for a few beats—then silence as they continue folding clothes. Dolores is crying, to herself. She sits*)

Kinda sick, huh?

(*They hold eye contact for a moment. Sandra breaks it*)

You were tellin' me about Jerry an' the bra thing an' it made me think about me an' Vinnie, 'cause sometimes we get kinky like everybody must, an' he puts Brut lotion on his whole body 'cause that smell drives me crazy. I mean I get lost in the smell when we're touchin' an' stuff an' I forget the kids an' my mother-in-law an' all the bills an' I just ... kinda lose myself. If they could make a Brut drink, I'd drink it. (*Silence*) What is the bra thing he ... that you an' he do? Now that I told ya' my little secret.

DOLORES: (*Wiping her eyes*) It's stupid is all, an' I got so sick a' doing stupid things, Sandra ...

SANDRA: But how can it be any worse than Tommy the mailman tyin' you up to trees?

DOLORES: That was nothin'. Only doin' it for the covers of dirty books. (*Pause*) Sandra ... do you ... do you hit your kids a lot?

SANDRA: Of course not. I love my brats even though it's tougher bringin' up kids than I thought 'cause they want an' want an' get sick an' fight an' you're always seein' things of yourself in them an' that can piss ya' off if you let it, but ... I, uh, try not to let them bother Vinnie too much. They know they have to be quiet when he's here.

(*Pause. Sandra sits*)

Look ... I'm afraid a' losin' something just like everybody else ... I don't know.

(*A beat*)

An' I lied before about when I said that, uh, Vinnie only shoved me. He's hit me. It started with the dog. He really used to go bullshit on the dog an' sometimes for no reason. Just start beltin' it an' gettin' mean. I figured out that the dog is man's best friend 'cause it doesn't say "go fuck ya'self" afta' it gets hit!

(*A beat*)

One time last year me an' Vinnie was drivin' back from his mother's an' we were at a light over on Atwells Avenue, an' this motorcycle pulled up next to my window and I looked over an' saw this good-lookin' guy on the bike ... kinda like Al Pacino with blue eyes an' he had on a brown leather jacket, pair a' ripped-up jeans an' boots. His brown hair was pushed all the way back an'—an' he was so close I coulda' grabbed his arm. He turned an' looked at me with those eyes, great cheekbones he had an' he smiled at me, then winked ... just like in fucken' TV commercials! I couldn't take my eyes off a' him ... I tried,

cause I knew I was goin' too long, but I just couldn't help it, an'
then ... I felt my hair bein' pulled an' before I knew it, my head
was on the fucken' seat, an' I was bein' punched in the face!
Not slapped, but punched! Same way he used to hit the dog and
I ... I could hear the motorcycle way off in the distance ...
(*Pause*) Something went away with that guy ... (*Sandra shakes
it off, rubbing her eyes*) What ... what am I talkin' about?!
What the fuck is goin' on? This all seems so stupid now ...
hearin' it out, it all sounds silly or somethin'! I was yellin' at
you to get away 'cause my husband might be ... be mad at me
... (*Sandra stands and is pacing*) Oh, Dolores, I ...

DOLORES: Don't worry about it ...

SANDRA: That's it! You're staying here!

DOLORES: (*Stands*) No, no ...

SANDRA: I'll take care a' Vinnie ... I'll take care a' him ...

DOLORES: (*Facing Sandra*) Sandra ...

SANDRA: (*Angry, upset*) I mean you're my sista', damn it!
(*A beat*) If we can't even ... (*A beat*) What's the fucken' point?!

DOLORES: (*Wanting to calm Sandra down*) You got any
asp'rin?

SANDRA: What?

DOLORES: Asp'rin. You got any?

SANDRA: (*Grabs Dolores's hand*) Yeah, yeah ... but, uh,
listen ... do you want money? I got money saved for ... for
somethin' special someday an' ... you can have it.

DOLORES: (*Holding back her emotion*) I don't want your
money, Sandra. (*A beat*) Some asp'rin be good.

SANDRA: Asp'rin. Okay.

(*Sandra leaves the kitchen. Dolores wipes her eyes with a
Kleenex. She proceeds to the wall phone, takes a deep
breath and picks up receiver. She dials, then suddenly
stops—dropping the phone to the floor*)

DOLORES: (*Trembling, backing away from phone*) HE'S IN
THE HOUSE! HE CUT THE PHONE OFF! (*She pulls out a
small handgun from her coat pocket*) THE FUCKA' IS IN THE
HOUSE! C'MON YOU FUCKEN' JERK! C'MON,
ASSHOLE, 'CAUSE I'LL KILL YOU NOW! (*Sandra comes
running into kitchen*)

SANDRA: (*Drops the bottle of aspirin*) What the ... ?!

DOLORES: (*Waving gun around kitchen*) HE'S IN THE HOUSE! HE CUT THE PHONE OFF! BUT I CAUGHT IT JUST IN TIME!

SANDRA: (*Getting out of the way of gun*) NO! OH, GOD! PUT THE GUN DOWN!

DOLORES: (*Doesn't hear Sandra*) C'MON OUT! I'LL FINISH IT RIGHT HERE, YOU MOTHER-FUCKA'! C'MON OUT!

SANDRA: (*Pleadingly*) DOLORES! Listen to me! I unplugged the phone! I do it every Sunday! (*Sandra shows Dolores phone plug*) Look ... see? I just pull the plug out! (*Sandra plugs phone cord back in. Dolores lowers the gun*) Put that thing away ... c'mon, put it down.

(*Dolores drops the gun and collapses in a chair*)

DOLORES: I ... I shot him, Sandra. This mornin' I shot him. He hit me too many times, an' he won't let me outta his sight ...

SANDRA: No, you didn't ... tell me ya' didn't ...

DOLORES: I couldn't take it no more an' Jerry was readin' the paper at the table an' I had his gun that I took from his coat an' I aimed it at a picture of Reagan that was on the front page, and I shot through the picture an' Jerry went flyin' back onto the floor an' he ... he was laughin' ... his shoulder was bleedin' and I ran out an' heard him say that he could kill me now, and I ran down the middle of Holmewood Street an' heard him in the car beepin' the horn and I kept runnin' an' could see people goin' to church and pickin' up their papers an' I cut ... I cut through the Kentucky Fried Chicken place an' ran up the hill to Whitmarsh Street an' got on a bus an' went to Kathy's but ... nobody home an' then I came here ...

SANDRA: (*Stunned*) Are you shittin' me? Did you really ...

DOLORES: Yes. I ...

SANDRA: Holy shit ... uh ... oh, God ... (*Sandra is confused*) Uh ... why didn't you ... (*Dolores looks up at Sandra*) I didn't know it was that bad. (*Silence*) Shit, Dolores ... I don't know what to say ... I ... (*Phone rings. Sandra is shocked for a beat. She answers*) Hello ... (*A beat*) Yeah ... I ... she's here ... what? (*Sandra takes a deep breath*) I guess so ... right, right ... I know ... I'll bring her an' ... shut up, Mary Ann! 'Cause I'm bringin' her! Fine ... right ... bye ... (*Hangs up phone and turns to Dolores, who appears drained of all emotion*) That was

Mary Ann. Police found Jerry in his car ... dead. Bled to death on Broad street.
(*A chill passes through Dolores. She takes a deep breath and slowly exhales*)
DOLORES: (*Softly*) Broad Street ...
SANDRA: I'm gonna take you over to Mary Ann's. (*Sandra stares at her sister. Silence. After a beat or two—Sandra opens a kitchen drawer and takes out a hairbrush. She gets behind Dolores and slowly begins brushing her hair*) Sit up a little straighter. (*Dolores does. Sandra bends and turns on tape player and immediately song "Will You Love Me Tomorrow?" comes on. Sandra returns to working on her sister's hair. Both women crying, openly. Lights fade to black*)

The End

Romulus Linney

APRIL SNOW

Romulus Linney

Romulus Linney makes his fifth appearance in the *Best Short Plays* series with the sophisticated, trenchant character study *April Snow*. First presented in New York City's Ensemble Studio Theatre's (E.S.T.) Marathon '87, *April Snow* was subsequently produced by the Manhattan Theatre Club in the spring of 1988. Mimi Kramer, reviewer for *The New Yorker*, praising the E.S.T. production, raves, *"April Snow* is probably the best play I've seen in New York all year." *New York Times* reviewer Mel Gussow characterizes the play as "a sophisticated study of artists, love and loneliness, as exemplified by a 61-year-old author-screenwriter (Harris Yulin) who, through the exercise of his charm, ineluctably damages lives, beginning with his own ... [T]he drama shifts ... until each character is seen in deep, sympathetic focus. Then the playwright brings in three minor characters for a late-night soiree, and they have a catalytic, comic effect on the principals. The writing has Mr. Linney's customary intelligence, as well as a mysterious, enigmatic quality."

The 1987 edition of *Best Short Plays* included Mr. Linney's play *Why the Lord Come to Sand Mountain*, a Biblical tall tale based on his book, *Jesus Tales*. In a review of that play as directed by the author and presented by the Whole Theatre of Montclair, New Jersey, *New York Times* reviewer Mel Gussow describes the tale: " ... Jesus and Saint Peter, in humanly guise, visit a 'hard-time family' in a lonely shack." As the characters sip brandy and exchange stories, "what might in some hands seem blasphemous—or precious—is comic in Mr. Linney's patented mountain Gothic style." The tall tales "eventually lead to a testament of faith, as late at night, Jesus reveals the true reason that he came to Sand Mountain."

In the 1986 edition of *Best Short Plays,* Mr. Linney's *The Love Suicide at Schofield Barracks* presented a rivoting and searing drama in the inquiry on a major general and his wife who have carried out a murder-suicide pact. Two earlier plays in this series from Mr. Linney are *F.M.*, published in the 1984 edition, and the Obie winner, *Tennessee*, which appeared in the 1980 edition.

Mr. Linney's most widely produced play, *The Sorrows of Frederick*, is a psychological drama about Frederick the Great. Its many stage productions include the 1967 premiere at the Mark Taper Forum in Los Angeles with Fritz Weaver in the title role. Subsequent productions of the play were presented in New York with Austin Pendleton, in Canada with Donald Davis, in Great Britain with John Wood, and later, Tom Conti. It also was performed at the Dusseldorf Schauspielhaus in Germany and at the Burgtheater in Vienna, where it successfully played in classical repertory through the season of 1969–70 in a production that won two Austrian theatre awards.

Born in Philadelphia, Pennsylvania, in 1930, Romulus Linney grew up in Madison, Tennessee, and spent his summers in North Carolina. He was educated at Oberlin College, where he received his B.A. in 1953, and the Yale School of Drama, earning a Master of Fine Arts degree there in 1958. He has taught playwriting at many schools, including Columbia University, Brooklyn College, the University of Pennsylvania, Connecticut College, Princeton, Hunter College, and most recently at the University of Pennsylvania.

Mr. Linney received two fellowships from the National Endowment for the Arts, and from 1976 until 1979 served on its literary panel. In 1980 he was awarded a fellowship from the Guggenheim Foundation, and in 1984 he received the Award in Literature from the American Academy and Institute of Arts and Letters.

He is also the author of two highly regarded novels, *Heathen Valley* and *Slowly, by Thy Hand Unfurled,* and has recently written a third novel. In addition, he has written numerous other plays, including *Democracy, Holy Ghosts, Old Man Joseph and His Family,* and *Laughing Stock*, picked by *Time* magazine as one of the best plays of 1984. Mr. Linney has written extensively for television, had an opera made from a short play, *The Death of King Phillip*, and has published a number of short plays and fiction in numerous literary magazines.

As a director, Mr. Linney has staged his own plays for the Philadelphia Festival of New Plays; the Actors Studio; the Alley Theatre in Houston; the Bay Area Playwrights Festival in

California; the Milwaukee Repertory; the Whole Theatre Company in Montclair, New Jersey; and the Circle Repertory Theatre in Manhattan.

Other plays by Mr. Linney include *Childe Byron*, produced in New York by the Circle Repertory Company, in Louisville by the Actors Theatre, in Costa Mesa, California, by the South Coast Repertory, and in London by the Young Vic; *The Captivity of Pixie Shedman*, at the New York Phoenix Theatre and the Detroit Repertory Theatre; *El Hermano* and *Goodbye, Howard* at the Ensemble Studio Theatre in New York; *A Woman Without a Name* at the Empire State Theatre in Albany, New York, and at the Denver Center Theatre Company; *Sand Mountain* at the Philadelphia Festival for New Plays and the Whole Theatre in Montclair, New Jersey; and *Pops* at the Whole Theatre and at the Bay Area Playwrights Festival in California.

Characters:

GORDON TATE, *sixty-one, a writer*
GRADY GUNN, *fifty-eight, a woman writer*
MILLICENT BECK, *twenty, a student*
LUCIEN FIELD, *forty, a painter*
BILL DRYER, *twenty-five, an actor*
THOMAS HARDY, *forty-five, a lawyer*

Time:

April, 1982.

Setting:

Gordon Tate's loft. Bookcases. A writer's desk. A warm rug, some stuffed chairs. A small bar, with an electric Crock pot. A small wooden statue of Don Quixote on the desk.

Scene One:

Morning: Gordon, Grady.
Gordon is stirring soup in the electric Crock pot on the bar

GORDON: So why are you giving only six readings next year?
(*Pause*)
GRADY: Mona's come back to me.
GORDON: Again?
GRADY: For good.
GORDON: When?
GRADY: A month ago. Mona's twenty-eight now. Little Fred is nine. This week, there had to be a visit. So, there was. Doorbell rang. There was Fred, coat and tie, hair slicked down, looking angelic. Behind him stood Richard, the injured father,

looking innocent. The little boy and I faced each other. "Hi, Grady," he said. "Hi, Fred." "Mama here?" "Yep." "Bye, Dad." Richard left. Mona came out of my kitchen. "Hi, Mama," said Fred. "Am I in the maid's room again?"

(Pause)

In the morning, I got up first. How to work? Think clearly about Madame de Stael, Madame Recamier and Madame Krudener? Read Sainte-Beuve, oh, please! I studied a paragraph. Madame Krudener dying, floating down the Volga on a houseboat with her coffin by her side. She was ridiculous. All my work confronted me like a coffin. My home felt like a tomb. I felt like a corpse, and I was afraid of Mona's child.

(Pause)

They got up, made breakfast. I worked, pretending diligence. They tiptoed past my study, shushing each other. Utter silence. I hollered. "Oh, come in!" They did. Both, staring. Fred and I smiled. Like this. God. Two hypocrites. I wondered why he didn't leap over the desk, grab my throat and throttle me. It's what I wanted to do to him. But the little boy whose mother left his father for me, *again*, he didn't do that. He tried to talk, coughed, blew his nose, as wretched as I was. Then he said, "Can I watch tv in the bedroom?" I said, "Sure." He kissed me, and he went into the room where his mother and I sleep, and watched his cartoons. He's with us every other weekend now. He says he loves me. I believe him. I want to believe him. I must. Madame de Stael, Madame Recamier, Madame Krudener, all talk happily at once. I just take it down. I love Mona. I love Fred. I stay home now. I will give only six readings next year. Do you see?

GORDON: I do. Potato soup in the Crock pot. Want some?

GRADY: Oh, God no. I'm never hungry now. I'm in love!

Scene Two:

Noon: Gordon, Milly.
Milly sits in Gordon's lap, arms around his neck.

GORDON: The American pig, we are told, loves to hide. But not thinking he is very big, he will peer at you from behind a stick, sure he can't be seen. Like this. Hello.

(*He peers at Milly, like a pig behind a stick. Milly laughs and kisses him. They kiss for some time. Pause*)

MILLY: Do you *have* to have lunch with that man?

GORDON: I'll be back. Four o'clock. Not a moment later.

MILLY: Why did you tell me that story?

GORDON: Thought it was funny.

MILLY: About the pig.

GORDON: Yes.

MILLY: You aren't a pig.

GORDON: It was a story.

MILLY: Nothing is just a story. I'd like some wine. May I?

GORDON: Sure. There's soup in the pot.

MILLY: Just wine. I don't eat much. You want some?

GORDON: No.

(*Milly pours some wine for herself at Gordon's bar*)

MILLY: Always the same, this room. Your desk, Don Quixote. You had two cots, for Jimmy and me.

GORDON: I remember.

MILLY: We slept out here, watching The Late Show. Down from Riverdale, with Alice and John, to SoHo, where nobody lived then but you. With your beautiful young wife and Ruby. Who would be what, Ruby, sixteen now?

GORDON: Eighteen. Living in California.

MILLY: I know. When do you see her?

GORDON: Twice a year.

MILLY: You worry about her?

GORDON: Some.

MILLY: You worry about me?

GORDON: Some.

MILLY: I'm stronger now. Being crazy can do that for you. It taught me things.

GORDON: What?

MILLY: Things. How to live without eating. I do now but not much. When people tell stories for hidden reasons.

(*Pause*)

I was eighteen when I went in the hospital. In Minnesota, the treatment was—conservative. They gave me insulin shock

and wrapped me in bedsheets. I was there ten long months.
You sent me that book. *Grimm's Fairy Tales*. An ugly Scottish
edition with scary illustrations. Just right for a girl in a mad-
house. I read and read. Giants, and monsters. Wicked step-
mothers, heartless kings, and little runaways. Stand-ins, I
knew. Momma, Daddy, Brother, me. You. There was one good
book in the hospital library. The plays of Strindberg. Strindberg,
Grimm, and me.

(*Pause*)
Maybe I can be crazy in a book some day.

(*She laughs*)
About a sane brother and a crazy sister and the crazy sister
survives and the sane brother might not. I'd write it now but it
wouldn't be believable.

(*Pause*)
When we were all together, and we came here, the family, do
you remember the day I kidnapped you? Toothbrush, paste, my
sweater in a bag. Off to the river, pulling you along, swinging my
little bottom and batting my eyes. I was running away with you.

GORDON: I remember.

MILLY: Who packs a bag now, to run away with you?

GORDON: I go nowhere now, with anyone. I sleep here, with
a nice friend once in awhile, not often. To tell you the truth,
recently at depressing intervals ominously increasing in length.

MILLY: Did I make you happy last night?

(*Gordon shrugs, then smiles*)
GORDON: My God, darling, yes. But when it's time to go,
you go.

MILLY: Just like that. Not one word. You'll be proud of me.

GORDON: Right. You will find your young man. I will go
back to my Medocs and Marsalas and haute cuisine, which I
hardly taste anyway, since I never seem to be hungry anymore.
My sex life will once again be a kind of after-brandy
afterthought. I'm too old to change that.

(*Pause. Gordon grins*)
You have a beady look in your eye. Found him already?
Time to go? I'm philosophical. Go.

MILLY: I love you. (*Pause*) I adore you. (*Pause*) I have
since I was a child. I always will, as long a I live. There can
never be anyone for me but you.

GORDON: You take my breath away. (*Pause*) Do you want another drink?

MILLY: If you do. Another drink, I mean.

GORDON: (*Simultaneous*) I don't.

(*Pause*)

MILLY: What do you want, Gordon?

GORDON: I want you to come to Spain with me.

MILLY: With you?

GORDON: For the summer. I've got to work on this movie. It's called *A Day in the Life of Nero*.

MILLY: Won't you like that?

GORDON: It pays. Blood and sex and everything like that. Come with me. Please.

MILLY: To Spain with you?

GORDON: Leave May fifteenth. Well?

MILLY: May fifteen! Blood and sex and everything like that! Spain?

Scene Three:

> *Afternoon: Milly, Grady.*
> *Outside the window, snow begins to fall.*
> *Music. Milly is curled in a chair, reading a book. Pot of tea beside her. A fire burns in the fireplace. A radio is playing a Christmas carol:* Christmas Bells.
> *Enter Grady, covered with snow.*

GRADY: Oh.

MILLY: Hello. You have keys, too.

GRADY: Yes. So do you, evidently.

MILLY: Yes.

GRADY: Snow in April. Not since the 1880's, I hear.

MILLY: Yes. They're playing Christmas carols on the radio. (*She turns the radio off*) I'm Millicent Beck. Gordon lets me study here sometimes.

GRADY: Grady Gunn.

MILLY: Oh! Sorry. I study you in school. Gordon has all your books here. He talks about you.

GRADY: Really.

MILLY: Want some tea? There's potato soup, too, in this pot. Not very fancy. Here's a teacup, just waiting.

GRADY: For Gordon.

MILLY: I don't mind. Please. He said he'd be back around four.

GRADY: No soup. I couldn't eat anything.

MILLY: Gordon said he'd be back around four.

GRADY: All right. A cup of tea. I won't stay long.

MILLY: You can if you want to. Gordon will be glad to see you. He likes you.

GRADY: Oh, *does* he?

MILLY: That was patronizing. I'm sorry again. Here. (*Milly gives Grady some tea*) It's just that Gordon talks about you all the time.

(*Grady takes a flask from her purse, pours whiskey into her tea*)

GRADY: I'll need a little of this, hope you don't mind. What does Gordon say about me all the time? I can just imagine.

MILLY: Maybe not. He says you've worked hard all your life, and deserve your success.

GRADY: Did he tell you I was married to him once?

(*Pause*)

MILLY: No, he didn't.

GRADY: Well, I was.

MILLY: When?

GRADY: In the summer of 1954.

(*Pause*)

MILLY: Eight years before I was born. For how long?

GRADY: Six months.

MILLY: All right, then?

GRADY: It was long enough.

MILLY: I knew his other wife. I just didn't know you'd been one, too.

GRADY: One of four.

MILLY: Four? I thought there was only one.

GRADY: Four. Estelle, me, Betty Jean, and Lucy. Four. Which of us did you know?

MILLY: Lucy.

GRADY: Health, home and children. Lasted four years. I was the fellow artist—six months. Estelle the buxom mother—one year, and Betty Jean the socialite—two. This man is sixty-one years old. He has been married four times, for a sum total of seven and one-half years. For fifty-four years of his life, he has lived alone, with crushed ice in empty rooms, and his throbbing heart. What do you think that means?

MILLY: I don't care.

GRADY: You'd better. He might marry you someday.

MILLY: Estelle for her bosom, you for your talent, Betty Ann ...

GRADY: Betty Jean ...

MILLY: ... for her money, Lucy for home and children and me—for my youth. Is that it?

GRADY: I'm glad you were listening.

MILLY: Well, you're wrong. He isn't like that now.

GRADY: What is he like now?

MILLY: He's my contemporary. By magic.

GRADY: Really? (*She takes a large gulp of tea, chokes*)

MILLY: Are you all right?

GRADY: Yes. Snow. Fire. Whiskey and tea. Christmas carols on the radio. All in the springtime. It's confusing.

MILLY: You're in real trouble.

GRADY: You can see.

MILLY: I know what that is. I'm sorry.

GRADY: How nice.

MILLY: Gordon said you were living with a young woman who was very important to you. Who had a little boy.

GRADY: What do you think about that?

MILLY: I was crazy once. I learned not to judge other people.

GRADY: Oh, just this once. Do it.

MILLY: Maybe you feel she came to you out of prison. With her little boy.

GRADY: You aren't crazy now. You're quite right. She did. (*With bitterness*) She was sitting under a fir tree. In a white summer dress, on a white iron bench, reading my book about Colette. The weather, it was summer, was dazzling. Teal blue skies, air like spring water. She was pregnant. Separated from her husband, torturing him, beautiful, and we became lovers. She had her baby with me. I took her to that little hospital, waited. I thought I was the father! Well, I saw it first! Before he did! I named him. Frederick. That was that. They came to live with me, for a year. Then left. Came back. Left again. This was the third time.

MILLY: She's left you again. When?

GRADY: An hour ago.

MILLY: You came here to talk to Gordon. I'll get out.

GRADY: Thank you.

MILLY: Gordon will understand. He always does.

GRADY: Yes, he *will!*

MILLY: I'm sorry!

GRADY: No, I am.

MILLY: What can I say? You have your career?

GRADY: That will do.

(*Milly gets her coat*)

MILLY: So talk to Gordon. He listens. He can help. I heard you once, on the radio. Everybody cheered. It was heaven!

GRADY: I was at my best, no doubt.

MILLY: Don't be so bitter. I don't know how you feel, but really, what do you want, love *and* literature?

GRADY: Well, yes. Once you've had it, you see, you keep trying to keep it. You don't understand that yet.

MILLY: Because I haven't been to heaven! I've been to Fifth Floor, Ward Six! I'm trying NOT to have any more of THAT!

GRADY: Really? Well, if anybody can put you back in Ward Six, it's Gordon.

MILLY: You're bitter and you're wrong.

GRADY: Find out for yourself.

MILLY: Gordon Tate is my teacher and my lover and my friend! I'm sorry you're upset, but leave us alone!

GRADY: With pleasure! (*Pause*) I beg your pardon.

MILLY: I beg yours.

GRADY: About Gordon, I do hope you're right.

MILLY: No, you don't. You know you are.

GRADY: Maybe!

MILLY: I was in an asylum! I know that look!

(*Pause*)

GRADY: It's still snowing.
(*Exit Milly*)

Scene Four:

Afternoon: Grady, Gordon.

GORDON: You think I'm behaving badly. Right?
GRADY: Right.
GORDON: The spectacle of an aging egotist consorting with an orphan out of a mental institution *revolts* you. Say it.
GRADY: She tells me you are contempories by magic. Really?
GORDON: You didn't see her when Alice died. John first, then Alice. She was in pieces. She could hardly talk.
GRADY: She can talk now.
GORDON: Yes!
GRADY: Fine! She's twenty-one ...
GORDON: Twenty!
GRADY: Twenty, and she can take care of herself. Bless you both.
(*Pause*)
GORDON: Then what is the matter with you?
GRADY: Fred is the matter with me!
GORDON: Mona?
GRADY: Yes.
GORDON: She left you? *Again?*
GRADY: Of course.
(*Pause*)
GORDON: Really?
GRADY: Really.
GORDON: Why?
GRADY: Figure it out.
GORDON: Fred?
GRADY: Little Fred. The little bastard.
GORDON: What?
GRADY: My darling Fred! He was lying! He was telling me he loved me, wanted to come see me *every* weekend, and telling

her, "Mommy, we want you back. Leave this old witch and come home." I mean, the nine year old little *bastard*.

GORDON: How can you know he said that?

GRADY: Mona told me. On the floor, hugging my knees, crying, saying goodbye! He said exactly that!!

GORDON: Oh.

GRADY: Yes.

GORDON: I'm sorry.

GRADY: Not really. But you will be.

GORDON: Sorry about Fred?

GRADY: About Milly.

GORDON: Maybe not.

GRADY: The trouble with you is, you won't face what's happening.

GORDON: What is?

GRADY: You want that child to live with you.

GORDON: Watch out, Grady!

GRADY: I've just been *left!* You watch out! GORDON, LOOK AT US! Our dazzling lives! Our brilliant work! Our ferocious dedication! These scrupulous, loveless lives!! We were blooming in childhood, thrilling in youth, underwhelming in development, lost in maturity and competent in age. It is almost over. So what do we do? We hunger and thirst and turn to the young, as once we turned to the sun.

GORDON: I did ask Milly to go to Spain with me.

GRADY: Will she?

GORDON: Yes, I think she will.

GRADY: If you take her, you're a son of a bitch.

GORDON: You'd have taken Mona to Spain.

GRADY: No, Gordon, I wouldn't have taken Mona to Spain. That's the difference between us. I love Mona.

GORDON: And I love Milly! Decently!

GRADY: In bed, decently, a child?

GORDON: Yes, in bed, decently, God damn you, and she's not a child! And last night was the first time, after years and ...

GRADY: After what, Gordon?

GORDON: I loved Milly the first day I saw her. When Alice and John brought her here, on a visit, to this loft, she was three years old, I think. Her brother, a lumpy little sorehead, I even liked him, but Milly was just enchantment. The minute we saw each other, we delighted each other. She's jump on me, hug me, I'd melt. She's laugh. We'd play. She grew up. She was sick, very sick for awhile. She doesn't and won't ever know how I kept up with that, what it did to me. John died. Alice died. She was hanging on by a thread, and she came to me. Christ! And now, when she looks at me, and when she says she—oh, loves me, and I know, I know, she'll grow out of that—but—you're right, it's the sun! Happiness!

GRADY: But you don't love her.

GORDON: Grady!!

GRADY: Not if you take her to Spain, you don't! As your baggage? An old man's *thing?* You don't!

Scene Five:

Evening: Milly, Gordon.
Embers glow in the fireplace. The snow has stopped. Gordon sits on a pillow by the fire. Milly is looking out the window, a book in her hand.

MILLY: A few people, moving through snow. Too many. They could all come up here. (*Pause*) Know what Faust did when he first made his pact with the Devil?

GORDON: He corrupted an innocent child.

MILLY: That came later. Anyway, she wasn't a child. She was a buxom lass who went to bed with a good-looking man. It usually happens without supernatural assistance. No, in the old German books, the first thing Faustus did was go to a tavern and order a big dinner. Then, when it came, because the place was so crowded, people jammed in back to back, eating shoulder to shoulder—well, by God, Faustus for the first time invoked the powers of hell. He waved his arms and every single person in that whole nasty medieval diner turned to stone. And he ate his supper in peace. Would you do that?

GORDON: Of course.

MILLY: So would I. I'm Faustus. You're the devil. I've signed in blood. (*She waves her arms*) There. I just did it. Now nobody else can move. Just you, just me. In that snow down there, they've all turned to stone, and no one will be coming up here until I say so. No doorbells. The telephone can't ring. Life waits on us, and my soul is yours. (*Pause*) Where will you be, next Christmas?

GORDON: Right here, no doubt. And you?

MILLY: Somewhere else. Learning useful things.

GORDON: How to write?

MILLY: How to live, without you. It won't be hard. I'll find other teachers. Get another degree. Teach, myself. Marry a professor. Have a baby. Get divorced. Love a woman. Drink. Be mean. Write a book about it. The full life.

GORDON: I don't like to think of you like that.

MILLY: You'll just have to. My life is my life. I'm a grubby little intellectual moth, climbing up out of old books. I'll be a moth forever. My little bag of hopes will stand empty. I will blame my husband for it, and yell at my children. Then I'll tie my hair in knots. (*Pause. Gordon doesn't look at her. She goes to him, kneels behind him*) Tell me about yourself. When you were a moth. (*She puts her hands over his eyes*) No, close your eyes. Tell me. Who was he?

(*Gordon leans back against her, eyes closed. She rubs his temples*)

GORDON: He was a Knoxville paperboy, wanting to be a writer. Learned worshipping *Tarzan, The Shadow*. Holes in his socks. Gets through his paper route by six in the morning, has time to smoke Lucky Strikes, from a green pack, read *Tarzan, The Shadow*. That what you mean?

MILLY: Yes. More what you see.

GORDON: (*Gordon leans back in her arms*) No. Your thoughts are so much more vivid than mine. Compared to you, I'm shopworn.

(*Milly holds him against her, smiles*)

MILLY: I love you. I love you. I can't *stop* saying it now. I won't bother you with it. But do you hear me? I love you. When I've vanished—no, keep your eyes shut—vanished into my life, all gone, don't forget me. You've made me so happy. To come into this room. To see you walk into it, where I wait for you. You make me forget what I am.

(*Suddenly, Gordon gets up, pulling himself out of her arms. He goes to the window*)

GORDON: I'm not taking you to Spain.

MILLY: Oh. You're not?

GORDON: I thought I could, but I can't.

MILLY: Oh.

GORDON: I don't want you like baggage, living off me.

MILLY: I don't care about that.

GORDON: You would. People staring at you. Bad enough at lunch and dinner. At breakfast we'd look like something out of a Bunuel movie together. You would get tired of me. I might get tired of you.

MILLY: Tired?

GORDON: That's the best thing that could happen.

MILLY: What's the worst?

GORDON: I couldn't come back without you. You'd marry me. You'd turn into a nurse. Oh, all right for awhile. Fun. But I'm sixty-one years old. You'd be a princess for a year. Then a friend. Then a secretary. Then a nurse. And then a slave.

MILLY: Stop.

GORDON: At the end, you'd put me in a nursing home and wait to collect.

MILLY: Oh.

GORDON: It's the truth.

(*A long pause*)

MILLY: Oh, I believe it. I wouldn't want us looking like a Bunuel movie together. O.K. (*She smiles. She looks at her book*) "Poor Old Henry."

GORDON: What?

MILLY: A book, look, a book. Not Spanish. German. *Der Arme Heinrich. Poor Old Henry.* Not read much any more, but I think it would make a terrific movie. Maybe you can sell it to somebody.

(*Pause. She smiles*)

It's about a medieval knight. Very honest, decent and brave. Not because Henry worships God or anything, he just likes being wonderful. Smooth and elegant, and in shape and witty and smart, and vain. So God punishes Henry. With leprosy. Instant old age. His eyeballs fall into his highballs, plop, like that.

GORDON: Milly.

MILLY: His supermanhood rots right away on his bones. His nose? God! A hole in his face! His fingers? Horrors! All calcified into claws! His feet? Well, Henry can't feel his feet at all, so he stumps around bending over, like an old man climbing the stairs.

GORDON: Now please. Calm down.

MILLY: I'm not going to calm down! I'm going to tell you this story! (*Pause*) Henry consults specialists. Doctors, wizards, magicians. They all say there's only one cure. The leper's body must be washed in the blood of a virgin. Enter a little girl.

GORDON: I'm not surprised.

MILLY: You will be. Her name was Sigrid. She was as sick as Henry. She wanted to be a saint. So when she realized she could have her veins cut open and her blood donated to famous Knight-Leper Henry, she was happy. They were both proud. Two of a kind.

GORDON: *The Leper and the Virgin.*

MILLY: The title already! Knew you'd catch on! Well, no fool Heinrich. If a crazy virgin wants to give him a bath in her blood, can't hurt, can it? Doctors strip the girl naked! Hang her upside down over pots and pans! Slit her veins! Drain her blood! Ah! He sees her! All innocence and purity! All sexy and bloody! The end!

GORDON: She dies?

MILLY: What do you think? Once the toothpaste is out of the tube, it's a little hard to get it back in again.

GORDON: Milly!

MILLY: No, she doesn't die. Henry stops the doctors. He'll stay a leper before he'll bathe in her blood. She did that to him. She made out of this selfish rotten old leper a real man. He didn't want her to die. He didn't want to hurt her. Or maybe he couldn't take the sight of all that blood. Anyway, miracle! He gets better. His nose grows back. His fingers move. All those rotten scales fall from his skin and his soul. God gives him back his life, and he enjoys a long and honorable old age.

GORDON: And the virgin?

MILLY: She doesn't stay that way because he marries her, you see. (*She runs to him, sits in his lap*) Just a minute! Let me sit here just a minute, like a little girl! (*She jumps up, pushes him away*) No! Just never mind!

GORDON: Milly, listen to me!

MILLY: Not one word! You didn't have to worry about me! I would have left Spain anytime. I would have said goodbye, made you proud of me. I would have married you, too, *been* your wife and your nurse. You could have had my blood, and dipped your pen in it. (*She kisses him. He leans forward, embracing her. She backs away, so that Gordon falls to his knees*) Old man. (*She runs out*)

GORDON: For Christ's sake!

Scene Five:

Four a.m.: Gordon, Grady, Lucien, Bill, Thomas.
    They are all very very drunk, fighting to be sober, alert and lucid. Lucien, Bill and Thomas are in dressy evening clothes.

LUCIEN: It's four a.m. My goodness.

BILL: Everybody's asleep. Shhh.

THOMAS: Right.

LUCIEN: Everybody.

GRADY: Me. Gordon. Milly and Mona.

(*All groan*)

LUCIEN: Grady, not again! Spare us the scene!

THOMAS: We've been through it eighteen times with both of you! Oh, Mona! You don't know what you're doing to me, Mona!

LUCIEN: Milly! Little Milly! The pain! The anguish! Write it! "He knew she could be his daughter, and she knew he could be her father, but it didn't seem to matter at all then." Lyrical see, not too much. Dignity, calm. "It was snowing when they met, and it covered, oh, both their heads in white, so that they looked neither young nor old but alike. Very much alike." There. Just beautiful.

GRADY: You are unfeeling, Lucien. What I mean is, you don't feel. You stopped doing that. Wish I could. (*She laughs*)

THOMAS: Gordon. Grady. Lucien's here, isn't he? So am I?

GRADY: And so is Bill. Bill who?

BILL: Never mind, Grady.

GRADY: O.K. (*Pause*) Mona needs me. She does.

LUCIEN: Oh, what the hell! The woman went back to her kid. What do you want us to do about it, say she shouldn't? We know how sensitive you are, darling, and oh God the suffering, but the woman went back to her kid. Gordon's nymphet went back to her schoolbooks. What a tragedy!

THOMAS: Make the best of it, Gordon, and find another Lolita. Make the best of it, Grady, and meet Mona for lunch at the Plaza.

GRADY: You don't care what's happening inside me!

THOMAS: Of course, I care! I'm your lawyer, I care. I'm Gordon's, I care! I'm Lucien's, I care!

BILL: You're not mine.

THOMAS: Maybe I will be. And I'll care!

LUCIEN: And if Mona cares, she'll come back. She'll have to come back. I mean, she got the royal treatment, didn't she? After years 'n' years of squalid marriage, dumb husband ...

THOMAS: What does the dumb do by the way?

GRADY: He's a lawyer.

THOMAS: Oh, he is not!

GRADY: Is too! For the sanitation department. I don't know just exactly how.

LUCIEN: All right! After years of squalid marriage with a sanitation department lawyer, cooking food and washing socks, then oh! Grady steps in, dripping Colette and mink? Two precious modern hearts, skipping beats like one? She'll come back.

THOMAS: Lesbians are intimacy junkies.

GRADY: What?

THOMAS: I said, lesbians are intimacy junkies. They get hooked on intimacy. If you really got intimate, she'll be back. Otherwise, forget it, she'll get intimate with somebody else.

GRADY: This evening has degenerated. I'm going home.

(*Grady lurches to her feet. Outside, snow begins to fall again*)

THOMAS: Whoa! Steady standing up!

GRADY: I'm perfectly all right. Goodnight, gentlemen. Lucien, Thomas, Bill. Which one of these killer fruits are you going home with, Bill?

LUCIEN: I didn't hear that, and neither did Thomas.

THOMAS: Yes, I did. Which one of us killer fruits are you coming home with, Bill?

BILL: Gotta know?

LUCIEN: Gotta know.

GRADY: The suspense is killing us.

BILL: A killer fruit, by definition in New York, is an elegant, rich, successful, powerful gentleman, or I suppose now, lady, of high, same sex inclination, who will wage ferocious war over youthful flesh. You cannot attack them verbally, they are too self-assured. You cannot hope to deflate them egotistically, they are protected by their achievements. You cannot even get mad at them. They are so profoundly infantile, they only smile at you, who cannot possibly understand them. Goo. Like that. Goo.

LUCIEN: All right, goo. What's the point?

BILL: Point is I am going home to my trundle bed, to pass out in isolation and freedom. The great gurus of India and I understand the superior virtues of semen retention. It is the path to God and co-ops. My best friend is my telephone. I trust dead writers, sometimes my agent, and the paychecks I get acting on soaps. My life and real love are incompatible, and I have the sense to see that and go to bed ONLY WHEN I PLEASE! Of course, you are all charming, and useful maybe someday, so I hope you will keep on asking me out. And that, in youthful candor, is what I think about New York!

GRADY: What a terrifying poverty level of experience. And who drinks a whole bottle of vodka tonight? Babyface does. What you and the great gurus of India really retain, Babyface, isn't frankly all that interesting. What is interesting is what will happen to YOU in thirty years! Why ARE YOU HERE anyway, batting your eyes at three weary SoHo bohemians and this old lesbian? You give me the willies! Goodnight, Gordon. At least *I* know how you feel!

THOMAS: Bravo!

LUCIEN: Sold!

THOMAS: What style!

LUCIEN: What class!

(*Bill gets up*)

BILL: I am *going* now. This has been real.

LUCIEN: Real what?

BILL: Oh, Jesus. Goodnight.

THOMAS: Last words.

LUCIEN: Famous.

GORDON: Get out.

LUCIEN: What?

GORDON: All of you, get out of here.

THOMAS: Oh, dear.

BILL: I knew I should have left ten minutes ago. Bye.

(*Bill goes to door, opens it*)

LUCIEN: Gordon, really!

THOMAS: *You* want to fuck Bill, too?

(*Gordon slaps Thomas. Thomas slugs Gordon*)

GORDON: Ow!

LUCIEN: (*Simultaneous*) Hold it!

GRADY: (*Simultaneous*) Gordon? You leave Gordon alone!

Ow! (*Grady gets an elbow in the eye*) My eye!

GORDON: My nose!

GRADY: Gordon, help. I can't see!

LUCIEN: Oh, boy!

(*Bill runs back in, jumps on them, pushing them apart*)

BILL: The door's open! Now let's GO! Break it UP!!!

LUCIEN: Bill, lay off!

GORDON: Bill?

BILL: Gordon!

(*Gordon swings at Bill. Bill slugs Gordon*)

GORDON: Ow! My NOSE

GRADY: (*Pushing Bill*) You GET OUT of here!

LUCIEN: Stop it, Grady!

BILL: Grady, let GO! (*Bill swings around, hitting Grady*)

GRADY: Ow! My eye! Again!! Damn you, I can't SEE!!!

THOMAS: EVERYBODY! STOP IT!

LUCIEN: RIGHT NOW!!!

(*Lucien jumps on them. There is a terrific wild sprawling
and a pileup on the floor by the front door. Enter Milly. She
has a large white bandage taped over her head and across her
left ear. She stares at them. The snow has stopped*)

GRADY: I can see! It's all right. I thought I was blind. Ow, it *hurts!*

LUCIEN: What happened?

THOMAS: Gordon had something to say, and couldn't say it.

LUCIEN: About that ridiculous girl?

BILL: Whatever it was, it's dumb to hit your lawyer. *I wouldn't do that!* (*He has a terrific coughing fit. They start getting off the floor*)

THOMAS: Gordon, really, sober up, can't you? (*He slips and falls, taking others with him. They are all on the floor*)

GORDON: Milly!

(*They stare at her. Gordon tries to get up, slips, falls. Everybody lies in a pile on the floor, with Milly staring at them*)

MILLY: I didn't know you were having a party. (*She turns to go. Gordon gets to his knees*)

GORDON: Milly! What's happened to you?

LUCIEN: (*Whisper*) That's Milly.

THOMAS: I bet.

GRADY: Milly? What?

MILLY: I didn't know how to do it. I went to a bar and got picked up by one man and I wouldn't go anywhere, then got picked up by another man and I wouldn't go anywhere, I then flirted with a married couple who got excited until I said I'm teasing, I'd never in my life do that with you, and were furious. After that I started home.

(*She gets the statue of Don Quixote, sits down and looks at it. Everybody else is still on the floor*)

The first man followed me, swore at me, hit me in the ear with his umbrella, yelling now "Go to Saint Vincent's, you little bitch," and ran off. It worked out the way I wanted it to. I got hurt and humiliated, went to a hospital to get my wounds treated, and saw the light still on here and came back, to make you feel as bad as I can.

GORDON: Do you *have* to play with Don Quixote right now?

GRADY: Madame de Stael, the only woman Napoleon was afraid of, spent her life passionate about a *wimp*. The elegant Madame Krudener's fashionable lover tipped his hat to her, had a heart attack, *died* on the spot, which converted her into a life-long, utterly *ridiculous* evangelist! Madame Recamier, greatest beauty in all the history of France, stayed *virgin* until she was forty, then died horribly in love with a pompous immortal named Chateaubriand, remembered today for a *steak!* Which I am going to need for this *eye!* My God, it'll turn yellow *and* purple! Sex makes fools of everybody.

MILLY: "In last year's nests, there are no birds this year. I once was mad but now am sane." That's what Don Quixote said, when he died.

GORDON: Just give him here, will you? (*Gordon gets up, puts Don Quixote down with his back turned*) There! Ow. My nose won't stop bleeding.

(*He sits again, bloody handkerchief to his nose. Bill, Thomas and Lucien observe Grady's eye, Milly's bandage and Gordon's nose. Bill gets up off the floor*)

BILL: Of course it was a marvelous party, and I was enchanted by the literary conversation, but you are all really just blockheads, you know. I mean, honestly, look at you. Black eye, busted ear, and bloody nose. Really. *I'm* going home alone!

(*Exit Bill. Lucien and Thomas pick themselves off the floor*)

THOMAS: Well, Lucien, that young man ...

LUCIEN: Sad.

THOMAS: You can have him.

LUCIEN: He's all yours. (*To Gordon*) When do you leave for Spain, Gordon?

MILLY: On May fifteenth. To write about Nero. And sex and blood and everything like that.

LUCIEN: Well, good. (*Pause*) Home alone. (*He starts out, comes back*) I wish I was famous. That would be something, anyway. Grady, did Madame de Stael say something profound about fame? And sunlight, the sun?

GRADY: She said it was the sun of the dead.

LUCIEN: "Fame is the sun of the dead." Goodnight.

(*Exit Lucien*)

THOMAS: Obviously, I must top that. Let's see. French maxim: "If loving is judged by what it looks like, it looks more like hating than anything else." That's what you all look like. Me too. Home alone. Goodnight.

(*Exit Thomas. Pause*)

GRADY:

"There once was a Pirate named Bates,

Who attempted to rhumba on skates.
He slipped on his cutlass,
Which rendered him nutless,
And practically useless on dates."
Now who wrote *that*, I wonder? And *why* is it running through my head?

GORDON: Old man and woman sat in a bar out West. "Want to?" said the old man. "Your place or mine?" said the old woman. "Well," said the old man, "if you're going to argue about it, let's just forget it." (*He shrugs. They look at Milly*)

MILLY: "In last year's nests, there are no birds this year. I once was mad but now am sane." (*They all nod. Grady gets up, examines her eye in a compact mirror. Outside, snow begins to fall*) Gordon, why are you staring at us?

GORDON: "In last year's nests, there are no birds this year."

MILLY: So?

GORDON: Spain.

GRADY: What?

GORDON: Spain. Let's all go to Spain!

GRADY: What a ridiculous idea.

GORDON: No, it isn't.

GRADY: Milly can't stand me.

MILLY: That's not true.

GRADY: I wasn't nice. I was mean. I told Gordon—if he really cared a thing about you—to take you nowhere.

MILLY: (*To Gordon*) Did she?

GORDON: Yes.

MILLY: Oh. (*Smiles*) I think I want something to eat.

GRADY: Where would we sleep?

GORDON: We'd vote.

GRADY: Is that possible?

GORDON: I don't know. Maybe.

MILLY: What happened to the potato soup?

(*Milly goes to the bar, opens the Crock pot*)

GRADY: Potato soup?

MILLY: It's still hot.

GRADY: Is it?

GORDON: I don't want to go to Spain by myself.

GRADY: One, two, three.

MILLY: We can look like a Bunuel movie together.

GRADY: No, we'd look like a family.

MILLY: You want soup?

GRADY: Yes, I think I do.

GORDON: There's bread and wine.

(*Gordon goes to help Milly*)

GRADY: Who pays for what?

GORDON: I'd pay for Milly. And the rent.

GRADY: I might do part of that.

GORDON: O.K.

MILLY: I have three hundred dollars in the bank, and I can type.

GRADY: Oh, you can?

MILLY: Sixty words a minute.

GRADY: Then I pay half.

GORDON: O.K. (*Milly and Gordon bring soup, bread and wine*) Maybe another log.

GRADY: I'm ravenously hungry.

MILLY: So am I.

(*Gordon puts a log on the fire. They eat the soup. The fire blazes up. The snow falls heavily*)

GRADY: God, this is good.

GORDON: Hot.

MILLY: Yum.

GRADY: Old Spanish house?

GORDON: Sure.

GRADY: Bedrooms?

GORDON: Three.

MILLY: Three.

GRADY: Three.

GORDON: My nose has stopped bleeding.

(*Grady turns Don Quixote around again*)

GRADY: He's still crazy.

MILLY: The radio. (*She turns on the radio. It plays* "Hark! How the Bells." *They look at each other, tentatively, listen to the Christmas carol, and look out the window. Gordon sets Don Quixote on the window ledge, where he stands against the falling snow. They look at each other again. They eat the bread and potato soup and drink the wine. The firelight glows*) More potato soup?

GRADY and GORDON: Yes!
MILLY: Here.
(*They hold out their soup bowls and she reaches for them. Tableau. Lights fade on the three of them, then on the April snow*)

The End

William R. Lewis

TROUT

> I have cast aside today's business,
> and have gone a' fishin'.
> Izaak Walton, *The Compleat Angler*

William R. Lewis

Trout, published here for the first time, is the tenth play written by William Lewis. It was one of a half dozen plays to be selected for a scene presentation at the Playwrights Workshop prior to the 1987 convention of the Association of Theatre in Higher Education. With a wit as dry as the flies floated by the fishermen in his play, Dr. Lewis nets a full string of philosophy on fishing, friendship, and personal freedom.

William R. Lewis was born in West Virginia in 1948. His formal education includes an A.B. in Speech and Art from Glenville State College, an M.A. in Theatre from West Virginia University, and a Ph.D. in Theatre from Southern Illinois University at Carbondale, where he studied playwriting with Dr. Christian H. Moe.

With a writing career starting in 1979, Dr. Lewis's credits include *Murphy's Law,* produced for PBS television in Illinois in 1981, and two stage plays, *Living the Straight Life Up in Connecticut* and *The Gravest Insult of Them All,* directed by Peter Frisch in an Equity Showcase in New York in 1984. Other short plays of his include: *Yikkin Vins, Loving Annie: A Journal, Up on Rolling Pine,* and *Loaves and Fishes.*

Dr. Lewis has taught playwriting, acting, and dramatic literature at several colleges, including Purdue University and the North Carolina School of the Arts. He has served on the Playwriting Awards Committee of the American College Theatre Festival and with the Playwrights' Program of the Association of Theatre in Higher Education. He is also a member of the Dramatists Guild.

Presently, Dr. Lewis lives with his family in Winston-Salem, North Carolina, where he was recently Artistic Director of the Mimesis Theatre Group, an organization he founded in 1988.

Characters:

BERT
CHARLIE

Place:

Up a creek.

Time:

Time for lunch.

Setting:

Before the play begins, the audience is seated before a drop upon which is painted an outdoor scene of two fishermen on a mountain trout stream. The painting is done in the style of calendars and sportings goods advertising. There are many large and small rocks in the stream. As the play begins, the painting comes to life. It is a scrim now backlit to reveal the actors.

During the course of the action, the "rocks" upstage the need for flowing water on the set. They may also serve to hide technicians or technology used to hook the fish in the play. At the end, the lights fade on the fishermen, who have returned to their original positions. The scene again becomes a painting.

Charlie and Bert are fishing. Charlie executes a few casts with his flyrod. Bert, who is fishing with bait, leaves his line in the water. Obviously, the two are some distance apart.

CHARLIE: So?
(*Long pause*)
BERT: Yes.

CHARLIE: So?

BERT: Yes.

CHARLIE: Catching any?

BERT: No. None today.

CHARLIE: Oh.

BERT: So?

(*Long Pause*)

CHARLIE: No.

BERT: No?

CHARLIE: Oh.

BERT: Go?

CHARLIE: Certainly not.

BERT: Fine.

CHARLIE: Lovely spot.

BERT: Hey?

CHARLIE: Lovely spot!

BERT: Oh. Yes. Yes, it is. So? How long ...

CHARLIE: Oh ...

BERT: How long have you been fishing?

CHARLIE: Well, ...

BERT: Yes?

CHARLIE: Since I was a boy. I first went with my father.

BERT: No, Charlie! No! How long today?

CHARLIE: Oh, since this morning. Since very early this morning.

BERT: Since right after breakfast, I suppose.

CHARLIE: Yes. Since about then.

BERT: Have you many?

CHARLIE: Hey?

BERT: You! Have you caught many?

CHARLIE: Fish?

BERT: Yes, Charlie, fish. Have you?

CHARLIE: Today?

BERT: Yes, Charlie. Today.

CHARLIE: No.

BERT: Oh.

CHARLIE: Not many. Not today. None, in fact. Today.

BERT: Well, ...

CHARLIE: Bertie?

BERT: Yes?

CHARLIE: Isn't this a lovely spot?

BERT: Oh yes. Lovely. A lovely spot.

CHARLIE: Yes.

(*Long pause*)

BERT: This way is better; you know that.

CHARLIE: Which?

BERT: This way, as opposed to that way.

CHARLIE: Better?

BERT: Much. Much better. Far more effective.

CHARLIE: This way is not effective?

BERT: "This way is not effective?"

CHARLIE: Well?

BERT: No. This way is not effective. I mean, that way is not effective. It is not nearly as effective a way as this.

CHARLIE: That way is better then?

BERT: Much. At least it is more effective.

CHARLIE: I'll be damned.

BERT: But it is lovely.

CHARLIE: Really?

BERT: Oh yes. More lovely by far than this way. Graceful. The motion. The form. It is very lovely.

CHARLIE: Quite the critic, are we?

BERT: Oh yes. Quite. I suppose.

CHARLIE: Lovely then.

BERT: Wonderfully so, Charlie.

CHARLIE: I'll be damned. Lovely was not a goal.

BERT: Is it ever?

CHARLIE: I don't know.

BERT: Does one ever?

CHARLIE: Effective. The original impulse was to be effective, not to be lovely.

BERT: That's the way it goes, I guess.

CHARLIE: I've been wasting my time then.

BERT: Oh no, Charlie. Don't ever think that.

CHARLIE: Of course! I've waited all this time trying to be effective and the result of my efforts is simple beauty.

BERT: It's not like that, Charlie.

CHARLIE: "It's not like that, Charlie." I should quit.

BERT: You won't.

CHARLIE: Yes. I know. All the same ...

BERT: You can't quit, Charlie. Not now.

CHARLIE: Yes.

(*Long pause*)

BERT: Charlie?

CHARLIE: Bertie?

BERT: I'm hungry.

CHARLIE: Yes.

BERT: Is it time?

CHARLIE: Time?

BERT: Yes.

CHARLIE: No.

BERT: No?

CHARLIE: Yes. No.

BERT: But I'm hungry.

CHARLIE: We could have a drink instead.

BERT: A drink instead of lunch?

CHARLIE: Yes. Whiskey.

BERT: Whiskey. That would put a whole, a completely different, well …

CHARLIE: On things. Yes. It would.

BERT: Whiskey.

CHARLIE: Ice.

BERT: Ice?

CHARLIE: Yes, Bertie. And a spot of water.

BERT: Neat.

CHARLIE: Neat then.

BERT: Is it time?

CHARLIE: I'd say. The leaves are turning. Gold and yellow.

BERT: Red. The snow will come soon. It's time, all right.

CHARLIE: Whiskey season. A good tonic. Hibernation.

BERT: Would they let us, do you think?

CHARLIE: I'd rather tend to think not.

BERT: Yes.

CHARLIE: No, they wouldn't.

BERT: All the same …

CHARLIE: Yes.

BERT: Let me know, will you?

CHARLIE: Yes. Of course.

BERT: When it's time.

CHARLIE: Yes. Certainly will. When it's time.

(*Long pause*)

BERT: Charlie?

CHARLIE: Yes, Bertie?

BERT: Why ... ?

CHARLIE: Yes?

BERT: Oh. Never mind.

CHARLIE: Go on. Go on.

BERT: No. It's silly.

CHARLIE: Silly? I doubt that. And besides, if I can be lovely, then surely you can be silly.

BERT: Why do I love this so much?

CHARLIE: Hmmmm.

BERT: See?

CHARLIE: No. Because it is so ... relaxing.

BERT: I detest relaxation. I'm a Protestant.

CHARLIE: Because of the challenge.

BERT: Surely living is challenge enough.

CHARLIE: The solitude then.

BERT: But I'm not alone. You're here.

CHARLIE: Should I give up or go on guessing?

BERT: "Should I give up or go on guessing?"

CHARLIE: Twit.

BERT: Son of a bitch!

CHARLIE: How dare you! Ass!

BERT: No, Charlie! Not you! There! There! I think I'm getting a bite!

CHARLIE: You mean ... ?!

BERT: Yes! A fish!

CHARLIE: Where? Where is it?

BERT: In the water, Charlie. In the water ... Come on ... come on ...

CHARLIE: Do you see him, Bertie?

BERT: No, but I feel him. Come on, you rascal.

CHARLIE: Hold him, Bert. Hold him! Keep the line tight. Put some pressure on him. Not too much. Easy, Bertie. Easy ...

BERT: He's a trout. Big as a house. Must be a five pounder. Come on, you son of a bitch ...

CHARLIE: Whoa! Here he comes ...

BERT: Here we go ...

CHARLIE: Easy! Up he goes ...

BERT: God Almighty ...

CHARLIE: No!

(*The line goes slack*)

BERT: No! No!!

CHARLIE: Damn!

BERT: He snapped the line! Damn.

CHARLIE: Too much pressure! You have to be careful!

BERT: It wasn't my fault!

CHARLIE: And you should use decent equipment! How in the world you can expect to land anything with *that* is beyond me!

BERT: Fishing snob!

CHARLIE: Antiquarian!

BERT: Fly-tying, fly-fishing, ... ELITIST!!!

CHARLIE: WORM DABBLER!!!!

BERT: That does it.

CHARLIE: Oh?

BERT: Oh. Over there. You fish over there.

CHARLIE: Over there?

BERT: Yes. And be quick about it for I may drown you right here and now. You are an effete, domineering equipment fetishist, and I do not wish to share this lovely spot with you any longer. Go!

CHARLIE: Effete.

BERT: Yes. Effete. I know your swimming skills aren't what they once were. You won't last long if I toss you in. Go.

CHARLIE: Toss me in?

BERT: You and your nymphs and yellow stone flies and your number ten Black Gnats and your snobbish attitude. Go quietly, my friend. That was my fish and you felt as if I had to be coached like some small child or old lady. It's a trait that I do not admire in you. Go now. Fish alone. And ...

CHARLIE: But ...

BERT: Piss off, Charlie.

CHARLIE: Fine. Just fine. I'll go. I'll go happily.

BERT: Good!

CHARLIE: Good.

BERT: Good.

CHARLIE: I admit that I am occasionally cursed with a sur-feit of enthusiasm. I admit it. But you learned to fish one way when you were a boy—MANY YEARS AGO—and you refuse to see new and better, more pleasing, ways of doing things. If the world looked to you for progress, we'd all be huddled around in some cave somewhere because we wouldn't even know how to make fire. "Certainly is an effective way of keeping warm," you say as you would rub your matted fur, shivering in the cold of night, bloody entrails dangling from your complacent chin as you shivered and shook and admired the lack of progress in the world and fished with rusty hooks!

BERT: That hook is as good as the day I bought it!

CHARLIE: Twelve years ago, you borrowed it from me! You fish one way, Bert, because you're cheap!

BERT: Frugal!

CHARLIE: Cheap!

BERT: All right, so I understand full well that upon green trees money does not grow. But at least I'm a gentleman about other men's fish! Not that I get many opportunities to be otherwise when I fish with you! NOW GO!!!!

CHARLIE: Fine. I'll go over there. Good. That's a lovely spot just over there. Not so much rust in the water. Head of the hole. Brimming with trout. Very effete trout. Good, good.

(*Charlie crosses to another spot. The two ignore each other pointedly. Charlie makes it a point to talk to himself loud enough for Bert to hear*)

CHARLIE: So. Here we go. Lovely spot. Just lovely. Let's change the old bug. Can't go about fishing our entire life with the same little old thing tied to our leader. Let's see. What to use? Yellow stone fly? No ... Black Gnat ... No. Gosh, there are so many to choose from. Not the same at all. Ah, the Clark Special. Beautiful. Off with the old. Save for later. On with the new. There we are. Ah. (*He casts his fly into the wing*) Lovely. Lovely. Check cast. Strip. Strip. Stop. Strip ... strip ... stop. Clark Special ... strip ... stop.

BERT: Oh, will you please ...

(*Charlie's line goes tight. Flyline is immediately coming off the reel. The rod bends with the weight of a mighty trout*)

CHARLIE: Oh!! Oh no!! OH NO!!!

BERT: Big one? (*Bert rushes to Charlie*)

CHARLIE: Yes! Oh, hell yes!!! He's a whopper, Bertie! A giant!

BERT: Hold him!!!! Hold him-m-m!!!!!
CHARLIE: I can't! He's running!!
BERT: Play him, then! Play him!!! Keep your line tight!
CHARLIE: Yes! Yes!! Steady as we go ...
BERT: Easy, Charlie. Easy ...
(*The line breaks, falls free*)
CHARLIE: Hell's fire ...
BERT: Son of a ...
CHARLIE: Well.
BERT: Yes.
CHARLIE: So?
BERT: Use a worm.
CHARLIE: "Use a worm." A solution to everything.
BERT: Yes.
CHARLIE: Bah!
(*Long pause*)
BERT: Charlie. Tell me something.
CHARLIE: Yes?
BERT: Where did it come from?
CHARLIE: I don't know.
BERT: But you have several. Where did the first one come from?
CHARLIE: What? Are you sure you've no whiskey?
BERT: The Clark Specials, Charlie. Where did ... from where did they first originate?
CHARLIE: You mean the first one?
BERT: Yes.
CHARLIE: I don't know.
BERT: But you have several. Where did the first one come from?
CHARLIE: What? Are you sure you've no whiskey?
BERT: The Clark Specials, Charlie. Where did ... from where did they first originate?
CHARLIE: You mean the first one?
BERT: Yes.
CHARLIE: Oh, well, why didn't you just ask? Don't be reticent, Bertie. If you want to know the answer to a question, just ask. That's all you have to do.
BERT: Well, then?
CHARLIE: The Clark Special?

BERT: Yes.

CHARLIE: What about it?

BERT: You know.

CHARLIE: She's a beauty, that one. Red, like my wife. Dry fly. Never needs wax. Always dependable. Rock of Gibraltar or something like that. Easy movement. Discernible. Good as gold.

BERT: And the origin. From your wife, you say? What was her name?

CHARLIE: Sandra. Sandy. Her hair was red. I called her "Red." I never called her "Sandy."

BERT: And her maiden name was Clark?

CHARLIE: I believe so, yes.

BERT: Was she the first to tie the Special? The Clark Special?

CHARLIE: No. I was.

BERT: Oh. And you named it for her.

CHARLIE: Yes. I used some of her hair.

BERT: Oh?

CHARLIE: Yes. She clipped a bit for me now and then.

BERT: I see.

CHARLIE: A beautiful, flowing red; see it move? Isn't that just exquisite?

BERT: Oh yes. Exquisite.

CHARLIE: She clipped a bit for me ever so often. I saved it. Used some. Saved some for later. Old Red's been gone for several seasons, but her immortality is assured.

BERT: Yes.

CHARLIE: She floats on flowing water, season after season. I hope I can do as much after I go, that's for certain.

BERT: Well ...

CHARLIE: Ah.

(*Long pause*)

BERT: An exercise in futility.

CHARLIE: There you go again. Off and running. Complain. Complain.

BERT: All I meant was that I'm having trouble with this knot.

CHARLIE: Oh. Never mind then.

BERT: Right.

(*Long pause*)

CHARLIE: Fine, fine. You go first.

BERT: What?

CHARLIE: You go first.

BERT: With what? I may have missed a bit. I was broadsided by technology.

CHARLIE: Hook in your thumb, eh?

BERT: Right.

CHARLIE: Happened to me once on a trip in Canada. Right after breakfast I stuck a number six Blue Hackled Nymph in the web of my hand. The hook was barbed and I was alone. The pain was excruciating. Had to fish one-handed until lunch.

(*Long pause*)

CHARLIE: Things ...

BERT: Yes.

CHARLIE: They aren't ... are not ...

BERT: Yes, Charlie. What they seem ...

CHARLIE: ... to be.

BERT: What they seem to be.

CHARLIE: You're terribly smug.

BERT: Yes. Terribly smug. Yes, I suppose I am.

CHARLIE: Tell me. What do you do when things do not go well? When things do not follow a smug little plan.

BERT: Oh, I remain smug. Vary the depth. Change worms. Maybe switch to larger or smaller worms. Consider going with minnows, crickets, whatever they're feeding on. If they aren't feeding at all, I just enjoy the scenery. It's very simple really.

CHARLIE: I don't think anything is simple.

BERT: And you have no patience. You have to be in the spotlight.

CHARLIE: Do I?

BERT: You're a regular John Barrymore.

CHARLIE: Yes. He was quite talented, you know.

BERT: I suppose.

CHARLIE: Dead.

BERT: Yes. That too.

CHARLIE: I saw Gandhi once. Did you know that?

BERT: No, Charlie. I didn't know that.

CHARLIE: Yes. I was just a boy. He touched my mother's hand as he passed. Everyone wanted to touch him. For him to touch them. He was the smallest man I ever saw ... and the largest.

BERT: Did he touch you?

CHARLIE: No ... not physically.

BERT: Did he say anything to you?

CHARLIE: No. Not in words.

BERT: Gandhi. Hmmmm.

CHARLIE: It was right after that that I took up fishing.

BERT: Hmmmm. Gandhi. (*Long pause*) I used to hunt. My father taught me. He was quite a hunter, my father. Birds, mostly. Oh, he fished, too. But he was in the main a hunter. Of course, fishing is a form of hunting. Fishing is a form of hunting, but not hunting in the strict sense. There are two reasons why this is true. Firstly, the hunter seeks his prey on the prey's own ground and in a sporting manner suitable to the prey's own rules of the game. The angler, on the other hand, does not enter the water with the fish, that is to say that although the angler might be *in* the water, he is not *under* the water ... under the surface of the water ... with his prey. So, a whole new set of rules apply. Secondly, the hunter has one ultimate goal: to find his prey and kill it. There is no doubt about the fact that the prey comes up short in that regard. The angler will, upon capturing his prey, have the choice of killing it or releasing it. Setting it free in the water to live. To breathe through its gills, to reproduce, to eat and grow and thrive. Or at least to be captured by a less charitable angler or another larger creature further up on the old food chain. Knowing that simple fact, being aware of it, no matter how subtly, makes the angler smug. Are there questions?

CHARLIE: No.

BERT: Good. Dismissed.

(*Long pause*)

CHARLIE: Bert, did you know that the common brook trout has not evolved one whit in approximately three million years?

BERT: Yes. I knew that.

CHARLIE: Don't you think that is amazing? Just wonderfully amazing?

BERT: Actually, no. But it does reflect a certain lack of progress, that's for certain.

(*Long pause*)

CHARLIE: After Sandra passed away, I drank quite a bit. Far too much for far too long. I finally realized that I was supposed to live, not to die. Not to join my wife in whatever great or narrow water lies upstream. Then, I came to realize one other thing. That to fish, to be an angler, a true angler, was to be a kind of priest. I am a shepherd of the water. My soul flows and ebbs and moves in this impermeable current that is, in fact, my self. I am not a fisher of men, for that is what I was taught when I was a boy. Now, I am a man, and I am obligated to throw away many of the things I learned when I was young. Fishers of men have built-in excuses for pulling in empty nets. And they have precious little free time for real fishing. No, I am an angler. The highest form of life above the water. And practicing my craft keeps me keenly aware of my responsibilities. I am a piscatorial nimrod! A magician, a scorcerer and conjurer of images on flowing water wherein dwells my sober soul. I am shaman, Bertie! This bamboo wand is my pen, my staff, and my sword! I exist, by God. I am, Bertie, A FISHERMAN!!!!!

(*Pause*)

BERT: I like fishing because, just as the fish strikes, I get an erection.

(*Pause*)

CHARLIE: Yes. There's that too.

(*Long pause*)

BERT: Carp. Now there's a topic.

CHARLIE: A whole new kettle of fish.

BERT: Salt of the earth. A fine specimen. Noble.

CHARLIE: The dregs. The lowest rung on the piscatorial ladder. A giant amoeba.

BERT: Most powerful of the freshwater species. A prey worthy of the fear it generates.

CHARLIE: It devours the eggs of bass and trout. It eats offal and dead frogs.

BERT: A frugal fish.

CHARLIE: A trash fish.

BERT: Dogs.

CHARLIE: Right then. A mongrel man, no?

BERT: Definitely. Use the world's creatures. Save the lost. And you?

CHARLIE: Retrievers. Setters. Registered stock only. Nothing else is worth the trouble. A dog should be at least as smart as its master.

BERT: Bah. Elitist poppycock. Shotguns.

CHARLIE: Doubles. Nothing but doubles. Side by side, not the new kind. You?

BERT: Autoloaders. Best you can find. Very efficient.

CHARLIE: To use on ... birds.

BERT: Squirrels. The odd rabbit. Varmints.

CHARLIE: Anything moving, in other words. I knew it.

BERT: Spincasters. Now there's the stuff.

CHARLIE: Too easy. Too common. Anybody can use a spincaster. Press a button.

BERT: Exactly. Proletarian stuff, this. A spincaster on a fiberglass will catch anything worth catching.

CHARLIE: Like carp?

BERT: Oh yes. You?

CHARLIE: Split bamboo. Or at least the new graphite. Eight and a half feet. Floating line only. Dry flies. Hand-tied. Good, well-blooded dogs. Scotch.

BERT: Gin. Even though a dram of the whiskey is healthful.

CHARLIE: But only in whiskey season.

BERT: Yes. Temperance.

CHARLIE: Leather. Clean air. Horses.

BERT: God ...

CHARLIE: Nature!

BERT: Management!

CHARLIE: Labor!

BERT: Worms!!

CHARLIE: FLIES!

BERT: *COUNTRY!!*

CHARLIE: *WORLD!!*

BERT: Bah!

CHARLIE: Bah! Bah! Bah!!! (*Makes a raspberry*)

BERT: Aristotle!

CHARLIE: Plato.

BERT: Meat pie!

CHARLIE: Fish.

BERT: White bread!

CHARLIE: Brown.

BERT: Red wine!

CHARLIE: White.

BERT: New Testament!

CHARLIE: Old.

BERT: Rembrandt!
CHARLIE: Klee.
BERT: Hemingway!
CHARLIE: Fitzgerald.
BERT: Wagner!
CHARLIE: Ives.
BERT: EMILY GODDAMN DICKINSON!!!
CHARLIE: Virginia Woolf.
BERT: AHRGGGGAAAAAHHHHHHH!!!!!!!!!
CHARLIE: Careful, Bertie. You might scare away the carp.
BERT: You haven't changed a bit.
CHARLIE: Oh. (*Long pause*) Catgut.
BERT: What?
CHARLIE: Catgut. Cat gut. The guts, as it were, of a cat.
BERT: Oh. Yes.
CHARLIE: Catgut. A virtuous and sturdy material.
BERT: Be quiet.
CHARLIE: Right.
(*Long pause*)
BERT: Structure: "Keys for Landing Whoppers." Structure is essential for the maintenance of the aquatic environment. Structure is anything that breaks the line of the surface of the bottom of the aquatic environment. This includes plants and submerged objects. Structure will provide a base for microscopic life forms which live in water. These tiny things will provide food for larger life forms, which may be seen with the naked eye. These forms will appear green and will feel slimy. This slime, if you will, will provide food for small aquatic creatures such as minnows, crawdads, and earthworms, which will be drawn toward it. Aquatic insects will also depend on this slime for food and even shelter. Larger fish will be attracted to the structure because it holds things for them to eat and, in the case of a fairly massive structural object, a place to hide from larger predators, a place from which to ambush the smaller life forms, and a place from which to seek shelter from the glaring rays of reflected sunlight which hurt the fish's eyes. Therefore, the angler wise enough to fish in and around known structure will encounter more fish than the angler who fishes in open water. This is the business of angling.
CHARLIE: In other words, Bertie ...

BERT: In short, fish around stumps, submerged timber, and any grass or lily pads you can find. That's where the fish are.

(*Long pause*)

CHARLIE: "The Zen of Angling."

BERT: Right then. Fish where you're going, not where you've been.

CHARLIE: Fish in the moment. Fish in the here and now.

BERT: Keep your line in the water. Maintain your equipment and know how to use it.

CHARLIE: Once the hook is set, the line must be kept tight or the fish will escape.

BERT: Never touch a fish that you plan to release, unless you have to touch the bottom of the fish's mouth to remove the hook.

CHARLIE: Release all bass over fourteen inches. If the bass is a trophy fish, then photograph it before release.

BERT: Kill all fish that are to be kept. Or, keep those fish alive in a clean, oxygenated livewell. If a fish is killed, it must be cleaned immediately and kept on ice.

CHARLIE: Tie all knots securely and effectively.

BERT: Keep all hooks as sharp as possible.

CHARLIE: Hypocrite.

BERT: I beg your pardon.

CHARLIE: Your hooks are covered with rust.

BERT: But they're sharp.

CHARLIE: Bunk.

BERT: Zen, Charlie. Zen.

(*Long pause*)

CHARLIE: Do you trust people who don't fish?

BERT: I hadn't thought about it. Do you?

CHARLIE: Think about it? Certainly. All the time. It's the first test I give a person. Say I need a clerk. I interview people. Inquiring about their various skills and so on. Discreetly, then, I ask if they enjoy the odd opportunity to go a' fishin'. To cast aside, as it were, the day's business and so forth. If they say no, then I refuse to trust them. I may in fact employ them. But I will never fully trust them. Non-anglers don't know the world, Bertie ...

BERT: They don't know about living and dying, Charlie ...

CHARLIE: About victory and defeat ...

BERT: About solitude. About the spiritual ... about hope.

CHARLIE: They think the world of the water and the forest, the wetland and the upland, that these worlds ...

BERT: And they are worlds ...

CHARLIE: Pastoral. Idyllic. Yet noisy. Full of sound ...

BERT: Symphonies. Poetry. The theatre of the flowing stream ...

CHARLIE: The literature of the gamecock ...

BERT: The non-angler by his fireside ...

CHARLIE: With his important media, blaring forth the important matters of the smaller world ...

BERT: Has no idea, cannot begin to comprehend ...

CHARLIE: The moment. The here. The now ...

BERT: The life ...

CHARLIE: The responsibility ...

BERT: Yes ...

CHARLIE: Yes ...

BERT: Yes. (*Long pause*) You're a liar, Charlie.

CHARLIE: Am I?

BERT: Yes.

CHARLIE: Let me tell you a story. This really happened. Once, I was fishing a lake in the high mountains. A small lake. More of a pond, really. The water was very cold. And the sky and the mountains were reflected on the surface. Often it was very difficult to tell which was water and which was sky. I had been fishing all day, and the sun was about to set. The sky was red, and the air was taking on the chill of evening. A flock of geese, their silhouettes honking and streaming, passed overhead, heading for structure. I was drinking whiskey—ancient autumnal, peat-inspired whiskey. It was whiskey season. Whiskey seasons were longer then. I was fishing with a Clark Special, which hung on the surface like a small chunk of a leftover dream. Sandra had recently gone to her reward and I was feeling very blue. I spent a lot of time drinking and fishing, and crying. Often, all at the same time. But this time was different. Different and very special. The Clark Special would sail off through the crisp, thin air and land so gently on the water. Check cast. Wait. Count. Strip. Count. Strip. And so on. Then, without my totally noticing, the water began to show me things. People I hadn't seen in years. Sounds I hadn't heard. I saw Sandra on the still, glassy surface. In it. On it. Like a living person reflected in the water, but there was nothing to reflect. She smiled at me. She asked if they were biting, and if I wanted to eat dinner at home or to go out for a late supper. I saw myself as a young boy, helping my grandfather lay a fire in his fireplace. His hands would touch my small shoulders. He laughed and lit his pipe. I struck a match and my grandfather heaped on kindling. He peeled an apple for me with his pocketknife, and the sweet juice dribbled from my chin as I munched apples, and smelled my grandfather's pipe. I saw Sandra again, this time as a young bride who depended far too much on her stripling groom. She was very serious then. And I saw my father, sitting at another fireplace, doing what he did best in all the world. Holding the knife he had inherited from his father in his nimble, brown hands. He created flyrods. Split bamboo. White birch. Curls of wood piled at his feet by the fire. Once, and I saw this too—in the water of that lake in the mountains— my father was stripping the bark from a long branch that was to be my own first flyrod. The knife slipped off the wood and dug into the fleshy web of my father's gentle hand. Blood spurted and ran from the wound. But my father only held his hands together, folded as if in prayer, and he stared into the fire and smiled. All of this, I saw on the surface of a lake in the mountains of America. And, as the vision vanished, I snapped the Clark Special back off the surface in preparation for another cast, and ... and blood dripped from the fly. And I was not afraid.

(*Long pause*)

BERT: The most innocent of pastimes.

CHARLIE: That's why it must be taken seriously.

BERT: The rising of the moon, Charlie. The running of the deer.

CHARLIE: The blood of our fathers. The miracle of water.

BERT: Yes.

CHARLIE: Yes.

(*Bert and Charlie fish on without speaking. We hear the sounds of flowing water*)

The End

Lanford Wilson

A POSTER OF THE COSMOS

Lanford Wilson

"Lanford Wilson is probably our greatest functioning American playwright." Thus wrote Rob Baker of the New York *Daily News* in reviewing the Circle Repertory Company's production of Mr. Wilson's *Brontosaurus* (which appeared in *Best Short Plays 1979*).

Since that assessment in 1977, Mr. Wilson has written his most comprehensive project to date—three plays depicting the Talley family of Lebanon, Missouri. In 1979 New York's Circle Repertory Company produced *Talley's Folly*, a two character romance between Sally Talley and Matt Friedman set on July 4, 1944. Walter Kerr in the *New York Times* raved about the subsequent production on Broadway, "a charmer, filled to the brim with hope, humor and chutzpah." The play won the 1980 Pulitzer Prize for Drama, the Theatre Club Inc. Award for Best American Play and the New York Drama Critics' Circle Award. The second play in the series, *5th of July*, set in 1977, depicts the next generation of Talleys attempting to piece together their lives after a disruptive decade of social change. The third Talley play, *A Tale Told*—Wilson's 29th production directed by Marshall W. Mason—again takes place on July 4, 1944, showing the family that Sally Talley wanted to escape. Julius Novick in the *Village Voice* responded to *A Tale Told:* "What an old-fashioned play Lanford Wilson has written; and what a good one!" ... Mr. Wilson writes in his "customary Chekhovian fashion, bringing very specific selves and viewpoints and relationships with them ... the people of his trilogy go on living when they are offstage." A revised version of the play entitled *Talley & Son* was presented by the Circle Repertory Company in 1985.

Lanford Wilson was born in Lebanon, Missouri, in 1937, and was educated at San Diego State College and the University of Chicago, where he started writing plays. His professional career began at the now defunct Caffe Chino in Greenwich Village. After having had ten productions at this pioneer Off-off Broadway cafe-theatre and six at the Cafe La Mama, he moved to Off-Broadway in 1965 with the presentation of *Home Free!* at the Cherry Lane Theatre. In 1966, Mr. Wilson again was represented Off-Broadway, this time with a double bill, *The Madness of Lady Bright* and *Ludlow Fair*, at the uptown Theatre East. *This Is the Rill Speaking*, another of his short plays, was seen during that same season at the Martinique Theatre in a series of six works originally presented at the Cafe La Mama.

In 1967, Mr. Wilson won a Drama Desk-Vernon Rice Award for his play, *The Rimers of Eldritch*, a lyrical study of life in a small town in the Middle West. This was followed by another full-length play, *The Gingham Dog*, which opened in 1968 at the Washington Theatre Club, Washington, D.C., and was presented on Broadway the following year. The author returned to Broadway in 1970 with *Lemon Sky*, which drew the following comment from reviewer Clive Barnes: "Mr. Wilson can write; his characters spring alive on stage; he holds our attention, he engages our heart." A New York revival of *Lemon Sky* in December of 1985 presented by the Second Stage company won plaudits from critics and audience.

In 1972 Mr. Wilson received considerable praise for his libretto for the operatic version of Tennessee Williams' *Summer and Smoke*. The opera, with music by Lee Hoiby, was performed by the New York City Opera at Lincoln Center.

Mr. Wilson's highly acclaimed play, *The Hot L Baltimore*, written under a Guggenheim Fellowship, originally was presented by the Circle Repertory Company in January 1973, then transferred in March to Off-Broadway's Circle in the Square Downtown for a commercial engagement, ran for 1,166 performances, and won the New York Drama Critics' Circle Award for Best American Play of the 1972–73 season; the Outer Critics' Circle Award; and an Obie award for Best Play.

Among the author's other works for the theatre are *Balm in Gilead*, presented in a highly acclaimed revival in New York in 1985; *Wandering*; *So Long at the Fair*; *No Trespassing*; *Serenading Louie*; *The Mound Builders*; *The Great Nebula in Orion*, introduced in *Best Short Plays 1972*; *The Sand Castle* in *Best Short Plays 1975*; and *Thymus Vulgaris*, commissioned by Edward Albee for New York's Lincoln Center One-Act Festival at the Mitzi E. Newhouse Theatre and published in the *Best Short Plays 1982*. Another play, *Angel's Fall*, presented by Circle Rep in 1982, joined *Talley's Folly* and *5th of July* in receiving a nomination for the Tony Award. A new translation of Chekhov's *The Three Sisters* was commissioned and produced by the Hartford Stage Company in 1984. Mr. Wilson's most recent play, *Burn This*, starring John Malkovich and Joan Allen, opened at the Mark Taper Forum theatre in Los Angeles in 1987, and subsequently received critical acclaim when it opened on Broadway in October 1987 with the same cast.

Mr. Wilson has been the recipient of Rockefeller, Yale, and Guggenheim Fellowships, as well as an award from The American Academy of Arts and Letters for "the body of his work as a playwright." In the fall of 1981 the University of Missouri at Kansas City awarded Mr. Wilson the honorary degree Doctor of Humane Letters.

The 1987 edition of *Best Short Plays* was enhanced by his play *A Betrothal*, a charming romantic tale of two lonely flower enthusiasts. *A Poster of the Cosmos*, a dramatic monologue account of a desperate relationship with a victim of AIDS, was first presented on June 8, 1988, in Manhattan's Ensemble Studio Theatre's Marathon '88, where artistic director Curt Dempster has fostered an appreciation for the short play form through an annual series of one-act plays. The production, directed by Jonathan Hogan, starred Tom Noonan, who gave a stunning performance. The author dedicates this play: "To Tom Noonan."

Character:

TOM, *thirty-six, very large and brooding*

Setting:

A police station, New York City, 1987.

At Curtain:

Tom sits at an institutional table in an institutional chair. There is a tape recorder on the table. He sits in a white pool of light in a black void. He wears a white T-shirt, white work pants and sneakers.

He is addressing a cop who would be at the other end of the table, another off left or right would be slouching against a door. If he gets up, something in the cop's posture tells him he'd better sit back down.

When he smokes, the smoke rises up in the white downspot like a nebula.

TOM: (*He is standing and quite pissed-off*)
All right, I'm sitting down and I'm staying down. Okay?
(*He sits*)
Now, are you happy?
(*Glares at them in disgust*)
Jesus, you guys slay me with that crap. "You don't look like the kinna guy'd do somethin' like dat." You're a joke. Cops. Jesus. I mean you're some total cliché. I don't have to be here lookin' at you guys, I could turn on the TV. "What's that white stuff on your shirt?" Jesus. I'm a baker, it's flour. You want a sample, take to your lab?
(*Shaking his head in wonder*)
"You don't look like the kinna guy ... " What does dat kinna guy who'd do somethin' like dat look like to a cop, huh?

And what kinna *thing?* You don't know nothin'; you know what you think you know. You seen every kinna dirty business there is every night, lookin' under the covers, spend your workin' day in the fuckin' armpits of the city and still ain't learned shit about people. You're totally fuckin' blind and deaf like fish I heard about, spend their life back in some fuckin' cave.

(*He looks around, taps the tape recorder, looks at it*)

Is this on? You got your video cameras goin'? 'Cause I told you I'd tell you but this is the only time I'm tellin' this. So, you know, get out your proper equipment, I'm not doin' this twice.

(*He looks around, still disgusted*)

"You don't look like the kinna guy'd do somethin' like dat." Johnny said I didn't look like no kinna guy at all. Just a big ugly guy. Said I was like Kurt Vonnegut or somebody. Somebody had the good sense not to look like nobody else. He said that, I read every word Vonnegut wrote. He's good. He's got a perverted point of view, I like that. There was a time I wouldn't of understood that, but we change, which is what I'm sayin' here.

(*Beat*)

"You don't look like the kinna guy'd do dat." What kinna guy is *that? What* kinna guy? Oh, well, you're talkin' *dat* kinna guy. The kinna guy'd *do* that. *Dat* kinna guy ... Well, I *ain't* dat kinna guy. I'm a kinna guy like *you* kinna guys. That's why you make me want to puke sittin' here lookin' at you. "Hey, guys, dis guy is our kinna guy. I can't believe he's dat kinna guy." Well, I *ain't* that kinna guy.

(*Almost saddened by them*)

You guys move in the dark, inna doorways, if you didn't look right through people 'stead a' at 'em, you'd maybe know there ain't no *"Kinna guys."* You'd maybe know you can't sort guys out like vegetables. This is a potato, it goes wid the potatoes; this is a carrot, this here's celery—we got us an eggplant, goes wid the eggplant. That's vegetables, that ain't people. There's no kinna guys, cause guys can't be put in a shopping cart. 'Cause *guys*, if you used your *eyes*, you'd know, are V-8 juice, man. You don't know *what* kinna thing's in there.

(*Tom pauses, takes cigarettes from his pants pocket, puts them on the table with a Zippo lighter, takes one from the pack and lights it. He has a new thought that annoys him lightly*)

For all you know, Johnny was a junkie. Didn't see you lookin' for tracks, and you'd a' found 'em by the way, so what kinna guys are we talkin' about here? It depresses people to sit here and talk to this kinna massive stupidity.

(*Beat*)

Johnny'd love it. He'd laugh his ass, man. No shit, he'd wet himself over you guys. And I don't wanna make him sound simple. He was like this anything but easy sort of person. He used to, you know, when he was a kid, had this prescription for hypertension medication, but he said he didn't take it cause it messed up his bowels so bad. *Thinking* was Johnny's problem. Like 'cause his mind was goin' like on all these tracks, like it had all these connections and he was always re-pluggin' everything and crossin' over these wires, 'til you could almost like *see* this complicated mess of lines in his head. Like he'd wait 'till he was like fuckin' droppin', like his eyes had been closed for an hour before he'd even get in bed at night. And then he'd lay there and in a minute he'd be up again. And like, you know, you'd think, aw, shit, 'cause he's smokin' all these cigarettes and this shit and half the time he don't know if he's sittin' up or layin' down. The whole apartment could go up and he'd never know it. He'd just have to go on re-pluggin' those wires 'till finally, sorta totally unannounced, somethin' would short-out in his head. You could almost hear like his whole system shut down, and he'd be out cold somewhere. Maybe ona floor, ina chair.

(*Maybe a beat, but continues the same*)

Then, you know, he was a twitcher. Like a dog. Even in his sleep, which was something I never saw on a human being while they was sleepin'. Like a dog is chasing maybe a rabbit, or gettin' run after by a wolf, but you'd watch Johnny and say, Johnny what the hell are you dreamin' you're chasin'? Then he'd wake up and keep right on twitchin'. You know the foot is goin' or the fingers are goin'. He'd be biting at his lip or digging at his cheek like a fuckin' junkie, which I don't think he ever was, 'cause he worked for a hospital, procuring, and coulda brought anythin' home but never did, except stories about the fuckin' nurses and orderlies stealin' him blind, falsifying records on him, but he never said he was, and he'd lie, but his lies was always telling things on himself like he was worse than he was. Like he said he'd left his wife and kid back in Arkansas when he was seventeen, and really missed the little daughter, but like he fuckin' never had no kids. The wife, yeah, but—and a lot of shit like he'd been in jail, which he hadn't and all. But he, you know, used to shoot up but he never worked up a habit, 'cause probably he never, at that time, had the bread for it and you can't imagine a worse thief than Johnny, so he'd never make it as a junkie, 'less he had some john supportin' him in it. But he never said he was even an out-and-out user, so you can be pretty sure he wasn't. Which also he wasn't the type 'cause junkies don't want the responsibility of livin'. Anyway, you're not gonna catch no twitcher on the shit, 'cause it'd be like, you know, a waste of good shit. And Johnny was this, you know, he'd get his fingers goin' in his hair, I'd look over and say, "Aww, Jesus, Johnny," 'cause there'd be this like patch of red hair in the middle of all his like dirty blond and he'd say, "What, have I got myself bleedin' again?" And you couldn't figger what a basically nice-lookin' guy was always fuckin' himself over like that, but that was just all those wires he was re-pluggin' all the time. Like the only reason he had a good body was he had these weights, but he'd use 'em like to work off energy not to build himself up. That's what I say, his mom said he was born with it. But he like burned calories like nothin' I ever saw. Ate more than me and he's what? Five-eight, which he thought was short but it isn't like freakish or nothin' to worry about and weighed maybe a buck forty but he used to say like basically his body was a very inefficient machine. He was like a real gas-burner.

(*Beat. He thinks a minute*)

He was gonna open a delivery service. This from a guy who had a money job—and he'd be the only deliverer. On his bike. He used to sit and map out routes one place to another. He called himself the Manhattan Transit. Used to make practice runs; you know, during rush hour. But this was just a way to blow off that nervous stuff he had but it didn't work out 'cause he had no business sense. He could organize anything, but he couldn't start something. He went so far he made up this ad and put it in the *Village Voice* two weeks running with our phone number on it. This was during a two week vacation he had. We was goin' to go down to Petersburg, then he got this idea. Only the damnest thing, the phone never rung once. No, that's not true. Once about six months later I picked up the phone, said, hello, this guy says, "Is this the Manhattan Transit?" I said it used to be, but they sold their bicycle.

(*Beat*)

He would of been good at it. I said he should work at some place where they use messengers but he wasn't interested in workin' for somebody else. He was already doin' that, he had a regular job you'd think kept him so crazy he wouldn't have time to dream up some schemes, but you got to remember all those wires in his head—and he wasn't meant to work in a office. Twitchers are hell in a office. He was at St. Vincents first, then up to Doctors' Hospital and back to St. Vincents, runnin' procurements for like the whole hospital. Ordering truckloads of rubbing alcohol and all the prescription stuff, the bed pans and walkers, so you know it wasn't no snap, but one wire in his head was always out in the rain on his bike using this like photographic map of the city: The one-way streets, and places blocked off for school kids at recess time. You probably seen him. He's the guy goin' about five times faster than the traffic. And fightin' everythin'. Nothin' was easy. He went at everythin' crazy. He'd get off work, his face all red, you'd know he'd been diggin' at himself again. That he'd be up all night workin' on the bike. So I don't want to make him sound simple. He was anything but an easy sort of person. I was the easy one.

(*Pause. He stretches, or even gets up, then sits back down. He looks off, thinking*)

I was the easy one. He was always wantin' to change things, I didn't care how things was. Then he was always changin' jobs, or tryin' to. He'd blow up at somebody and walk out, they'd always ask him to come back and I been workin' at the same bakery twenty years. Since I was sixteen. And I like it 'cause they're old-fashioned and do it the same way they always did. You'd think bakin' bread is nothin' with the machines they use. Doin' all the measuring and mixin' and kneadin', what's to do but carry the trays to the ovens and back, but yeast is a livin' thing; it can't be taken for granted. One batch ain't like the next, and the humidity and temperature in the room makes a difference. Johnny liked it. I couldn't smell it on me but he liked the smell. He said people take on the character of their work and I figured I was gradually becoming this nice crusty loaf of Italian bread. But the way I think of it, it's good, 'cause, like I said, it's nourishing and it's a live thing. Bread. But I wasn't foolin' myself that it was a job that calls for a lot of thinkin'. Like Johnny's. Instinct, maybe. Also the money ain't bad and you always got fresh bread. Only thing, I didn't like was I worked nights and he worked days.

(*Pause. He looks at them*)

Hell, that got a reaction, didn't it? Now you're thinkin', "He ain't our kinna guy after all. Good, we ain't gotta worry about it." But I was, I used to be, I know all that. But circumstances are crazy things; the things that can happen all of a sudden change everything. Like I'd never thought much of myself as a part of anything. I was, you know, I thought I was above everything. I just watched it. But really, I didn't know how to get involved in it.

(*Beat*)

So, I get off work at seven, I'm eatin' at this place I always did, Johnny's havin' breakfast. He's depressed 'cause the Cosmos folded. I think they'd folded about five years back but he'd got to thinkin' about it again. And we're talkin' about atmospheric pressure, which is something it happens I've read a lot about, and we're both readers that only read factual stuff. Only I read slow and forget it and he reads like tearin' through things and remembers. And we'd both been married when we was kids, and had a kid of our own, only, you know, it turned out he didn't. And he said he was gay now and he'd been like fuckin' everythin' in sight for five years only he'd got frustrated with it and hadn't been laid in a month, and we're bitchin' our jobs and he got up and goes off for a minute and comes back and says why don't we go around the corner to his apartment 'cause we're takin' up two seats at the counter and this is a business based on volume and I said, no, you got to go to work and he said ... "I just called in sick."

(*He smiles, then thinks about it. A frown, a troubled pause*)

That's funny. He really did, first time I met him, called in sick. I never thought about that 'til right now.

(*Beat*)

Jesus, all that talkin' about food makes me realize I ain't eaten anything in two days.

(*A beat. He looks at them expectantly. Apparently there is no reaction*)

Fuck it, skip it. So anyway, if you'da said I'd be livin' wid a guy I'da said, you know, go fuck yourself. And it stayed like that. It was somethin' that always surprised me, you know? Well, of course you don't. Assholes. But I'd wake up, go in the livin' room, he'd be in a chair or somethin', you know, twitchin' like he was deliverin' somethin' somewhere. Or actually sometimes he'd be in bed there. And it always like surprised me. I'd think, what the hell do you know about this? If he'd been like a big old hairy guy or something probably nothing would have happened, but Johnny didn't have hair on his body, he had like this peach fuzz all over him that made him feel like … skip it. I'm your kinna guy, right? I don't think. I don't analyze. So you know … we had like … three years. We did go down to Petersburg. He'd heard about it, he'd always wanted to go. We didn't like it. We went on down to Key West, he'd heard about that, too. That was worse. We come back, rented a car, went up to Vermont. And that was good. Except for Johnny drivin', I couldn't let him drive 'cause he'd go crazy. We'd get behind a tractor or somethin', he'd go ape. Also I'd get dizzy on the roads all up and down and curvin' and Johnny being this aerobic driver.

(*Pause*)

So after three years, when he started gettin' sick—they was very good about it at the hospital. They let him come to work for a while. Then, you know, like I said, he'd dig at himself and bleed, so that wasn't possible. That'd be real bad. So then I started being the one that was crazy all the time and I'd get off and come home in the morning, he'd be starin' out the window or somethin'. He'd say, "I slept fourteen hours." It was like this blessing for him; like this miracle, he couldn't believe it. I guess everything that was goin' on in him, I guess was interesting to him. He was like studying it. I'd say, "What?" And he'd hold up his hand for me to be quiet for a long time and then he'd say, "I'd never have believed pain could be that bad. This is amazing." You know, he had like his intestines all eaten out and that and he had insurance and the hospital was good to him. They all visited him, but he didn't take the pain killers. He was curious about it.

(*He looks around, then goes on rather flatly*)
Then he got worse and started takin' 'em.
(*Beat*)
You could see by his expression that he hadn't thought he
was gonna do that. The staff, the nurses and, you know, the
volunteers, the ghouls that get off on that, they were okay. They
didn't get in our way much.
(*Searching, becoming frustrated*)
What I couldn't believe was that I didn't have it. I got the
fuckin' test, it was negative. I couldn't believe that. Twice. I
couldn't figger that, 'cause like the first time I was with him, I
just fucked him and he like laid up against me and jerked off.
And that was sorta what we did for a while. That was our pattern; you know, you fall into routines. But after a while, you get
familiar with someone, I was all over him. No way I wasn't exposed to that like three times a week for three years. What the
hell was goin' on? I got to thinkin' maybe he didn't really have
it, maybe it was somethin' else, but ...
(*He settles down, pauses, thinks of something else*)
He had these friends at the hospital, offered him somethin', I
don't know what, take him out of his misery, he didn't take it, he
wanted to see it through to the end like.
(*A little frustration creeps back*)
See, my problem was I didn't really know what he was goin'
through. You help and you watch and it tears you up, sure, but
you don't know *what*, you know, whatta you know?
(*Beat*)
He wanted to come home, but ... uh ...
(*Pause. He regards them*)
This is the only part you fucks care about, so listen up. We
wanted him to be home for the end, but it slipped up on us. We
thought he'd come home another time but he went into this like
semi-coma and just went right outta sight, he just sank. I didn't
know if he recognized me or not. I got this old poster of the
Cosmos and put it up on the wall across from the bed. They had
him propped up in bed, but he just looked scared. He saw it and
he said, "What's that?" You know, you know you know everythin' in the room and it's all familiar, and he hadn't seen that
before. Probably it was just this big dark thing in front of him

that he couldn't tell what it was and it scared him. He didn't understand it.

(*Looking around*)

This gets bloody, so if you're faint of heart or anything ...

(*Looking up*)

All you fuckers out in TV land, recordin' this shit for fuckin' posterity; check your focus, this is hot shit, they're gonna wanna know this.

(*Pause*)

So the nurse comes by, I said he's restin'. She was glad to skip him. And I took off my clothes and held him. He was sayin', it sounded like, "This is curious." And there was just like nothin' to him.

(*Pause*)

See the problem is, like I said, I was the one who was crazy now. And, uh, well, to hell with it. I'm your kinna guy, fellas, I won't think about it. We do what we do, we do what's gotta be done.

(*And rather coldly, or that is what he tries for*)

So he died in my arms and I held him a long time and then I cut a place on his cheek where he used to dig and on his chest where he used to gouge out these red marks and in his hair. And when the blood came, I licked it off him. Cleaned him up. So then the nurse come, you know, and shit a brick and called you guys. But they let me hold him 'til you come. I guess they was afraid of me. Or maybe of all the blood. Then they knew I had to be crazy, 'cause like we agreed, I'm not the kinna guy'd do somethin' like dat. What they thought, I think, was that I'd killed him, but that wasn't what he wanted and what I had to consider now was myself. And what I wanted.

(*Pause*)

So if it don't take again, then I'm like fucked, which wouldn't be the first time. I guess there's gonna be maybe some compensation in knowin' I did what I could.

(*A long wandering pause, then he looks at them*)

So. Are you happy now?

(*A pause. Eight counts. Blackout*)

The End

RAMON DELGADO, EDITOR

This publication is the ninth edition of *The Best Short Plays* edited by Ramon Delgado, who has continued the series made famous by the late Stanley Richards, and established earlier by Margaret Mayorga.

An experienced literary advisor, Dr. Delgado has served as chairman for new plays at the Dallas Theater Center, as a literary advisor to The Whole Theatre Company in Montclair, New Jersey, and as theatre consultant to Scholastic Magazine's *Literary Cavalcade*. Dr. Delgado has also been script judge for the Playwrights' Program of the American Theatre Association, the International Biennial Play Competition sponsored by Southern Illinois University at Carbondale, the Illinois Arts Council, and has adjudicated for the American College Theatre Festival.

Born in Tampa, Florida, and raised in nearby Winter Haven, Ramon Delgado started writing plays for marionette shows when he was eleven years old. By the time he had finished high school he had written two full-length plays and several one-act plays. Recognition as a playwright has been received with honors in five regional and twelve national playwriting competitions, including those sponsored by Theta Alpha Phi, the University of Missouri, EARPLAY, and Samuel French. Three of his full-length plays—*Listen, My Children*; *A Little Holy Water*, and *The Fabulous Jeromes*—received honors in the David Library American Freedom division of the American College Theatre Festival. Seven of his short plays have been published, notably "Waiting for the Bus" in *Ten Great One Act Plays* and *Themes in the One Act Play*, and "Once Below a Lighthouse" in *The Best Short Plays 1972*. His full-length play *A Little Holy Water*, a Cuban-American romantic comedy, was published in 1983.

In 1978 Dr. Delgado's one-act play *The Jerusalem Thorn* was chosen for the Dale Wasserman Midwest Professional Playwrights Workshop, and after expansion into a full-length script, the play was produced Off-off Broadway by the Acting Wing, Inc., at the Shandol Theatre. Two of his short plays have had Equity showcase productions at the No Smoking Playhouse and at The Glines. The New York Hispanic theatre INTAR selected him as a Playwright-in-Residence in 1980. Three of his short television plays have been aired over PBS, Channel WSIU, Carbondale, Illinois.

Dr. Delgado began his education at Stetson University in Deland, Florida, then studied with Paul Baker and Eugene McKinney at the Dallas Theater Center. He received a Master of Fine Arts degree in 1967 from Yale School of Drama, studying playwriting there with the late John Gassner, and later with Christian H. Moe at Southern Illinois University at Carbondale, where he received his Ph.D. in 1976.

Cited twice by *Outstanding Educators of America*, Dr. Delgado has taught acting, directing, playwriting, and dramatic literature at Kentucky Wesleyan College; Hardin-Simmons University in Abilene, Texas; St. Cloud State College, Minnesota; and Montclair State College, New Jersey, where he is presently Professor of Speech-Theatre. Dr. Delgado holds memberships in the Association for Theatre in Higher Education, the Dramatists Guild, and the Nashville Songwriters Association International.

Dr. Delgado's full-length play, *Stones*, produced at Montclair State College in 1983, stimulated discussion on the toxic waste problems of the environment. His acting textbook, *Acting With Both Sides of Your Brain*, published in 1986, has been adopted by colleges nationwide. His lyric "Grandpa's Watch" shared a first place award in the 1988 Music City Song Festival competition. At present he is working on an acting styles book, an introductory text for theatre appreciation, and a one-man show on the nineteenth century actor Edwin Booth.